BIZARRO among the SAVAGES

Also by Dan Piraro

BIZARRO among the SAVAGES

A Relatively Famous Guy's Experiences on the Road
and in the Homes of Strangers

Dan Piraro

**Andrews McMeel
Publishing**

Kansas City

Library of Congress Cataloging-in-Publication Data

Piraro, Dan.
  Bizarro among the savages : a relatively famous guy's
experiences on the road and in the homes of strangers /
by Dan Piraro.
    p. cm.
  ISBN 0-8362-2173-7
    1. Piraro, Dan—Journeys—United States. 2. United States—
Social life and customs—Caricatures and cartoons. 3. American wit
and humor, Pictorial. I. Title.
NC1429.P58A2   1997
741.5'092—dc20
                                              96-33267
                                              CIP

*To Katie Berry and Bart Odom,
my round-the-clock friends,
when I was no fun to be friends with.*

*Special thanks to Bart Odom for his
invaluable suggestions and critique.*

Contents

Preface

In the fall of 1995, motivated by a dark cloud of discontent and a lust for fame and fortune, I embarked on a tour of North America to promote my latest book of cartoons. What I thought would be an entertaining series of free vacations and parties disguised as a publicity gimmick turned into a spiritual pilgrimage of life-shattering proportions that would change me forever.

Bizarro among the Savages is the true-life account of that unique trip across the continent—and one or two dozen other completely irrelevant events as well.

ONE

The Truth from the Gutter

These days, most of your popular big-time cartoonists are completely inaccessible to their readers. They don't do interviews, they don't answer their fan mail, they don't even answer their front door when you stand there patiently and ring the bell nonstop for three days. Most people don't even know what these guys look like. Those who do frequently wish they didn't.

Bill Watterson, creator of *Calvin and Hobbes,* hasn't been heard from or seen in public since he signed his last syndication contract in 1990. Even TV's *Unsolved Mysteries* has failed to locate him. Gary Larson, creator of *The Far Side,* has taken to wearing an Afro wig and sundress in public to avoid being recognized (according to an unnamed source). And perhaps the most conspicuous example is Scott Adams, creator of *Dilbert,* who, for a number of years, masqueraded as a computer nerd at a major corporation until he was discovered and forced into hiding. And, although he *appears* to communicate with his fans via E-mail, an unnamed source (the same cowardly worm who told me about Larson's cross-dressing) informed me that Adams's responses are merely mechanical form letters, sorted and sent out by a rhesus monkey.

So why all the secrecy?

I may be able to shed some light on this sore spot with American comics fans, for I, too, for the first ten years of my career, hid from my readers. So here, for the first time, is . . .

The Shocking and Sordid Truth About Life as a Cartoonist!

Have you ever met a syndicated cartoonist? Of course not! Almost no one has! What are they hiding? Why do they go to such great lengths to avoid the public? What are they trying so desperately to keep you from finding out?!

Sure, everyone has run into countless small-time impostors and wanna-bes.

But why don't your favorite cartoonists, the "big shots," ever hang out where you can find them? If the big shots had their way, you'd never find out, but now, because of the courage and stupidity of one such big-time cartoonist—me—the unvarnished cat will be ripped from the bag, kicking and screaming! And, man, is the poop* gonna hit the fan†.

The ugly truth is that the biggest reason we big guys avoid our public is because we're having way too much fun. Our greatest fear is that boring, everyday peasants like you would only ruin it. Most of us don't even get out of bed until 1:00 P.M. We have coffee, martinis, and cigarettes for breakfast, then stumble over to our drawing table, where we spend about twenty minutes drawing our one little cartoon for the day, then we blow the rest of the afternoon running over windsurfers with our speedboat. (Almost all cartoonists live near water.)

We also typically stay out all night partying at secret places with celebrities and power brokers. Six or eight times a year, we go on elaborate vacations, traveling to exotic lands, drinking, fighting, and gambling heavily.

Now that I've spilled the beans, I will most likely be ostracized by my fellow cartoonists, and I may even have trouble getting into the next party at the Playboy Mansion. But I wanted you to know because I feel it's important that you, the reader, understand why we cartoonists have shunned you.

It's not because we don't appreciate your loyal readership and undying adoration. It's because personally acknowledging your existence and making ourselves available to you would ruin the fun of celebrity for us. If you're honest with yourselves, I think you'll admit that if you were in our shoes, you'd do the same thing. After all, what good is fame and fortune if you can't selfishly shut yourself off from the common rabble and feel superior to others?

But I, for one, have recently been made to see the error of my ways. Thanks to spiritual intervention, personal hardship,

---

*Substitute "poop" for another word *only* if over eighteen.
†"Fan" refers to you, the reader—not the wind-making, rotating blade variety.

and the icy, unlubricated hand of tragedy, the life of the money-grubbing celebrity recluse is over for me. I am a changed man and now gladly count myself among the peasants I used to abuse. Put on a helmet and grab a couple of beach towels, for the story I am about to tell you will leave you bruised, battered, and damp with sin.

A little over two years ago, I woke up in a gutter in Monte Carlo (one reserved for celebrity recluses) and couldn't remember for the life of me how I'd gotten there. I looked at the calendar on what was left of my diamond Rolex watch and realized that four days were missing from my memory. I was hungry, cold, and scared to death.

Having been raised in Oklahoma, my first inclination was to attribute this time lapse to alien abduction. But deep down inside, I knew that the real cause was that life in the fast lane was catching up with me. I stumbled to my feet, wiped the spittle from my chin, and dusted off my evening gown. By the light of a street lamp, I could see my watch said 12:10, but in my pitiful stupor I had no idea if it was noon or midnight. A wave of disgust washed over me as I contemplated my pathetic state. After a few moments it occurred to me that if it was dark, it would *have* to be midnight. Duh. Now I felt a little less pathetic, but no less disgusted. I shuffled aimlessly down the narrow street, wanting to be anywhere else but in my own skin.

As I passed by the darkened shops along the street, something in a window caught my eye. It was a face, staring accusingly at me from some other dimension not yet cataloged by modern-day occultists. Not a real face, of course, but a smear of window cleaner that had dried in the *shape* of a face. I stared in disbelief as I realized whose face it was staring back at me in silence.

It was the image of *Wheel of Fortune* game-show host Pat Sajak, and I felt certain he was trying to tell me something.

Transfixed, I met his glare with fear and humility. His lips did not move, but I could hear him speaking nonetheless. His message was simple, but it cut through me like a John Tesh sonata. "It's time to spin the wheel," he said.

Pat's message was multileveled and powerful. He knew of which he spake, for he, too, had ridden the wave of the ego-intoxicated megalomaniac. Not long ago, he had abandoned the filthy throngs of toothless American game-show watchers who had made him a star and moved into the powerful talk-show host arena. Leaving his fans to choke on the dust of his departure, he ruled over the talk-show genre like Idi Amin for a brief but dark period of American pop-culture history.

Eventually, as is frequently the case with the fans of the big-haired and power-mad, his millions of spurned constituents revolted. They snatched his ratings out from under him like a gallows trapdoor, sending him plummeting back to Earth and reality.

"It's time to spin the wheel." No one knew the meaning of those words better than Pat Sajak when he returned to his rightful place as this continent's most beloved game-show host. And as I stood disoriented, disheveled, and lost, staring at Pat's face in that window in Monte Carlo, the full meaning of those words hit me like a Hollywood freight train. I knew what I had to do.

I needed to get back to the people. I needed to meet my readers, to smell their cheap cologne, shake their sweaty hands, and laugh at their amateurish jokes. That was what it was all about. That was where I would find peace. I headed for home no less arrogant, but with a renewed sense of purpose.

In seat 29A, thirty thousand feet above the Atlantic Ocean, a tall, handsome, dark stranger told me of the resplendent wonders of E-mail. He expounded at length about the pleasure he experienced on a daily basis as strangers from all over the country wrote to him and complimented his efforts. I tried to ignore him, pretending to read a book, but he wouldn't take the hint. I took out headphones and a tape player, but he continued. Even my request to the flight attendant for a pillow and my subsequent melodramatic snoring and drooling didn't stop him. "Who the hell *is* this guy?" I shouted at first to myself and eventually to him.

He was (and still is, at this writing) Jim Toomey, affable and talented creator of *Sherman's Lagoon,* a popular syndicated comic strip about fish. He was one of the first few cartoonists to publish his E-mail address in his daily strip, and he spoke so glowingly about the daily letters from his readers that he managed to convince me I should try it. After all, I had just promised myself I was going to get in touch with my readers, and this could be the first step to fulfilling that promise.

Some hours later, after Jim had talked himself to sleep, I was thinking about this whole E-mail thing while idly flipping through an in-flight magazine. I happened across a full-color ad for a soft drink featuring a large, glistening, ice-filled glass of dark liquid. An unseen force seemed to draw me into the picture, to the myriad reflections and shadows in the ice cubes. And there, to my astonishment, was Sajak's face once again.

The plane was dark and quiet. Only the distant humming of the engines could be heard. Most of the passengers were asleep. My reading lamp was a lone beacon in the mechanical hush of this metal tube hurtling through the sky so far above the ocean. I looked over at the dozing Jim Toomey, his head slumped over, hair pointing in impossible directions, mouth agape, probably dreaming of fish. Of course it was true. He had been sent by Sajak.

TWO

The Art of the Mooch

S etting up my E-mail account was as easy as anything electronic can be for an MDA (Mechanically Disadvantaged Adult) like me. I followed the directions, called the help line, called my computer-geek friend, Bobby, whined a lot, used every profanity I knew, invented new profanities, asked my kids what profanities *they* knew, and eventually had someone else come over and do it for me. That's pretty much the way I accomplish everything mechanical.

So while setting up my account was relatively simple, knowing what to do with it was not. I had begun putting my address in my cartoon panel and was getting mail on a daily basis, but reaching out to strangers was not something I was very good at. I have always been the sort of person who considers himself shy but whom no one else believes is shy. Perhaps you know someone like this. While I would typically rather eat bees than talk to a stranger or call someone I don't know on the phone, once I get to know people, I'm reasonably verbose and uninhibited. E-mail turned out to be the perfect medium for me.

With the anonymity of the mail, but the immediacy of a phone call, I quickly came to feel very comfortable with my new E-mail acquaintances. I was able to be witty, charming, and outgoing without any of the fear or insecurity I typically feel when face to face with strangers. My letters became longer and more elaborate, and my correspondents were usually thrilled and surprised by the ornate and prompt responses they received from me. Many of them wrote to me numerous times, and, with some, I felt I was forming a relationship remarkably similar to friendship.

A number of them made comments like "If you're ever in Southern California, my husband and I would love to take you to dinner" or "If you find yourself in Pittsburgh, you're welcome to our guest room and some good home cooking." At the other end of the spectrum, one reader, upset over a satire I had done about *Family Circus*, said that he would very much enjoy supervising my slow and painful death. But his feelings were in the minority, by far.

A typical letter was something like this:

Dude, you rock! I've been reading your comics every day for blah, blah, blah. I think you're better than blah, blah, blah, and my favorite was the one about blah, blah, blah. Do you have any books out or a screen saver, blah, blah?

To which I would typically reply something like:

Thanks for the groovy letter. I'm as happy as a chimp with a new haircut that you're enjoying my comics, blah, blah, blah. Since you asked about books, you may be interested to know there are now eight books of BIZARRO in print. Because of evil plots to end my career, they are sometimes hard to find, but can be easily and legally ordered from any bookstore. Please feel free to buy 100 copies of each, and encourage a thousand of your closest friends to do the same. If you do this small favor for me, I will be that much closer to being able to quit my job as a yard-ornament salesman. Thanks again for writing, I wish you the best of everything, and that includes the entire family of polyester-related products. Your latter 20th century friend from Earth, Blah.

To which they would frequently respond:

Wow! You have books? I had no idea. I've been looking through the humor sections of bookstores thrice weekly for the past decade, and have never come across a BIZARRO book, or anyone who has ever even heard of one!

After a few months of this sort of riveting electronic exchange, I began to realize that I had a marketing problem. I had known for years that my books weren't being ordered by bookstores and had recently chased down what I have come to accept as the primary reason for this.

My first eight books were published by Chronicle Books of San Francisco, a company that specialized in really cool gift books and big coffee-table books. Mine were the only cartoon books they carried. Accordingly, when bookstore owners went to order books to fill their humor shelf, they weren't reaching for Chronicle Books' catalog. They would grab the Andrews McMeel Publishing catalog, the biggest publisher of cartoon books on the planet, and fill their section from that. If they wanted more, they'd order a few from a couple of other publishers that carried a number of cartoon books. As far as the average bookstore owner knew, Chronicle Books didn't even carry cartoonists. Consequently, after eight books of *Bizarro* cartoons with Chronicle Books and fairly disappointing sales, I switched to Andrews McMeel.

Only a few months after I began my daily E-mail correspondence, it was time to put together material for my ninth book of cartoons, and first book with Andrews McMeel. I cleverly decided to title it *Bizarro Number 9* in an attempt to alert my readers that there were eight others they'd perhaps never seen. I assumed that this book would make it into stores where my work had previously never been offered, but I wanted to do something more to promote it. I immediately started thinking about my commitment to getting in touch with my fans. Then I thought of my E-mail pals.

I asked myself this simple question: What if I travel around to some of the cities from which I get a lot of E-mail, do some book signings, and meet some of my readers?

I gave myself this simple answer: You can't afford it.

I asked my new publisher if they'd like to pay for it. They asked me did I know how many $6.95 cartoon books I would have to sell to pay for a trip of that sort. I asked if money was really the bottom line. They asked me if I'd been drinking.

So it was back to the drawing board: What could I do to promote my new book that wouldn't cost a fortune, but would be newsworthy enough to grab a little media attention?

I was sitting in front of my computer terminal one night, thinking about this very question and watching the little wheel on my screen spinning as my computer was trying to bring up that day's E-mail list. I had already ruled out an assassination attempt of some sort—that always lands you in the headlines, but usually also behind bars. I was completely out of ideas, and my computer was still frozen in its "thinking" mode, so I decided to go to the kitchen for a snack. I stood up and felt a sharp, stabbing sensation piercing my brain. It wasn't really painful, but it certainly wasn't the comfortable sort of numbness I was used to feeling between my ears. As I staggered to maintain my balance, I suddenly became aware that someone in a distant room of the house was watching *Wheel of Fortune*.

"It's a sign!" I thought to myself. "Pat is trying to tell me something!"

But I couldn't hear the TV well enough to understand what was being said—only every fifth word or so was coming through. I concentrated to make sense of it. "Mooch," someone said. "Beg," said another. "Sponge," came the third. What did it mean?

I looked back at my computer screen at the list of E-mail letters for that day that had finally come up. "Mooch. Beg. Sponge." I repeated the words, looked at the screen, and repeated the words again. Then all of a sudden, there was the answer I'd been looking for! I could ask my *readers* if they'd help me travel around the country. I could ask them to pick me up at the airport, drive me around, put me up for the night. As long as I was at it, I could even ask them for plane tickets! What's the worst that could happen? They could say no and I'd be no worse off than I already was.

I decided to target California first and quickly constructed the following letter:

Greetings Golden State Bizarro Reader,

Please excuse the impersonal nature of this form letter, but the following important message requires me to send the same epistle to all my California E-mail pals at once.

My new book, BIZARRO NUMBER 9, will be appearing in stores in the very near future. I would very much like to take this opportunity to visit as many BIZARRO cities as possible, sign books, kiss hands, shake babies, make speeches, and meet as many of my readers as I can tolerate. That is why I am proud to announce the nationwide 1995 BIZARRO LAP OF LUXURY BOOK TOUR. But I need your help.

Because I want to do everything within my power to combat the stereotypical aloof-millionaire-celebrity-snob-hermit image that we cartoonists have, I have opted to turn down the publisher's offer to whisk me around the country with a crowd of bodyguards from Lear Jet to limo to five-star hotel to bookstore and back again. Instead, I want to meet and greet you, my semiadoring, semiconscious public up close and personal.

Accordingly, I am looking for a few dozen good-hearted, fun-loving BIZARRO fans in the Los Angeles and San Francisco Bay areas to volunteer their homes and/or services during the second week and weekend of November

(8th–13th) to make this book tour a reality. It's a wonderful opportunity for you to do something positive for your family and your community, and have a little fun, too. Here's how:

If you would like to donate a plane ticket, pick me up at the airport, drive me to a book signing, act as personal bodyguard during said signing, put me up for a night at your house, feed me dinner, drag me to parties, or any one or combination of the above, let me know A.S.A.P. and I will send you details on how to apply.

At this moment you may be saying, "It sounds like fun, Dan, but what if you turn out to be a chain-smoking egomaniac who teases my dog and scares the children? How do I know I really want to get involved in this revolutionary public relations gimmick and maybe end up with my picture in People *magazine with my arm around your shoulder?" Well, that's a fair question and one I could very well ask of you, too. But let me assure you that while I am visually unusual and an avid nonconformist, I am an exceptionally polite house guest who has excellent hygiene, does not drink to excess, does not smoke, does not use illegal drugs of any kind, and is invariably loved by animals, children, and the elderly alike.*

If you or anyone you know is interested in donating any or all of the above-mentioned goods or services and would like more information on the application process, please E-mail me at the above AOL address.

Hurry! For obvious tactical reasons, only a limited number of applicants will be chosen!

Until we speak again, best wishes and fine dining.

Your talking-mammal friend,
Dan Piraro

I pulled the entire group of addresses from L.A. and San Francisco out of my address book and sent the E-mail letter off that very night. To my great surprise and glee, I began receiving replies within an hour. Within a few days I had more volunteers than I could possibly use and the idea was snowballing out of control. I called my publicist at Andrews McMeel to let her know what I was up to and to brag about my brilliance.

"I had a great idea about a way to go on a book tour without having to pay for it, Eunice!" I exclaimed.

"Oh great! What is it?" she replied in her usual exuberant and cheerful way.

I told her all about it, and she loved the idea. It seemed to both of us that the strangeness of the whole scheme would be a sure publicity-getter.

The next day, however, she called back with a different story. As always, she spoke cheerfully and exuberantly.

"Dan, I talked to the Head Honcho [head of AMP books] and the Big Enchilada [head of syndication], and they thought your E-mail book tour is a neat idea, but they'd like you to let *us* fly you out to California and put you up in a *hotel*. Then you can still meet your E-mail fans for lunch or something."

"What?" I was flabbergasted. "I appreciate the offer, but that defeats the whole purpose," I protested. "I'm not going to get any media attention *that* way. What's their objection?"

"Well," she continued in a serious and conciliatory version of her usual cheerful exuberance, "Head Honcho is worried that it will make AMP look cheap if you ask your fans to pay for the trip, and Big Enchilada is afraid you'll be killed by a psycho."

"It's a bit ironic that they won't pay for a book tour, but they don't want someone else to pay for it because it makes them look cheap," I whined sarcastically. I thought for a moment and decided I didn't want to give up the idea that easily.

"Go back to them one more time and tell them this: It doesn't have to make AMP look cheap. They aren't being cheap. Anyone who understands anything about capitalism knows that it just isn't good economics to spend a fortune traveling around the country to sell a handful of $6.95 cartoon books. In fact, I'll tell people you *offered* to pay for it (which they just had) but that I turned you down and insisted on doing it my way (which I was). We'll tell them I'm a lunatic loose cannon with some wacky idea about getting in touch with my readers, which shouldn't be too hard for anyone to believe considering I'm willing to stay in the homes of strangers." I thought for a moment more about the Big Enchilada's concerns about psychos.

"And tell Big Ench [as his friends call him] he's been watching too many David Lynch movies," I said.

"I don't think that's going to make him feel any better," Eunice countered.

"Then tell him that no one is more concerned about my health and safety than I am. I'm not going to put myself in any unnecessary danger. I wear a helmet when I *shower*, for crying out loud." I reasoned. "Plus, these are mostly people I've talked to at length on E-mail, and some by phone, and they're just normal, everyday people who think it would be fun to have a cartoonist in their home for a night. Besides, if psychos were that easy to come across, the police wouldn't have so much trouble finding them."

"All right, I'll give it one more try," she said a bit less cheerfully and a little exasperated.

"Thanks, Eunice. Let me know what they say." I knew I could go on the trip without their blessings if I wanted, but I also knew that it would be that much less effective and more difficult if I didn't have their cooperation in scheduling book signings and media. I needed to talk them into it if it was going to be a success.

A few days later Eunice called back and told me that Honcho and Enchilada had acquiesced. For once we were both cheerful and exuberant. In the back of my mind, however, I couldn't help thinking about the bitter irony of it all should I actually encounter a psycho (or ten) and end up in some serial killer's refrigerator as a cartoonist casserole. But I had already opened my big mouth, and now I had to go through with it. To chase away the shadows, I busied myself with arranging the details of the California trip and deciding what cities I would target next with my "Mooch" letter.

I sent similar letters to Cleveland and Raleigh, North Carolina, with similar results. Almost immediately I had offers of plane tickets, places to stay, free lunches, parties. One guy in Cleveland said he was a pilot with his own plane and would be willing to fly me to Pittsburgh if I wanted. I'd gotten a fair amount of E-mail from Pittsburgh, so I accepted his offer. Another guy from Cleveland wrote to say he was a liquor distributor and though he couldn't give me plane tickets, he would throw in a case of gourmet wine to anyone who would.

A woman in Raleigh wrote to say she had plenty of frequent flyer miles and would love to send me a voucher. She was also willing to let me stay at her house, set up the book signings for me, and solicit the local media.

My book tour idea actually seemed to be working. Who would've thought so many people would be willing to cough up plane tickets, rides, and guest rooms for a veritable stranger? I was beginning to get a trickle of media attention in the form of newspapers wanting to do articles about it when I came to their town. I sensed I was on to something big, and it looked as though it could quite possibly get a good deal bigger. I was so proud of myself.

I'd never been known as a marketing genius. In fact, I've always considered myself to be too "artistic" to do anything that made good business sense. I'd always been the sort of person who has trouble turning two nickels into a dime, much less coming up with a good nationwide marketing idea. So now that my kooky mooch tour idea was working, I was stoked! I was still convinced the whole thing was a fluke, that when I had stood up unexpectedly from my computer table and felt that stabbing sensation in my brain, I'd accidentally intercepted an idea on its way to someone else's head. I was certain that somewhere in Dallas was a guy whose livelihood depended on his marketing creativity who was on the verge of suicide because he couldn't think of a damned thing.

Who knows, maybe the whole thing was a supernaturally

engineered switch. Maybe when I came up with this tour idea, he was sitting at his computer terminal across town, hypnotized by a slowly rotating image of Pat Sajak where his screen saver should be. Wherever the idea came from, and however sorry I felt for this hypothetical schlub across town, I wasn't going to lose sleep over it. For once, I had done something smart, and I was going to revel in it!

I started working like mad to make arrangements, and, little by little, everything was falling into place. But as the first dates of my tour approached, I began to have trouble sleeping.

THREE

Cannibals, Zombies, Wackos, & the Power of Fruit

L ike mildew on the walls of a shower, my lifelong fear of strangers began to creep back into my mind. No matter how hard I tried, I couldn't eradicate it completely. Sure, the main phobia was gone from the smooth surfaces of my psyche, but it wouldn't come out of the grout between the tiles, no matter how hard I scrubbed. I was beginning to have nightmares about the sort of people I would be staying with.

With my nights filled with these and other images of catastrophe, my thoughts during the day were not much different. What if some of the people are flakes and don't show up? What if they are crazed drug addicts and assume I'm the same? And what if they *aren't* wackos, but completely boring, mindless zombies? What will I say to them? How can I bear to be face to face with nothing but random, unpredictable strangers for more than a week? I'll have to use other people's bathrooms! They'll see me with my hair wet! What if I accidentally leave a pair of underpants under someone's bed? What if pictures of me in the shower suddenly appear on the Internet?

As the days crawled by, I was coming closer to meltdown.

The toilet is out behind the munitions shed and there's plenty of field rations in the kitchen if you're hungry — make yourself at home. If you need anything, I'll be out in the woods shooting at lifesize cut outs of the President...

GIVE ME LIBERTY

OR GIVE YOU DEATH.

I had constant thoughts of canceling the entire trip, claiming I'd gotten sick. "I'll just stay home!" I thought.

But as tempting and comforting as that seemed, it filled me with feelings of inadequacy and self-loathing. I had finally come up with a cool idea and I wasn't going to throw it away out of fear! What kind of a pathetic worm would do a thing like that? *I'm going!*

But how could I put myself in the hands of a nine-day parade of virtual strangers and potential lunatics? What if one of them *is* a serial killer or a pervert? What if I am captured by a cult of suburban cannibals? *I'm staying home!*

But people were expecting me. They were excited about my visit. They'd planned parties! They'd spent their hard-earned money on chips and salsa, for God's sake! How could I look at myself in the mirror knowing I had disappointed them? *I'm going!*

But what if I disappeared and ended up on *Unsolved Mysteries and Practical Jokes*? My children were too young to be left fatherless! *I'm staying!*

This waffling worthy of the International House of Pancakes went on hour after hour, day after day. I drove my wife nuts with my constant analysis and reanalysis of the situation. At one point, she threatened to go on the trip herself, just to get away from me.

To a mentally healthy person, putting oneself through such an ordeal over "shyness" probably seems like a ludicrous waste of valuable brain cells. But like any panic attack due to phobia, logic and common sense have no place in the process. Clearly, I needed major psychoanalysis to uncover the root of my fears, but with only a few days to go before I was to leave, there simply wasn't time. I had to make up my mind.

Not surprisingly, the resolution to my problem came from beyond the realm of the normal.

I was foraging for something to eat one afternoon through the stacks of clutter and carnage that is my kitchen, when, to my pleasant surprise, I found a piece of fruit that didn't seem too far past its prime. I thought it was a peach, although in retrospect I think it was more likely a nectarine with a newly acquired coat of fur. As I inspected it for signs of edibility, I noticed a large, soft, brown spot on one side with a strange, but familiar shape to it. Sure enough, it was the face of Sajak, attempting to contact me through the miracle of biological decay.

Whereas I might normally have thrown the peach (or whatever it was) into the trash, deeming it unfit for human consumption, in this case I took Pat's visage as a sign that I should indeed eat the fruit, thus gaining courage, or insight, or some other useful quality that might help me solve my dilemma. So I closed my eyes, whispered what had become my mantra, "Time to spin the wheel," and bit into Sajak's face.

What happened next was four blocks the other side of weird. I dropped to the floor in a trance and was instantly thrown back into my childhood; reliving the years in a matter of moments, reviewing the formative events of my past, seeing with supernatural clarity the interlocking influences of my youth. In this way, I was able to achieve in a single afternoon what would have taken years of therapy and hypnotic regression to attain. Finally, the roots of my fear of strangers was laid out before me like a photo spread in *People* magazine.

To put this revelation into proper perspective, it will be necessary for you to attempt to see what I saw as I lay in a semiconscious state on my kitchen floor. Though what I experienced was highly visual and as realistic as any three-dimensional image in a Viewmaster, what you will see will be mostly words on a page and a few drawings. I don't think it will be necessary for you to lie on the floor as I take you back in time and recount the events that led to my present condition. (But if you have your heart set on it, be my guest.) So indulge me, if you will, and shield your eyes if needed, for I am about to divulge certain facts about myself that *no one* should have to read.

FOUR

In the Shadow of the Pterodactyl

On the morning of October 7, 1958, the sun rose slowly over the hideous specter of another day in the Bible Belt. In a small apartment in Kansas City, a city once called "Cowtown" because of some relationship it probably had with cows, a young woman sat up in bed and said, "Fred, I think it's time."

My mother was that woman, and "Fred" was her husband, as well as the man she believed to be my father. She cried out to him as she was feeling the first of many pains I would give her over the next several decades. What she didn't know, however, was that I was about to be born. Well, she knew *someone* was about to be born, but she didn't know that it was me, specifically. For instance, a year and a half earlier, on April 9, the same thing had happened, and it turned out to be my older sister. But this time, it was my turn.

My birth was a great embarrassment to everyone involved. It was the first (and I wish I could say the only) time I appeared in a room full of strangers, soaking wet and buck naked. It took my mother nearly three days in bed to recover from the shame, and even then she had to be taken out of the hospital in a wheelchair.

And so it came to pass that October 10, 1958, was the first time I put myself in the care of relative strangers and attempted to make myself at home. That first time was so traumatic I have no recollection of it, or of the next few years.

My memories begin at the age of three or four, but most of the images are spotty and incomplete. I recall numerous early experiences with an older, white-haired man in a dark uniform who was trapped inside a big, glowing, electronic box. He sometimes entertained me with a puppet or a dancing bear, and Ping-Pong balls used to regularly rain down upon him. I don't recall his name but have since come to refer to him as "Colonel Kangaroo."

My earliest cohesive memories are of church. Elaborate stained-glass windows, massive statues, vaulted ceilings, the stench of smoking incense, the long, hard, wooden benches called "pews" (a name that derives from the sound people often make the first time they encounter the incense).

As a five-year-old I started the first grade at Our Lady of Misery, Oppression, and Bingo Catholic School in a small town called Boredom, Oklahoma. We were required to attend an hour-long mass given in Latin each morning before school. The classes themselves were taught by priests (called "Father") and nuns (called "Sister"). Part of our regular curriculum each day was catechism, which is religion class, so it wasn't too far removed from church, except that it was in English. On Sunday, my parents gagged my sisters and me, shackled us in our finest clothes, and dragged us back to church again. For years, I thought my sisters and I actually lived at church and were occasionally sent to this other place to visit our parents. It seemed a logical assumption—there were numerous fathers and sisters at school and church, only one father and a few sisters at home. There was only one mother in either location, but the one at school and church was called "Mother Superior," so surely she *had* to be boss over the one at home.

Saturdays, for some reason, had slipped through the system. My sisters and I were convinced this was an oversight of some sort and never discussed this phenomenon out loud for fear that calling attention to it would make someone come up with a reason to get us to church on that day, too. On Saturdays we got up early, walked through the house quietly and reverently, eyes to the ground, hands folded in front of us, not wishing to draw attention to ourselves. We gave each other breakfast quickly and silently by standing facing each other, tilting our heads back with our eyes closed and our mouths open. We would then take turns placing a single corn flake on the other person's tongue, until we'd each finished a bowl. (It seems strange now, but at the time it was simply a habit that seemed as natural as kneeling before plaster replicas of Bible characters.)

That ritual behind us, we left to play at *other* kids' houses until dark, not daring to return home even for lunch. If no other kid could play, we would spend the day skulking through the neighborhood, moving silently through the shadows, avoiding open spaces of any kind for fear we'd be spotted, captured, bathed, and dragged back to church.

One might be inclined to wonder if my kitchen-floor vision was exaggerating the amount of time I spent in church as a child. I must confess I wondered the same thing. True, the vision was fundamentally a consolidation of my own memories of my life, but couldn't these memories have been inflated with time? To get to the bottom of this question, I have since spent a great deal of time in therapy trying to determine the accuracy of these memories. But as a result of the quality time and hard-earned cash I spent with some of our nation's finest mental health care professionals, I have indeed come to trust my memories as authentic and accurate.

The deciding moment for me came only a few months ago when I was in very heavy hypno-regression therapy three times a week at the North American Psychiatric Center for the Chronically Self-Absorbed. During a particularly grisly session, I successfully regressed all the way back to 1964 and finally came face to face with what is now commonly called the "inner child." It was a major breakthrough in my treatment, and the entire team of psychiatrists involved in my case were on pins and needles as they anxiously waited for me to ask said child the important questions we'd all waited so long to be answered. The exhilaration evaporated, however, as my inner child said only, "Can't talk. In church."

I pressed on in an urgent whisper, asking about just a few of the more pivotal issues in my life, but Sister Mary Pterodactyl flashed a look at us that would have snapped the rusty lock off a tool-shed door, and we had to shut up.

Not ready to give up, I ventured back a few more times, but it was always the same story. "Can't talk. In church." I began to notice during these later visits that each time my inner child had been moved closer to where Sister Mary Pterodactyl sat. I knew from experience that if he continued to draw her attention in church, he would eventually be sitting *right next* to Sister. Once this had happened, you were one infraction away from being taken to the convent and eaten by the nuns. Rumor had it that they were not just strict, they were carnivorous.

But back to my fruit-induced vision:

As a result of a technicality due to our recent move to Oklahoma, I was to skip kindergarten and start first grade. The previous fall, in Missouri, I wasn't quite old enough to start kindergarten. In this new town, at five years old, I was just barely old enough to start the first grade, so I did, even though I had never been left in the care of strangers in my life. But in my family, no one was ever allowed to take second best or the easy way out, so first grade it was to be. I suppose my dad figured it would get me to the White House that much sooner. They would have sent me straight to Oklahoma State University had the law allowed (but that would have entailed the installation of shorter drinking fountains and urinals, and funds for public education in Oklahoma were scarce).

I remembered the profound sense of abandonment I felt as my mother led me into the damp, cold, dark, torch-lit school-room that first day and introduced me to my new keeper, who was dressed in black and had a face like a flesh-eating dinosaur. I begged my mother to stay; she said she couldn't. I pleaded with her to stand out in the hall where I could see her through the tiny food slot in the massive iron door; she said it wasn't allowed. I beseeched her to take me back home with her; she said it was out of her hands. I cried as they shackled me to my desk and the moss-covered door clanged shut behind her. I didn't fully understand then, but it was the last time I would see her. Until nearly 3:30 P.M.

My horror only intensified in the coming days as I learned that I was not only expected to endure this agony quietly and politely, I was also expected to learn to decode and decipher a complex system of glyphs and scribbles and convert them into meaningful language. Sister Mary Pterodactyl called this mysterious and ancient practice "reading," and as near as I could tell it was a system she employed specifically to blow out the cerebral cortex of small children.

And it didn't end there. Once I had given in and learned this little reading game, these so-called educators still wouldn't let me go. No matter how much useless information I stored in my gradually swelling brain, there was always one more thing I was supposed to know before I would be released, and after I'd learn *that*, there was one more. And so on, and so on, in a never-ending parade of information, for twelve years. It was enough to knock the childish glee out of any small boy, and knock it out of me it did. By the time I had been paroled, or "graduated" as they called it, I was bitter, cynical, depressed, and tired most of the time. I had begun to act like an adult.

A very prominent aspect of my life since my earliest years has always been my desire to draw. Since I was very young,

drawing was my favorite pastime (next to thoughts of Julie
Newmar as Catwoman), so back in the first grade, when Sister
Mary Pterodactyl said, "Take out your crayons, it's time for
art," I was off and running without any need for further
instruction. She would then drone on about that day's assignment (because God forbid you would allow an impressionable
youngster the sinful experience of unrestrained creativity) and
I would be midway through a visual representation of an epic
tale of the Old West before anyone else had even started. She
would usually say something like, "Today I want you to draw a
picture of the way you think Jesus might look after you've lied
to your parents," and I'd never hear a word of what she'd said.
I was already lost in my own little world of cowboys and
Indians (and Julie Newmar).

So while every other kid in class was drawing a picture of a
handsome, well-groomed, bearded, Caucasian Jesus with
bloody thorns sticking into his head and big, doughnut-sized
tears rolling down his cheeks, I was drawing the gunfight at the
OK Corral. In all fairness, there was one other kid who never
followed the assignment, either. He was Lenny Abismo, who
never drew anything but overlapping blue and orange circles
and squares of various sizes until the paper was completely
filled and no more white was showing. It looked like some
hideous modern-art interpretation of a violent accident involving the Miami Dolphins. Lenny drew this same picture every
time, robotically, no matter how the nuns talked to him, pun-
ished him, beat him, or dragged him around the parking lot tied
to the back of the convent station wagon. (I ran into Lenny
years later in prison, but that's another story.)

Once, during just such an art class, I was happily working
away on my depiction of an Old West bronc' bustin', when
Sister Mary Pterodactyl came slithering up the aisle from
behind me like a black mamba, grabbed my picture off my
desk, and began hissing questions into my startled ear.

"What Bible story does this represent?" she spit.

Too frightened to respond, I called on one of the alternate personalities I had developed to endure verbal abuse from members

of the clergy. I believe it was "Ricky, the crippled slave boy" who answered in this instance. "I don't know. It's just a bunch of horses," he quavered.

"Why is this one so big?!" she belched, flames lapping at the edge of my ear as she pointed to a horse I had drawn in the extreme foreground.

"I don't know," Ricky cleverly replied for me.

She proceeded to hiss one of her stock lectures about the importance of listening carefully and following directions and how it could only lead to eternal torture in the fiery abyss if I didn't, and then she goose-stepped away from my desk with the drawing clasped tightly in her claw.

Despite the magnitude of terror I had experienced during this one-on-one confrontation with authority incarnate, all I could think of was that she had taken my drawing!

I was wounded! I was incensed! True, she was the autonomous, all-powerful, supreme dictator of my life while I was at school, but it just didn't seem right that she would just grab my drawing and walk away with it! How would she feel if I snuck up behind her while she was grading papers and grabbed that giant rosary she wore around her waist?

"What kind of fashion statement are you trying to make with this!" I would shout.

"I don't know . . . I . . . all the nuns wear one."

"If 'all the nuns' were swallowing rusty nails, would you do that, too?"

"I don't know . . . I guess not," she would cower.

I'd snatch the rosary from around her waist and hold it in my tiny fist. "Next time, wear a belt!" I'd command, and storm away.

I was so upset by this art-snatching episode that I sat at my desk like a stone until I was suddenly awakened by her chilling and malevolent voice calling me from the front of the class.

"Mr. Piraro, you'll stay after school today until you've learned to follow directions."

As far as I had always known, Mr. Piraro was my dad. But a quick glance around the room told me that he was nowhere to be found, and I figured out quickly that she must have meant me.

"Come and sit in this chair for the rest of the afternoon, please," she commanded smugly.

"This chair" was an uncomfortable, kid-sized, wooden seat without a back, positioned next to Sister's desk, facing the class. It was as close to the Colonial "stocks" as 1960s Oklahoma law would allow for children. (Luckily for me, I had started school one year after the new law had been passed and the stocks were removed from the classrooms.)

I was further mortified by this latest development. Not even Julie Newmar could calm me now. Sister M.P. had always used "staying after school" as a threat. On many occasions she had explained to the class that she didn't care *how* long we had to stay after school, she *lived* at the convent (which adjoined the school and church) so she was *already home*. You could just *stay all night* if that's what it took for you to learn your lesson.

All I could think of was how furious my parents would be if, at the age of five, I came staggering through the front door of our house at dawn after having spent the night at school. I had to think fast, and, for a first-grader, that can only be achieved with the aid of massive amounts of adrenaline (or a really big candy bar). By this time, I had plenty enough of that to do the job. My eyes were as big as sewer pipes, sweat shot off my face like industrial irrigation sprinklers, the buzz-cut hair on my head stood out like the fur on the back of a rabid Chihuahua.

Sister was a couple of feet to my right, grading papers, while I sat facing the class, the ticking of the clock echoing through the room. The other kids looked at me soberly as one might gaze upon a man being strapped into the electric chair. I stared blankly past them, wheels almost visibly turning in my brain.

Suddenly, I had a plan!

My hand shot up. (Step one of my plan.)

"Yes, Mr. Piraro?"

"May I use the rest room, please?" I squeaked. (Step two.)

"Yes, but be quick about it," she answered calmly, hardly looking up from her desk.

I stood up and walked steadily out the door and down the school's empty hallway. I turned left at the library and headed for the bathrooms. I held my breath, passed the bathrooms without ever looking back, and went straight through the doors at the end of the hall to the outside. (Step three was complete!)

I was free!

I skirted from bush to tree to shadow all the way home. I was good at moving through the neighborhood silently and secretly from the Saturdays I'd spent avoiding the church patrol. When I arrived at the edge of my yard, some ten blocks from the school, I suddenly realized I had run out of steps in my plan.

What did I do now? I needed a step four! I couldn't just walk into the house and pretend nothing was wrong—it was the middle of the day. In fact, I didn't really know what time it was, as I couldn't tell time yet. On top of all that, I had left my jacket and my Daniel Boone Starring Fess Parker lunch box at school. I needed a new plan. Life as a fugitive was harder than I'd thought it would be.

I stayed crouched in the bushes next to my house for who knows how long, waiting for something to occur to me. Eventually, I spotted other children heading up the sidewalks. Salvation! School was out! I waited for my sister to come by, then just slipped into the house behind her unnoticed. So far, so good. I could simply pretend I'd forgotten my jacket and lunch box at school, something I would typically do in those days, and no one would be the wiser. My plan had been perfect, step four had taken care of itself. Step five was in full swing: Enjoy the rest of my life.

Around 4:30 that afternoon, I witnessed in horror the surprise emergence of step six, which entailed explaining to my mother why Sister Mary Pterodactyl had called to report I had disappeared from school an hour early after having gotten in trouble and being told to stay after.

Now I was really on the spot. I had less than a few seconds to hatch a new plan and execute it with calm, cool precision. But after my success earlier that day, I had built up a little confidence. I *knew* I could do it. The seconds ticked by. My mind raced. My mother waited. I opened my mouth. I began to speak.

I burst into tears and collapsed against my mother and confessed the entire sordid event, from the beginning of art class and the theft of my drawing to the image of walking home at daybreak through Boredom's goblin-infested streets. It was then that I discovered the classic defense technique of "extreme self-deprecation," that wondrous thing that happens when you're so hard on yourself your parents don't have the heart to punish you. It was to become my favorite tactic throughout my childhood and adolescence (and wasn't abandoned for good until I realized its ineffectiveness in the real world at the age of twenty-four, after a visit to traffic court).

But on that tragic afternoon in 1964, it worked like a charm! Mother felt too sorry for me to punish me any further. Instead, she calmed me down, went back to the phone, and came back a while later with a compromise: I was to stay after school the next day, quietly and politely for just a few minutes, and all would be forgiven. And Mom was even going to go to school, have a chat with Sister M.P., and get my drawing back. And also, I was supposed to do my best to listen to Sister in the future and follow instructions or something like that. I don't remember that part very well.

The ridiculous end to this turgid tale is that, although Sister M.P. was upset that I had once again ignored her art assignment, the real reason she had taken the drawing from me was to show my parents what she believed was evidence of a burgeoning talent in art. Having run into me around the house once or twice during the previous five years, this was something of which they were already vaguely aware.

When faced with the choice between encouraging a child to develop his talent or attempting to beat him down to the level of the average kid, Sister M.P. didn't have to think twice about which course of action to pursue. To people like her in those days, blind conformity was the greatest virtue to which anyone could aspire. For her, the choice was simple: Chastise me publicly and immediately, praise me in private to a third party later.

But I bear no resentment toward her now, and seek no revenge. I'm too big a person for that. She was just a woman in a black dress, her head wrapped up tightly (perhaps a little *too* tightly) with only her face showing, living a celibate life with a bunch of other women dressed the same way in a bleak, austere, little building in the corner of a parking lot outside a church in Boredom, Oklahoma, talking several times each day to invisible beings, trying to teach the heathen children of strangers the value of mindless compliance to authority, and doing the best job she knew how.

I wish her well and wonder sometimes what became of her and if she is still alive. I even sometimes regret all those years that I had the gay porno magazines delivered monthly to the convent in her name.

So began the six years of parochial school I was to endure at the hands of rigid, authoritarian celibates. Growing up in this manner, in this part of the country, wasn't a cakewalk. In fact, there was very little cake involved at all, as I remember.

But somehow I managed to avoid the outward appearance of what most people have come to expect from those of us raised in this region. When I meet my readers on the road, whether at bookstores during signings or in airport rest rooms between flights, they frequently ask me, "Where are you from?" When I tell them I grew up in Oklahoma but now live in Dallas, the reaction is always the same. Somewhere between "Really?" and "Liar!"

This reaction is particularly pronounced on the coasts, where people tend to think that everyone from Oklahoma and Texas is an illiterate, toothless, pickup-truck-driving, goat-roping, cowboy-hat-wearing, trailer-park-residing, gay-bashing, UFO-spotting believer in the resurrection of Elvis.

This is, of course, a complete misconception. Every person in an area the size of Oklahoma and Texas could not possibly be exactly alike, and having lived here for more than thirty years, I can personally attest to this. In my life, I have known nearly *two dozen* native Texahomans who do not fit the above description at all. And there are probably even more.

Stereotypes of this sort about the good people of Oklahoma and Texas are unfair and un-American, in my opinion. And I believe I speak for everyone from this part of the country when I say that we resent this sort of bigoted snobbery and would very much appreciate it if you'd open your eyes and minds and stop confusing us with Arkansas.

In truth, this part of the country *is* a tad conservative. They don't call it the Bible Belt for nothing, and many people here do, in fact, wear Bibles on their belts, which is where the name came from. Everyone is familiar with the large, hubcap-sized, metal belt buckles that good ol' boys wear, but what many out-siders fail to realize is that these familiar accessories actually harbor Bibles inside. This handy accessory has a variety of on-the-spot uses, from settling complex theological disputes to propping open a barn door while you put your hay bailer away.

Being raised as I was in the epicenter of this deeply spiri-tual environment, during my rebellious adolescence I became fascinated with the religious beliefs of some of my Protestant schoolmates. By this time we had moved to Tulsa, and I was attending a public high school.

Completely disenchanted with my Catholic roots and feel-ing typically rebellious, at the age of sixteen or so I found great satisfaction in defying my parents and seeking spiritual answers elsewhere. While at that time Catholicism was still very much a secondhand experience—the priest performing all religious functions while the congregation watched in silence—my friends belonged to churches that purported to conjure up all sorts of cool special effects. Faith healing, speaking in tongues, miracles of all sorts, these were the spectacles my friends claimed to witness on a regular basis. In the pre-video-game era of the early seventies, I found the prospect of this kind of action to be mighty appealing. The more they talked, the more I wanted to hear. But the one thing they didn't tell me about their churches was the heavy emphasis they placed on evangelism, which was, of course, exactly what they were doing to me.

This period of spiritual investigation on my part did not sit well with my parents. The first time I came home from school and announced that I was going to attend a Protestant "Bible" church with a friend, they spontaneously burst into flames.

Eleven months later, when they were released from the hospital, fully recovered albeit unrecognizable, we resumed our discussion. By this time I had been going to the special effects church a couple of times a week for a good while and had become something of a "teen for Jesus." My parents soon realized there wasn't much they could do to stop me and resigned themselves to riding it out, hoping it was just a phase. After all, I was still celebrating the same holidays (Christmas, Easter), wearing the same jewelry (cross), and using the same instruction manual (Bible), and they figured it could have been a lot worse. I could have been hopping up and down at the airport with a shaved head and an orange dress, banging a tambourine.

For the short time that I enlisted in this evangelical army, however, the one thing I was never comfortable with was the evangelizing. My friends had sold the church to me with the promise of special effects, faith healing and miracles and such. But on a daily basis there was a great deal of pressure to proselytize and very little in the way of actual, before-your-eyes, show-stopping miracles. There was Jo Beth Morgan, who came forward at the end of just about every sermon to be healed of an undiagnosable pain in her shoulder blade, or some far more nebulous location, and she did cry and faint an awful lot, but it was hardly like watching a beggar's leg grow back or a leper's sores disappear before your eyes. In all fairness, much of the problem was due to the conspicuous lack of lepers and one-legged beggars in the upper middle-class suburbs of twentieth-century Tulsa, but I still went home hungry for entertainment.

Superfly & the Goddess

Hurtling back from my fruit-prompted vision to the present day, I regained consciousness briefly to find myself lying on the kitchen floor of my Dallas home. My eight-year-old daughter was standing over me, shaking me frantically, a shriek of desperation and panic spewing from her mouth.

"Daddy! Daddy! Wake up!" she cried.

I opened my eyes and looked at her as she bent over me, but I was powerless to speak. I made a grunting sound that resembled a camel being punched in the stomach.

"Daddy, wake up! I need you!"

Parental alarms went off in my head, and I struggled to focus my eyes and leap to her aid. Ancient instincts of offspring preservation came screaming to the front of my cranium and urged me to immediate action.

In my mind I was shouting, "What is it, honey? Tell me! Daddy's here!" But all I could manage to blurt out was "Glurgh!"

"Where are the Oreos?" she shouted, her eyes wide.

I grunted again as if to say "I don't know" and let my head

fall back onto the linoleum floor. Satisfied that I would be of no further use, she stepped over me and returned to her daily television-watching marathon (for which she currently holds several North American records).

I let my eyes fall slowly closed as I drifted back into my trance, focusing on the soothing smile on Pat Sajak's face that seemed permanently burned on the insides of my eyelids.

The next memory Pat brought me was from my glorious high school days in the now deservedly ridiculed early seventies. I was attending one of the first magnet school programs in the country, which Tulsa had started as a court-ordered, experimental alternative to busing.

For you younger readers who aren't old enough to remember when communities all over the country were experimenting with forced busing as an answer to racial unrest, and for you older readers who've taken too many recreational drugs to remember anything at all, busing worked like this: Cities would discuss the disparity between rich, predominantly white school districts and poor, predominantly black school districts. They would agree that this disparity was unfair and detrimental to the entire community. They recognized that offering an inferior education to the poor would only serve to perpetuate poverty and racial unrest in the future. They readily agreed that something must be done.

As a result, they mysteriously concluded that the solution would be to take an arbitrarily chosen number of children from both school districts and swap them. In this way, a handful of minority children would get a decent education in a socially stressful environment, while a handful of white children got a lousy education in a socially stressful environment. (Sure. That would clearly solve everything!) Redrawing bus routes is certainly a more permanent answer to racial discrimination than bringing the inferior schools up to standard. And a lot less expensive, too, come to think of it.

In a fit of mass antilogic, cities all over America began doing this. But in Oklahoma, for equally illogical reasons, they did something else.

A very big and powerful judge, probably the king of the judges, said that if Tulsa created one racially balanced school, open to the entire city by application, the city wouldn't have to do anything to any of the other schools or bus anyone against his or her will. At the time, this passed as good news to everyone.

So what Tulsa did was take an old, run-down high school called Booker T. Washington on the black side of town (as late as the early seventies, Tulsa was still remarkably segregated; nearly all whites lived on the south side and all blacks on the north) and turn it into a really cool high school that everyone would want to go to. The city hired the best teachers it could find (many with college degrees), equipped the school with the latest technology of the day (electric typewriters instead of manual, film projectors with sound instead of slide projectors with accompanying record players, indoor rest rooms, electric ovens in the cafeteria to replace the wood-burning stoves), and set up an avant-garde curriculum (photography, where you could walk around the campus every day and take pictures of stuff; TV production, where you could learn to point a video camera at something stationary and push a button; psychology, where you could talk about how much you hated your parents and pretend you were taking a science class; creative writing, where you could write anything you wanted without regard to grammar or punctuation and pretend you were in an English class; and pottery, or "ashtray making class," as it was more commonly called).

You had to apply to get in and have fairly decent grades, and the school had to be kept racially balanced at half white, half black. (Bear in mind that this was before local authorities had discovered or named any other racial groups.) Since Booker T. Washington was already the home school for some eight hundred black students, the challenge was to get rid of half of them and attract a balancing number of white students from the city's south side.

The experiment worked perfectly, as the white kids who didn't fit in at their home school for whatever reason scrambled to get into Booker T. On opening day in the fall of 1973, the school was attended by four hundred white and four hundred black students. There were news crews from all of the local TV stations and newspapers, as well as a couple of the big networks. We were told we were making history as the country's first voluntarily integrated "magnet" school, a brilliant new alternative to forced busing.

What they didn't mention was the four hundred disgruntled, displaced black students who were bused against their will to other schools in the city to make room for the white kids. These kids often found themselves to be nearly hopelessly disadvantaged academically and socially. But few people seemed to notice the irony of how large a role forced busing was playing in the brilliant new alternative to forced busing.

That skeleton aside, Booker T. was a paradise for the gifted, the talented, the unathletic, the fashion-challenged, and a number of other categories for geekoid misfits. I, personally, was looking for a more artistic and creative environment than the heavily regulated, all-white, socialite and/or jock-driven high school in my own neighborhood. While I wasn't exactly a misfit, I certainly wasn't a candidate for prom king or varsity quarterback, either, and had no qualms about trying out the experimental new school at the other end of town, sight unseen. I approached the decision with complete confidence and nonchalance until my bus pulled up in front of the school on the first day.

As I sat looking at the campus and its student population milling around out front, I was suddenly stricken with an all too familiar fear. While most of my friends were walking through a familiar neighborhood to a crowd of familiar kids in front of a familiar school, I had been riding a bus into a part of town I'd never seen before, to a school I hadn't even heard of just six months earlier, and was about to negotiate with a crowd of strange kids of a different race.

I felt remarkably as I did on the first day of first grade when my mother dropped me off at Catholic school. I asked the bus driver if he would stand out in the hall all day where I could see him, but his response was fairly similar to what my mother's had been, with less sugar coating. So I got off the bus and made my way through the crowd of Afros, shag haircuts, and bell-bottoms, hoping no one would notice how scared I was.

I hadn't thought it would matter, but I was suddenly acutely aware of the fact that in my sheltered, white, suburban existence, I had never been in a situation where whites were anything but a daunting majority. In fact, I don't think I'd ever seen more than a single family of black people at one time. Then something even stranger occurred to me: I couldn't remember ever actually having *met* a black person. (I use the term "black" here because in the early seventies that was the socially acceptable term of choice. At that time, it had been fairly recently updated from "Negro," the approved moniker of the fifties and early sixties. At this writing, "African-American" is the politically correct title, but by the time you read this book, it may well be "melanin advantaged.")

Crossing the schoolyard slowly but steadily, I felt ashamed to be so nervous and disoriented. "Am I a racist?" I asked myself. "No, I'm a chicken," I countered, "I'd be just as nervous on the first day of *any* new school." And I knew I was right. "But these black kids intimidate me more than the white kids." "They're more unfamiliar, that's all," I reasoned with myself. "And cut yourself some slack; these are poor, urban, streetwise teenagers. You've grown up in small towns and suburbs, you've never been around large numbers of kids like that of *any* color." That, too, was true.

On top of all that was the fact that at 5'6" (I had yet to attain my full, towering height of 5'8"), I was shorter than the average fifteen-year-old male Homo sapiens. Walking through a crowd of large, unfamiliar mammals of any race, species, or economic status was always a little daunting. The problem was particularly pronounced in this crowd because it was 1973 and virtually every black kid in attendance was wearing platform shoes and as big an Afro as he or she could muster. These fashion accessories could easily bring the average male to a height of seven feet or more.

I moved on to my first class and began school with a mixed sense of nausea and excitement (which is, come to think of it, pretty much the way I face every day of my life, even now). But very soon I became adjusted to the new environment and even began to relish it.

As the weeks of the first semester slipped by, I experienced a growing sense of accomplishment. I had conquered a strange new school in a formerly forbidden part of town! I was getting lots of extra attention, as my friends back in my home neighborhood constantly asked me about it. What was it like? Were there fights? Did I have any cool classes? Did I have any black friends? Some of them had wanted to go to Booker T., too, but their parents wouldn't let them. We all knew what that meant, but we didn't talk about it.

As this was only a few years after the social revolution of the late sixties, teenagers identified racism as a problem of the "older generation." The proper attitude of the young, would-be hipster was one of complete and utter (and often completely pretentious) acceptance and love of all people. Except racists. We honestly believed that racism in America would be wiped out completely as soon as our parents' generation died off. The more into "peace" and "love" you were, the cooler you were. We wanted this so much that we even went to the extent of pretending to be oblivious to race entirely.

I played this role to the hilt. When asked by my parents or a friend if a particular person I had mentioned was black or white, I would look wistfully into the sky and say, "I . . . I don't know. I haven't noticed." My friends pretended to buy this answer with the appropriate nonchalance, but my parents were not so easily fooled.

"What do you mean you *don't know?*" they would snap,

justifiably feeling their intelligence had been insulted. "Do you remember what he looks like, or don't you?"

"Ye-e-eah . . . ," I would say slowly, as if I didn't know what they were getting at.

"Can you picture him in your mind?"

"I guess so . . . ," still pretending I hadn't quite understood their point.

"When you see his face in your mind, is it *dark* brown or *light* brown?" they would ask in their best trial lawyer demeanor.

Armed with the face of one who is lost in the oblivious ecstasy of peace and love, I would reply melodramatically, "Does it really matter?"

It was a difficult time for my parents. It wasn't important to them if my friends were black or white, but they just could not stand my ludicrous charade of racial naiveté. But while my parents worried I was becoming a total buffoon, to my neighborhood friends I was "one happening dude."

I was the brave, hip, liberal guy who went to an experimental school with black kids, helping to undo the hundreds of years of damage our evil ancestors had done. Glorifying this new, open-minded, antiestablishment institution was a very popular pastime among my neighborhood crowd. I added to the mystique by adopting what were considered black fashions and expressions. For months, I went around saying, "Wha's happ'nin', dude?" and speaking with a pseudoblack dialect. On the fashion front, I was among the first white kids in all of Tulsa to begin wearing five-inch-high platform shoes. This brought me to a grand total of 5'11", and, for the first time in my life, I was beginning to feel like a real man.

I also had a newfound sense of pride in my genetic makeup. Being half Sicilian and plagued since birth with stubbornly curly hair, I could never manage a decent British Invasion hairdo. I had spent my junior high years trying to comb it down into some sort of Beatles look, only to end up with a frizzy, poofy hair helmet that made me look much more like a local TV weatherman than Paul McCartney. And forget trying to grow it really long like Gregg Allman or the guys in Grand

Funk Railroad; I'd have had more luck growing antlers. My hair didn't get "longer," it got "bigger." But at Booker T. I discovered a hairstyle that I had been *born* to wear: the Afro.

This spherical mass of protein projectiles not only added to my growing reputation at home on the white side of town, it also got me noticed at school. I was the only Caucasian in the entire school that first year who had a "'fro." The black girls were fascinated with me and were always asking to touch my hair or braid it. This unsolicited attention from the opposite sex was like a bucket of gasoline on the raging fire of my adolescent hormones. My Afro also had the added benefit of increasing my height by five inches. Could life get any better than this?

As a matter of fact, it could. Very soon after my hair had grown to a length where it actually started looking more like an Afro and not so much like Greg Brady or Horshack from *Welcome Back Kotter*, I discovered an alternate use for it that added yet another dimension to my reputation as "that weird white kid."

Lord knows what made me think of this, but what I began to do was take a couple of dozen old pencils that had been sharpened down to a length of two or three inches and insert them into my Afro from the back, point facing forward, so that they were lying against my scalp horizontally. (See illustration on the following page) Invisible to the naked eye, I would leave them there until the right moment presented itself.

Later, when I was sitting at a table in the cafeteria, for instance, talking casually to a friend, I would suddenly jerk my head forward a couple of inches and stop abruptly, as when sneezing. This would send all twenty-some pencils hurling out of my hair onto the table in front of me like the Ping-Pong balls on the old Captain Kangaroo show. I used this gag sparingly so that no one ever expected it to happen, but I soon became known not only as "that weird white guy with the big 'fro" but "that weird white guy with the big 'fro that gots stuff falling all out of it and shit."

At the peak of my Afro, it was much bigger than a basket-

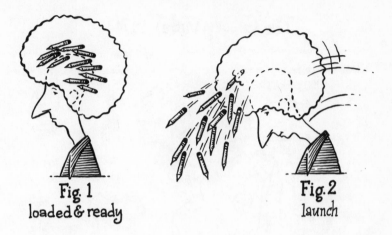

Fig. 1
loaded & ready

Fig. 2
launch

ball. To accessorize it I had taken to wearing a black, plastic Afro fork sticking up out of the back, the kind with a fist as a handle, meant to symbolize "black power." My wardrobe consisted of sparkly, "glitter-rock" shirts and satin, disco-style bell-bottoms. Dressed in this manner, and laboring under the misconception that I was somehow on the fashion vanguard, I was actually trying to get girls to go out with me.

I had failed to realize that only a handful of other whites at my school were subscribing to this look and that most people, both black and white, thought I was a complete idiot.

My folks, meanwhile, were once again experiencing daily seizures that probably took several years off the ends of their lives. While they certainly didn't want to seem bigoted or prejudiced in any way, and they knew enough to know that any substantial objection on their part was bound to be met by reinforced determination on mine, their son was turning into one of the Jackson Five before their very eyes. They dropped gentle hints from time to time about "not following the crowd" and "having the courage to be yourself," but these were lost on me. All along I thought they were complimenting my growth. Inside I was thinking, "Yeah! I'm finally discovering the *real* me!"

The "Groovy Dude", 1974

The "Fro"

Blue sunglasses, especially cool at night

Black, plastic afro fork with molded, 3-D "Black Power" fist.

(insert tab "A" into slot "B" for added grooviness)

Lime green, polyester shirt. (Half-life: 20,000 years)

Home-made leather choker

Black, sparkly t-shirt. (As comfortable as a steel-wool bikini.)

Fist of defiance

Shiney, silver, satin, skin-tight, hip-hugger bell bottoms (say it 5 times, fast)

Bell bottom blue jeans with filthy, tattered cuffs that drag the ground.

6-inch, platform shoes, as worn on T.V. by both Sonny & Cher.

Fortunately for all mankind, that particular version of the real me only lasted about nine months. My *Superfly* phase came to an abrupt end on a Sunday afternoon the following spring, and it went out with a whimper, not a bang.

My art teacher had arranged for a friend of mine and me to have an art show in an upstairs room of a local art gallery.

We were the two best artists in the school, and the show was a very exciting opportunity for us. We each hung ten or fifteen examples of our work, then scheduled a reception for a Sunday afternoon and invited special friends and family to come. I used this opportunity to try to impress a girl I had been silently worshiping for some time.

Her name was Celia, she was a year older than I, a couple of inches taller, and gorgeous. I used to cruise the halls looking for her, then fabricate excuses to talk to her. I was so good at making these meetings seem accidental that I was sure she had no idea how I felt about her. Getting her to come to my art show would be my chance to impress her with my artistic abilities and advance our relationship. I spent countless sleepless nights rehearsing what I was going to say and how I would say it, until I finally found just the right moment, and invited her.

I was leaning against a wall outside the art room talking to somebody and she wandered up and asked me if I'd seen the art teacher. To the best of my recollection, this was the first time she had ever initiated a conversation, so I felt an uncontrollable surge of confidence. Plus, we were right outside the art room, talking about the art teacher, so this was a perfect time to act as though I had just thought of inviting her. I opened my mouth and launched into my rehearsed invitation.

"Hey, I'm having an art reshow . . . reception . . . art show at this gallery with a reception Sunday this afternoon . . . this Sunday afternoon. Would you like to come?" I barked. The words sounded vaguely familiar to the ones I had rehearsed, but the order was completely new.

"You're having an art show reception this Sunday?" she said, her words falling effortlessly on me like snowflakes of pure silver on a crisp, sunny day in spring.

"Uh-huh," I half shouted, my rancid presence filling the cavernous hallway of school like the stench of a slaughterhouse.

"Great. What time? Where?" she uttered with a voice more melodious than a chorus of angels, the force of which pinned me against the wall in sheer ecstasy.

Somehow I managed to belch out the details in a language she was able to decode, and she said she'd be there. I, of course, took this to mean she would love me forever, and I began planning our honeymoon destination and the names of our first eight children.

When the day of the big art show reception arrived, I waited in the upper room of the gallery with great anticipation for Celia to appear at my side. I made certain I was looking my best that day, wearing my favorite new outfit and teasing my hair into an Afro that would have intimidated Angela Davis. My parents and sisters were there, as was my art teacher and her husband, a few of my friends and their parents, and one or two strangers. I had that sick feeling inside that I was setting myself up for tremendous disappointment by putting so much emphasis on Celia's appearance. She had never shown any particular interest in me before, why should she now? Maybe she was just being polite when she said she'd come. But I couldn't help hoping.

I was staring blankly at the punch bowl full of Hi-C when my friend nudged me. I turned around, and there was all five feet, eight inches of Celia standing at the door. My heart leaped. Next to her, however, was six feet and several inches of some guy I'd never seen before. They were holding hands.

She walked over to me with the graceful smile and effortless glide of Botticelli's Venus and said hello. She then introduced me to this behemoth she called "boyfriend" and I shook his hairy paw with feigned good nature. He had long, straight hair, a scruffy beard, and was dressed as she was, in a sort of ragged-jeans, baggy shirt, San Francisco–art-school look. They looked around for a few minutes as I watched them in the stifling, slow-motion silence you feel when you've hyperventilated. They said a few nice things, smiled, and left.

I looked at myself. I was wearing a skintight, black and silver T-shirt made of sparkly threads; silver, satin bell-bottoms; gigantic gray platform shoes; a leather choker, and my trademark Afro with the black power fork protruding from the top. I wasn't just out of Celia's league, I was from another planet. And she hadn't come to my reception because she liked me, it was her way of telling me that I wasn't her type and she already had a boyfriend. A much *older* boyfriend.

The feeling of rejection was so profound that I wanted to evaporate on the spot. I was instantly ashamed of everything I had done or said in the past year since I started high school. I saw the attention I had been getting at school for being cool turning to ridicule behind my back. My parents' endless hints about "being yourself" assaulted me like a ten-foot wave of ice-cold seawater crashing against a rocky coastline. I *hated* it when they were right, especially when their remarks were accompanied by dramatic similes about nature.

I stood silently next to the punch bowl for a long time, trying to disappear into thin air, never to be seen again. Unable to achieve this, I resolved to reinvent myself completely. I was through with the "Funkadelic" look forever.

As I look back at the pictures of myself in those days, I realize that I looked remarkably like some sort of a pale and sickly shrubbery wearing a Bee Gees costume and his mother's shoes. In retrospect, it is hard for even me to believe that I thought I was the messiah of cool, but history is rarely kind to the fearlessly trendy.

Too Many Plumbing Supplies, Not Enough College

I began to feel dizzy and groggy as I opened my eyes once again to find myself in the present day, still lying on my kitchen floor. This time it was my wife who was looming over me.

"Dan, are you all right? What happened, sweetheart?" she cooed as she knelt next to me and cradled my head in her arms.

"I must have passed out," I whispered, trying to focus on her face.

She leaned closer and brushed my face with her dark brown hair. "Wait a minute," I thought. "My wife has red hair" (this month).

"Are you okay, baby? Do you feel all right?" she said, as she smoothed the hair away from my face and kissed me gently on the forehead.

I looked at her face and brought it into focus.

"What are *you* doing here? You're not my wife!" I hissed in disbelief.

"No, I'm not your wife. And you're not awake yet, either," Celia said softly.

I began to feel dizzy and groggy as I opened my eyes once more to find myself in the present day, still lying on my kitchen floor. Again, it was my wife who was looming over me.

"Celia?" I said cautiously.

"Who the hell is 'Celia'?" my wife asked suspiciously, as she cradled my head in her arms.

"Just a girl I was in love with in high school," I explained.

"Well, fine then!" she snapped as she jumped up, letting my head drop to the linoleum floor once again, sending me reeling back into the past.

By the time I was a senior in high school, I had become much more lifelike. I was a little more true to myself, anyway, and by that I mean that I had stopped trying to be a tall black guy and had become content with being a short white guy. I'd gotten rid of the platform shoes and sparkly clothes, and, instead of forking my hair into an Afro, I was letting it do what it wanted to, which was to succumb to the forces of gravity and hang in long, phone cord–shaped ringlets.

Once again, fortune shined on my dubious gene pool as one of the most popular movies out at that time was Ken Russell's version of the Who's *Tommy*. Roger Daltrey was the latest sex symbol, and, when left to its own devices, my hair just naturally looked almost exactly as his did in the movie, except it was darker. For a short, skinny, big-nosed kid like me, a small coincidence like this can be the difference between a normal dating life and the life of a monk. Once again, my hair was a gateway to girls. But this time because they *liked* it, not because they found it a scientific curiosity.

In this manner I managed to snag a steady girlfriend, whom

I hung on to for dear life. We started dating during the summer between my sophomore and junior year and spent nearly every spare moment together throughout high school.

As my graduation drew near, I was ready to skip college entirely and go off and become a famous artist. I figured a guy with my incredible combination of talent, brains, and inherent value as a human being didn't need a college degree. I was just going to get an apartment somewhere, paint masterpieces, and wait to be discovered. Doubtless I would be a world-famous millionaire by the age of twenty-five.

My parents were not in the least impressed with this career plan, and so my mother began applying for scholarships on my behalf. She landed a fine arts scholarship for me at Washington University in St. Louis, and, after much pleading, badgering, and threats of bodily harm on her part, I agreed to go. I knew full well that I wouldn't like it, but I figured how tough could it be? It was only *art* school, after all, and maybe I'd get to see some nude models in life drawing class.

I saw nude models, all right, but they weren't the sort I was hoping for. They were more along the lines of something you spend the rest of your life trying to forget, like the images from that gory driver's education film they used to show kids to scare them out of driving too fast. A few of these models were enough to scare you out of being human.

Just being away from home, which for most college students is the single best reason for staying in school, was an almost unbearable pressure for me. It wasn't my parents or my family per se that I missed, it was familiarity. I simply could not adjust to living in a strange city, in a strange room, among strangers. I spent all of my time depressed on the inside, pretending on the outside not to be. Everyone around me was pursuing the sort of activities that college kids usually do their first year away from home, most of which involved alcohol, loud music, and nudity. But like the pathetic and immature dweeb I apparently was, I spent most of my time in my room brooding, philosophizing, and writing letters back home to my girlfriend and family. As parties raged on all around me, I often felt like the only sober person in Times Square on New Year's Eve, trying to work on his taxes.

My roommate, as fate would have it, was even quieter than I. He was a Japanese-American named Richard, and he gave new definition to the word "stoic." Richard almost never spoke, and, when he did, he showed absolutely no emotion. He never smiled, or grimaced, or knitted his brow, or even so much as blinked if he could help it. It took us weeks to accomplish even the most rudimentary small talk. The first week I learned he was an architecture major. The second week I found out he was from Colorado. And so on.

My self-imposed sense of loneliness was so profound that most of the time I found it generally difficult to keep from crying, especially late at night as I lay in bed, trying to fall asleep. It was a dreadfully humiliating situation, one I avoided as much as humanly possible by sheer force of will. Occasionally, when the urge was too strong to resist any longer, I would wait until I was sure Richard was asleep (which was difficult to judge as he was too stoic even to snore), crawl silently into my closet, slide the door shut, bury my face in a pile of laundry, and sob.

Once, Richard caught me doing this and I managed to save face by convincing him that it was an old family method of pretreating clothes before washing.

As the first semester wore on, Richard and I slowly became friends. He was an extremely intelligent person with a terrifically bizarre sense of humor, even though he never smiled or laughed. He was fond of being as mysterious and obtuse as possible, saying strange things that few people could understand without knowing him well and never divulging his intentions with his stone face. I came to enjoy and appreciate his humor immensely. It was he who introduced me to the cartoons of B. Kliban, who became my first and greatest influence as a cartoonist.

I staved off my depression and loneliness as long as I could, then dropped out of college after the Christmas break. That was December of 1976, and over twenty years later I'm still trying to forget a couple of those nude models.

My parents were none too thrilled to see me back in Tulsa, which did not surprise me, but I was still shocked to find that they had changed the rules. Whereas I used to live under the basic premise that Mom and Dad would give me a place to stay, clothes to wear, and food to eat in return for the mere pleasure of my company and my compliance with a few basic rules, they had now decided they would only provide me with these services in return for monetary compensation.

"We were willing to support you as long as you were in school" were Dad's exact words. "Now that you're not, you'll have to pay rent, just like in the real world. You're an adult now." And to add insult to injury, I was *still* required to comply with the house rules, notable among which were no staying out all night without telling them where I was going to be and no naked or drunken women in my room.

Now, I was no college graduate, but it didn't take me long to figure out that if I was going to be paying rent, I might just as well pay it to a stranger, who would not have so many concerns about my whereabouts and lifestyle.

This I did fairly quickly, renting an old but very cool little apartment near downtown using the money I was making from an unbearable job I'd gotten running a tiny plumbing supply store on the trailer-park side of town. It was a little more expensive than living at home and I didn't eat nearly as well, but there were no restrictions on my life. I was free to do as I pleased. Of course, I still didn't stay out all night because I really didn't have anywhere to go, and there were no naked or drunken women in my apartment; my girlfriend still lived with her parents and had a fairly strict curfew, but it was enough to know that the option was there.

The store I was running was called Plumbtown, and it was a job I had gotten through a friend of my girlfriend's parents who was looking for a responsible young man to run his new store while he continued to work his insurance job. Fulfilling two out of the three requirements, "young" and "man," and because he could find no one else, I got the job.

The claustrophobic little store was on a back street of a

remote, nearly rural part of town with no foot traffic and even fewer cars. It occupied a space that was formerly inhabited by a 7-11 that had gone out of business. (Something the owner of Plumbtown had missed was an age-old business axiom that is still being taught at Harvard to this day: "If a 7-11 can't survive in a given location, nothing can.")

I sat for nearly a year behind the store's counter, looking out the front windows at a godforsaken industrial wasteland of a neighborhood, dealing with an average of maybe one customer per week, and wondering if adulthood would always be that rewarding. Just like clockwork, the phone rang exactly once each day at ten minutes to closing.

"How'd we do today, Danny?" the owner would ask.

"Well, not too well, sir. No customers today," was my routine response.

I had an awful lot of time to think about my future as I sat behind that counter surrounded by toilet parts, and my prospects were grim. Like a prisoner who's spent too much time in solitary, occasionally I would begin to hallucinate. I sometimes imagined I was back in church with Sister Mary Pterodactyl, listening to Father Migraine droning on in Latin. They were chastising me for not having planned my career path more carefully, and, for once, I agreed with them.

After eleven months, and just in the nick of time, the owner decided to close the store for good. He called with the news at ten minutes to closing on a Friday, just as I was about to kick the chair out from under me, a rope tied around my neck.

"I know this is going to come as a great disappointment to you, Danny, but I've decided it's time to close down Plumbtown and cut my losses."

Based on his announcement, I took the noose from around my neck and decided to give myself another chance. That man saved my life that afternoon, and I will never forget him for it.

Narrowly escaping a gruesome death at my own hands changed the way I saw my life. I had no job, no education, no skills, no training, no money, and no naked women in my apartment. I was beginning to think I had misjudged my inherent marketability and would miss my goal of being a millionaire by the age of twenty-five by a few years, if not centuries. It had even begun to occur to me that my parents had been right (again!) in saying that I should have stayed in college. I had no direction to my life, and my prospects for a happy, functional adulthood were bleak. I was depressed and confused.

Then, with the timing of Satan himself, my girlfriend of nearly three years broke up with me suddenly and unexpectedly. It seems she was dating a small group of my friends behind my back and had waited as long as she could for me to notice. Too wrapped up in my exciting career at Plumbtown, I had somehow missed all the clues: broken dates, guys answering her phone, men's briefs falling out of her purse. The news of her betrayal hit me harder than Nixon's resignation, and I plummeted into a well of depression. I began hallucinating about Sister Mary Pterodactyl again, a fate worse than death. Weeks later, struggling to find some reason to get out of bed, I decided that if I wasn't going to kill myself, I at least needed to do something drastic to shake myself out of my childish delusions and force myself to grow up.

Some young people join the military when they reach this point, but I wasn't quite that delusional. I needed something else. Something that didn't involve daily emasculation at the hands of sadistic bald guys with guns. Something that had the potential of being fun as well as character building. Something that, if at all possible, might even involve women.

Oddly enough, the perfect solution came by way of my parents. A man my father had worked with some years earlier was living and working in Milan. He was an admirer of art and artists, and had run into my parents at a Christmas party in Tulsa while home for a visit. He'd remembered that I was an aspiring artist and had seen some of my work and offered to put me up at his apartment in Milan for a while if I was interested in seeing Europe and studying the art there. My parents encouraged me to go, and, after a great deal of fear and trepidation, I decided to take him up on his offer. I was tired of being ruled by my fears, desperate to find some direction to my life, and ready to take a chance and seek adventure.

I found a temporary job (one with other employees and customers and phones that rang more than once a day) and saved my money for several months. I arranged an open-ended trip with a one-way ticket and a three-month rail pass. The following spring I sold my car, moved my few remaining possessions into my parents' garage, and left for Europe. It was simultaneously the most frightening and exciting time in my life.

As my vision was taking me to the airport for my flight to London, everything went black. Pat Sajak's huge, floating face appeared before me.

"Pat, what's up? I'm thinking about my trip to Europe," I protested.

"It's time to spin the wheel, Dan," he uttered ominously.

"Yeah, I know. You said that a long time ago."

"Then do it."

"I *was* doing it," I explained frantically. "I was spinning the wheel and talking to my fans on the Internet and I was planning to travel around the country and meet people, but I got a panic attack and you started showing me my life and where my fears came from and I was just going to Europe and you pulled the plug! What gives?"

"You've seen enough for now," the game-show shaman urged. "It's time to move on."

"But I was just going to *Europe*! It was simultaneously the most frightening and exciting time in my life!" I shouted. "Plus, it was a hell of a lot of fun! C'mon!"

"You've been lying on your kitchen floor long enough,

Piraro!" Pat shot back, losing his patience. "If you don't wake up soon, you're going to miss your first flight!"

"I don't care! I'd rather go to Europe again!" I pleaded. "Plus, I need to find out where my fears come from! I haven't figured it all out yet!"

"A person only has so much time to spend on flashbacks, Dan. If you don't wake up occasionally and actually *live* life, you won't have anything to flash back to later."

"Just a few more minutes! Can't you hit the snooze button or something?" I pleaded.

"I'm afraid there are no snooze buttons in the spiritual world, pal. You'll begin to understand the point to all of this as you go along," he said.

"Wait!" I cried, but it was no use. Sajak's face began to fade and the darkness formed a swirling spiral around me like a cheesy TV movie about time travel. When I awoke, I was on the plane bound for L.A.

S E V E N

God Knows Where
with God Knows Whom

I pushed my call button and waited for the flight attendant to come.

"What day is it?" I asked timidly, trying not to sound too much like a soap opera amnesia victim.

"Why, Christmas Day, of course!" he replied in his best Cockney accent. I stared at him, confused and unamused. "It's the eighth, sir," he said with a polite smile.

"Of November?" I asked.

"Yes. Is there anything I can get you?"

"No, thanks," I said, and turned back toward the window. Once again, several days were missing from my life. How had I gotten from my kitchen to the airport and onto the plane? Was I on the correct plane? How much of my life was I going to lose to spiritual revelation?

I searched my pockets for my ticket and looked it over. The appropriate sections were missing, so I could only assume that I was on the right flight or the gate personnel would have told me. Feeling I had no other choice but to accept my fate, I resigned to settle in and make the best of it.

My flight from Dallas to Los Angeles was uneventful and tedious. I was having a fair amount of success fighting my usual thoughts of a fiery crash that would leave my wife and daughters grief-stricken and vulnerable in a cruel, crime-infested, male-dominated world. Instead, I was spending most of my time worrying about what sort of godawful jerks and insufferable creeps I would be stuck with on this trip and convincing myself that whatever sort of godawful jerks I got stuck with, I would only have to endure them for a few hours until I could move on to the next insufferable creep. Every so often, I tried to console myself with positive thoughts about how wonderful and interesting many of the people might be. How I might form friendships that would last a lifetime. But this was a difficult task given my fear of strangers and propensity for anxiety attacks and alarmist philosophy.

All rational thought having abandoned me, I calmed myself by closing my eyes, concentrating on Sajak's image, and repeating my mantra silently, "It's time to spin the wheel. It's time to spin the wheel."

Fortunately, we were about to land, and I was able to take my mind off my misgivings about the people I had chosen, and concentrate on my fear of landing in a fiery heap on the runway.

Like the pandemonium that accompanied the Beatles' landing at Kennedy Airport in the sixties, my arrival at LAX was nothing short of overwhelming. Nothing could have prepared me for the throng of people that was waiting there when I came out of the tunnel at my arrival gate. I stopped and took a moment to catch my breath, then raised my right hand above me like the pope, waving it papally and crying, "My flock! My flock!" My copassengers stared at me strangely, apparently unaware that they had been traveling with such an important celebrity.

I stood for a few moments at the gate, taking in the thousands of adoring fans crowding every corner of the airport. They were of all ages, races, genders, and economic classes. They were sitting, standing, running, walking, scratching themselves, ambling aimlessly. Some had luggage, some did not. Some were sitting in coffee shops or browsing through magazines at a newsstand; others stared blankly out the window or napped in a chair. It was perhaps the most Kodak moment I had ever experienced in my life, and I was deeply moved. A single tear crested my lower lid and streaked down my humble cheek.

"Thank you all!" I managed to choke out. The crowd sensed I was on a tight schedule, I think, and, not wishing to impede my progress, dispersed rather quickly, leaving me to look for my contact unmolested.

Unfortunately, the one person conspicuously missing from this incredible spectacle was my ride.

His name was Shane, and I had chosen him almost by default because he was one of the only people I had heard from who was available to pick me up at the airport on a Wednesday morning. Everyone else who had written had a job they couldn't get away from until at least lunchtime; Shane didn't. I began to wonder if the reason he was unemployed was the same reason he wasn't there to pick me up when he said he'd be.

So there I was wandering through the Los Angeles Airport looking for a guy I'd never seen before who had no idea what I looked like, either. What a perfect pair of idiots we are, I thought, as I stood there raising my eyebrows inquisitively at anyone who so much as glanced my way. Through all the planning, E-mailing, and phone calls, it never occurred to either of us to devise a way to recognize the other.

After a few minutes of posing nonchalantly by the arrival gate, I decided to move on to the baggage claim area to find my luggage. Once there, I parked myself against a wall, alternately watching the conveyor belt for my luggage and the crowd for someone who looked as if he might be unemployed and/or looking for me. Suddenly, I heard an announcement over the PA system:

"Would the party meeting Shane proceed to baggage claim area B, please?"

Now we were getting somewhere! I *was* at baggage claim area B! I looked around and immediately spotted a bank of white courtesy phones only a few feet away. Just hanging up was a young man with black hair, a goatee, a short-sleeved, green dress shirt, black docker-style trousers, black vans, black Ray Bans, and a huge sign taped to his back that read, DAN PIRARO YOUR FLY IS OPEN. I checked my fly quickly, walked over to him, and tapped him on the shoulder.

Shane and I hit it off immediately. I felt much better about my choice to go through with the trip within just a few minutes of riding in his dog-motif Jeep pickup truck, which had giant paw prints painted all over it and the words SLIMY DOG painted prominently across the sides. Shane was friendly and talkative, making me feel instantly comfortable. In fact, I was so relieved that he wasn't some creepy, unbathed, ultra-right- (or left-) wing fanatic with a dreadful comic strip he wanted me to help him get off the ground that I got momentarily carried away with myself and scooted over on the bench seat of his pickup and sat right next to him, "date-style."

He promptly slammed on the brakes, sending me crashing painfully into the dashboard. I realized my error, got back into my proper seat, and explained to him why I had behaved in such a strange manner. He understood, put the truck back in gear, and we moved on toward lunch, a little closer for the experience.

This being my first time in Los Angeles, I was awe-stricken by the scenery: traffic and brown sky, brown sky and traffic, everywhere you looked. Had it not been for the palm trees and unemployed actors lining the roadside, I would have thought I was in Dallas. But I was, in fact, in Los Angeles: land of myth and movies. And more important, *home of Pat Sajak*. I could feel the electricity in the air.

We drove a couple of miles to the beach, which, in the L.A. traffic, took most of the afternoon, and had lunch at a taco place.

Shane was not half the ne'er-do-well I had suspected. He was actually a highly motivated self-employed type, much like me. He made his living doing some kind of complicated computer graphics, writing articles about computer graphics, and creating and selling counterculture T-shirts under the company name "Slimy Dog." Earlier that year, when he had first written to me, he offered to trade me some of his T-shirts for an autographed copy of one of my books. I agreed, and he sent me a box of shirts and I sent him an autographed copy of *Bizarro Number 9*.

One of the shirts he'd sent was bright yellow with a very cool black logo on the front that said SLIMY DOG in sharp, gothic lettering. On the back, huge, bold type said MY DAD HATES YOU. I had no idea what this meant, but it made me laugh and the shirt instantly became one of my favorites. One place I had worn it was the "get-acquainted" beach party on the first night of the National Cartoonists Society's annual convention the previous May. In the ten years that I had been a professional cartoonist, I had never been to one of these conventions, so I knew almost no one there. All the old, famous guys were there, the *Family Circus* guy, the *Beetle Bailey* guy, the *Hagar the Horrible* guy, the *B.C.* guy, the *Peanuts* guy, as well as people from magazines like *Mad*. Also in attendance were any number of editors, salespeople, syndicate folks, cartoonists' family members, and so on. Most of these people, the cartoonists included, are pretty conservative. In fact, with few exceptions, the average mainstream syndicated cartoonist seems much more like a golfer than an artist.

There I was my first time to meet any of them, milling around on the beach with my goofy, white-boy dreadlocks hairdo, two earrings, and a T-shirt with MY DAD HATES YOU emblazoned across the back. And, to add stupidity to insult, I wasn't wearing my official NCS name tag. Not surprisingly, no one came up to me and introduced himself. I'm lucky someone didn't assume I was a drifter and throw me out. I wasn't completely without a sense of decorum, however. I did resist wearing one of the other shirts he had sent me with a huge picture of Snoopy decked out in punk-rock regalia, spiky Mohawk haircut, and giving "the finger."

I told Shane this story, and he seemed gratified to have been represented in absentia at the NCS convention in such a dubious manner.

The two of us bummed around for the afternoon joking incessantly and generally making nuisances of ourselves, walking along a pier, making fun of fishermen; going into a bookstore, making fun of the books; going to his house, making fun of the way the people who'd lived there before had decorated the kitchen. Typical, self-centered, male bonding kinds of activities.

Shane's house was very cool, with several fully operational pinball machines and arcade video games, electronic furniture of his own design and construction with flashing lights and sound, a topnotch computer graphics setup, and a dirt-track-racer obstacle course for remote-control cars in the backyard. What would normally have been a spare bedroom had a set of patio furniture, complete with four chairs, a table, and a giant umbrella in the center. This was covered with art projects of different sorts, mainly remote-control car bodies being repainted.

Shane's house was a grown-up's version of a kid's clubhouse. Clearly, this was the sort of guy who simply could not afford to get married. No woman worth having would agree to live in such a manner, and no man who'd gone to the trouble and expense to set up this kind of lifestyle could stand to give it up.

Up until recently, however, Shane had had a girlfriend. Or rather, he still had a girlfriend, but she had moved to San Francisco and wasn't sure about their relationship. Which is pretty much the same as not having a girlfriend at all, but at least you have someone to obsess over and concentrate your frustrations and jealousy on. Which is exactly what Shane had been doing.

As will often happen with strangers who meet under unusual circumstances, like being trapped in an elevator for several hours or stranded in a life raft at sea, we began to share with each other some of the more intimate details of our lives. We spoke of issues of the heart, the things in our lives that really mattered, things that went beyond video games, toy cars, cartoons, and computers: We talked about women and beer.

Shane told me an interesting morality tale that I believe

says a lot about how the relatively new phenomenon of cyber-space is affecting our lives. It is the tale of two people who shall remain nameless (him and his girlfriend) and the trouble they got into on the Internet. It went like this:

Once upon a time, a young woman decided that she needed some "space," some "time to herself," and so she left her boyfriend and her life in Los Angeles to try to "find herself." For reasons unknown, she thought San Francisco might be a good place to start looking, so she packed up her belongings, said her good-byes, and moved there promising to "stay in touch." In order to better achieve this promised state of "touch," the boyfriend, who knew a little something about computers, set up E-mail accounts for each of them so they could communicate more easily.

The young woman set up house in San Francisco and commenced "looking for herself." The boyfriend stayed in Los Angeles, writing to her regularly, offering to keep an eye out for her "self" should it happen to turn up around his house somewhere.

This went on for some time, each reporting to the other via E-mail until the young woman one day asked the boyfriend if he would go into her E-mail account and change her address to all caps, as she was not satisfied with its current version in upper and lower case. The boyfriend failed to see the logic in such a request, but readily agreed, went into the account under her name, and, while doing so, happened to notice for the first time a menu item called "Check Mail You've Sent."

Being a mere mortal, the boyfriend found himself unable to resist moving the cursor to this menu item and clicking on it. As it opened to a list of the mail the young woman had sent over the past months since she moved to San Francisco, the boyfriend was reminded of Pandora's box. He shrugged off the thought and read the list of addresses to which the young woman had written.

Included in the mail that the young woman had sent were a number of letters to another young person in San Francisco: a man. Wanting to give the young woman every benefit of the doubt, the boyfriend decided that he would not read the actual letters, but, rather, conduct a simple test. He would send the other young man an E-mail under his own name saying, basically, "Thanks for being a friend to [the young woman] while she is new in town. I am her boyfriend." The boyfriend saw this as a simple and honest way to "mark his territory," figuring if the other young man replied, "*Boyfriend!* She didn't tell me she had a *boyfriend*!" he would know that he had reason to be upset.

What happened next was nothing. The boyfriend checked every day for a week, and neither the other young man nor the young woman wrote anything in return. The boyfriend began to worry, letting his imagination get the best of him. At first he was concerned, then he was freaking, and eventually, he completely wigged out.

He went back into Pandora's box . . . er . . . the list of mail his girlfriend had sent, and began opening and reading the letters she'd mailed to the other young man. He was horrified to find that his worst fears were true. The letters, especially the most recent ones, were gushing with romance, lust, and decadence. Not only had the young woman found herself, but apparently herself had been spending a lot of time in this other guy's arms.

The boyfriend contemplated his options, including, but not limited to, homicide, suicide, hysteria, and alcoholism.

After a proper amount of time in reflection, the boyfriend confronted the young woman by phone, a call that began with a heated argument, escalated to vicious verbal assault, and culminated in the admission on the young woman's part that she had *intentionally planted* the lascivious letters after she had learned of the letter the boyfriend had sent introducing himself to the other young man. The young woman had assumed that the boyfriend had set the entire E-mail account up to monitor her behavior while she was away, and she had become angered at the prospect of being spied on. The boyfriend denied this vehemently, as he still does to this day.

Finally, the two of them worked everything out, reestablished a modicum of trust in one another, and then lost interest in each other completely.

The moral of this story, of course, is that all technology is bad and that we should live like the Amish, only with cable TV.

Enriched and morally elevated by the lesson we had learned, Shane and I went out for a beer and then proceeded on to the bookstore in West Hollywood where I was to sign books that evening. It was the first signing of my tour, and I was eager to get it off to a grand start. I was hoping that this first engagement would be fairly crowded and a big success.

We arrived a few minutes early and fought our way through the crowd of three people that had lined up ahead of time to see me. An audible hush moved through the trio as I passed, all three of them recognizing me from my picture on the back of my book. Sitting at the table the store had prepared for me, I addressed the assemblage of one man and two women.

"Hi, guys," I offered with a smile.

"Where is everyone?" one of my three adoring fans asked. "William Wegman was here last week and you couldn't get near the place!"

"Well, I don't know where everyone is, sir, but thanks for giving me a standard by which to compare myself," I said with a weak smile, my chin quivering.

I began to chat as amiably as I could through my tears, and the gentleman proceeded to console me.

"I guess people just don't know quality," he began. "Your comics are the only ones in the paper worth reading since Larson retired."

"Thanks," I sobbed gratefully. At least we were beginning to find common ground on which to communicate.

One of the women in attendance circumnavigated the author's table and put her arm around me, patting me gently on the shoulder. "There, there, let it all out. Yes, that's it. You'll feel much better."

I threw my arms around her waist and soaked the side of her blouse with my tears. When I had calmed down sufficiently, I began to sign the books of these three fans. When I have the time, I always write a strange little message of some sort and draw a picture in each book. The lighter the traffic, the longer the message and the more elaborate the picture. I had learned years ago that if the customers are scarce, the longer you keep each person at the table, the better it looks to passers-by. Most people are afraid to be the first person to wander up to a signing table for fear they will be embarrassed by the author's watery, pleading eyes into buying a book they don't really want.

After I finished the handful of books the trio had bought, they mercifully stuck around a few minutes more, too embarrassed to walk away and leave me sitting all alone. I was grateful for their kindness as the worst feeling in the world is to sit by yourself at a table in a bookstore with stacks of books all around you, a poster announcing your name and purpose for being there, and a pathetic look on your face.

This is what I call a "Forced Celebrity Backfire" situation. It occurs when someone, in this case a bookstore, places you in a situation where you are presented as a celebrity, but no one knows (or cares) who you are. In this situation, you are inevitably forced to explain to someone who you are and why they should know you. As you speak, you are struck with the absolute futility of the exercise because celebrity, we all know, is something that must be *given* to you by another and cannot be taken for oneself.

"What do you do?" a smiling woman browsing in the store will say as she wanders past my table with her child.

"I'm a syndicated cartoonist. These are books of my work,"

I answer politely, with a reluctant smile that shouts, "I *DON'T* feel sorry for myself, I REALLY *DON'T*!"

"Oh," she continues pleasantly as she flips idly through the books on the table between us. "Are you in the local paper?"

"Yes," I answer politely.

"What's the name of your comic?" she asks, staring at stacks of books that all have *Bizarro* written prominently on the cover.

"It's called *Bizarro*," I offer blandly, resisting the impulse to ask which she is, blind or illiterate.

"I don't think I've ever seen it. I don't really read the comics much." Her child is staring blankly at me. "Do *you* read the comics?" she asks the kid.

"Yeah," he says quietly, still staring.

"Have you ever seen this man's comics?"

"No," he says vacantly.

"Do you want me to buy you one of these books? He'll draw a funny picture in it for you," she coaxes.

"No," he answers coldly, with the artery-severing bluntness that only a child can deliver.

The woman smiles and takes the evil child by the hand. "Perhaps some other time," she says as she leads the little ego-sucking zombie away.

"Have a nice day," I offer affably as I struggle to stanch the river of blood flowing from my severed self-esteem.

When you hear of cartoonists or authors who refuse to do book signings, this is usually why. Gut-wrenching as it is, it is a situation that rears its ugly head with merciful rarity, as one learns to avoid engagements where you are likely to be completely devoid of fans, like a Sunday afternoon signing in the NFC champion's city on the day of the Super Bowl. Or in one of those gigantic, suburban, discount-club warehouses that sells everything from outboard motors and air conditioners to institutional-sized boxes of frozen burritos and suitcases of Cheerios, with a single table of books about military aircraft and the American Civil War somewhere amid the miles of concrete aisles and a nincompoop store manager who decides it would be "neat" to try something different, like a cartoonist sitting on a metal folding chair signing books on a board laid across two shipping crates in the middle of the aisle, only to discover that none of his customers can even fathom the concept of "reading for entertainment" when there's a perfectly good television within 100 miles. This actually happened to me once, in Vancouver.

The other, less devastating but more common sort of Forced Celebrity Backfire occurs when I am out with some well-meaning friend or acquaintance in public who runs into someone he knows. By way of introducing me to the other person, my friend will say, "Do you read the comics?"

"No," the other person answers.

This is when you know you're dead, but your friend's next words launch you irretrievably into the Backfire.

"Well, this is Dan Piraro. He does *Bizarro* in the newspaper!" my friend spouts with pride and glee. "Ever seen it?"

"No, I don't think I have, but I never really read the comics," he says apologetically as he shakes my hand.

"That's okay, I don't read them, either," I cough as I smile a smile that shouts, "I didn't ask to be introduced this way, I *REALLY DIDN'T!*"

But even though the bookstore Forced Celebrity Backfire is less common, it is all the more mortifying because it can last for up to an hour. In West Hollywood, I managed to keep my loyal trio at the table for around thirty minutes. As they finally pried my clutching fingers from their ankles and left the signing area, the store manager wandered over to the table, perhaps in response to my sobbing, and offered his apologies.

"I'm sorry there aren't more people here. We're usually pretty busy," he explained. (Oh, gee. *That* makes me feel better.) "L.A. is sort of a hard town to get attention in. There are so many celebrities here that people are kind of jaded and won't come out to see just anyone," he continued. (Just when you think you feel as low as is humanly possible . . .) "Plus, there's a rumor that Alec Baldwin and Kim Basinger are going to be strolling naked down the 'Walk of Fame' tonight."

It was just one of those nights.

As the hour drew to a close, I began looking for my host for the evening. Shane had only signed on to pick me up at the airport and schlep me around for the day. My overnight connection was to pick me up at the store that night. The feelings of insecurity and anxiety were predictably intense as I waited to see with whom I would be going home that first night. Shane had hung around the bookstore to wait with me and still had my bags in his dog truck.

A few minutes before I was scheduled to be finished, a man with neatly cut short hair and a goatee, two earrings, a tight, French-cut T-shirt, short shorts, and hiking boots came walking up to the table.

"Dan?" he asked as he extended his hand tentatively.

"Are you Bobby?" I asked as I offered my own.

"Yes, are you ready to go?" he said in a markedly effeminate voice.

Behind him, Shane looked at me with subtle amusement. Shane is an open-minded guy and meant no malice, but he flashed an expression that I perceived to mean: "Did you know you would be spending the night with a gay guy?"

Smiling wryly, I flashed an expression to him that said: "It's okay, man, I'm cool with it."

Shane responded in kind with a knowing glance as if to say: "Yeah, me, too. Some of my best friends are gay. It just isn't cool to be homophobic."

With a twinkle of approval in my eye, I nodded slightly and winked, telling Shane I was glad to know he was hip. Then I launched into a complicated sequence of facial spasms and gesticulations that said: "I'm glad to learn that you are not only educated and informed, but confident in your own sexuality, as am I. But if we're so open-minded and nonhomophobic, why have we just spent so much time and energy sending secret signals to each other?"

Shane's face twitched as he began to respond, but then he sneezed and it broke my concentration, bringing my attention back to Bobby.

As I continued to exchange pleasantries with my new host, I began to become aware that while I was cool, collected, and unalarmed outwardly, inside I was a little apprehensive. But not because he was gay. Thanks to my wife, who was born with what experts call the "Judy Garland gene," which causes most gay men to fall at her feet in adoration, we have always had plenty of gay friends. I was apprehensive because I was going home with God-knows-whom to spend the night God-knows-where. It was the fear-of-strangers problem again. On paper, the whole tour idea seemed workable, but now I was faced with the trial-by-fire first night. The much feared moment of truth had finally arrived, and it was nerve-racking.

But as weird as it was to be going home to spend the night in a foreign city with a veritable stranger, the thing that kept going through my mind was how I had imagined Bobby so completely wrong in my mind. From the numerous E-mail exchanges and the one phone conversation we had had, during which I had learned he worked for an African safari travel agency, I had erroneously pictured him to be a complete goof-ball, a thirty-something-year-old overweight comic-book nerd in a belted safari jacket and one of those hats with a leopard-print band and one side of the brim turned up who'd never been on a date in his life and still lived at home with his mom. In my predeparture psychotic cloud of paranoia and fear, I had envisioned him as some unwashed, obnoxious, totally macho goober-head who was going to drive me to suicide before dawn with his endless attempts to impress me with his hunting-knife collection, comic books, and video games. So when Bobby showed up and was the complete opposite of what I had imagined, I was very relieved.

Shane, Bobby, and I went out to the parking lot, switched my gear from Shane's dog truck to Bobby's Montero, I said my "thank yous" and "good-byes" to Shane, and we were off.

Bobby immediately announced that his ten-year-old son,

Dustin, was staying at the home of some friends for the evening in case we decided to go to a nightclub or something. In addition to hating nightclubs, I was dead tired, so I suggested we go pick up Dustin.

As we drove, I couldn't help but wonder where he'd gotten a son. Could he be one of those guys who seems from all outward appearances to be gay but is really straight and happily married? Or perhaps he had been married in the past, had a kid, then divorced and come out of the closet. But if he was openly gay, how had he gotten legal custody of his son? That sort of thing doesn't often happen where I came from, but maybe California was different. Or perhaps he'd been allowed to adopt, although that, too, seemed a long shot, at least it would be back in Texas. These were the best explanations I could come up with, but, as I later discovered, all three were wrong.

The home we went to was that of Jim and Andrea, a friendly, attractive couple who lived in the famous area of Los Angeles called Laurel Canyon. I was excited to see how the other half lived, as I had heard of the area and knew that a good many movie stars and show-business moguls lived there.

As we snaked our way up the narrow, steep road, Bobby provided what tourist information he could. "That's where Pete Rose lives . . . That big house there is where the Budget Rent-A-Car heiress lives . . . I think that house is where that blond chick from that movie *Species* lives."

We pulled into Jim and Andrea's impossibly steep driveway and went inside without knocking. Their house was built on the side of a sixty-five-degree incline and the street entrance was at the uppermost floor, so we entered at the top of a staircase overlooking the living room. As we descended the stairs, Bobby called out to the people below, "It's okay. He's normal!"

"What do you mean by *that*?" I inquired as I followed him down.

Bobby explained, "I was telling them that after I talked to you on the phone and agreed to let you stay at my house overnight, I thought, 'What if he's some big, fat, smelly, gross guy who still lives at home with his mother?'"

"You're kidding!" I laughed at the remarkable similarity of our fears.

"No," he continued. "I thought, 'I've never met a cartoonist. I don't know what they might be like. For all I know, you could've been some gross, dysfunctional nerd who still lives with his parents and has never been on a date in his life.'"

"I don't believe it! That's what I was worried *you'd* be like!" I confessed.

We had a good laugh over it and stayed for an hour or so, visiting with Jim and Andrea and watching Dustin fall asleep on the couch. Jim and Andrea told some amusing "rich people" stories about the frequent irritation of getting trapped in their neighborhood by the giant limos that come to pick someone up for a big movie premier and block the narrow road, sometimes for thirty or forty minutes. If the star isn't ready when the limo arrives (and a *real* star is *never* ready when the limo arrives), everyone living on the road above the star is held hostage.

It occurred to me that the rich are not so different from the rest of us, as this is Laurel Canyon's version of the guy at the end of *my* street who leaves rusted and wrecked cars parked in his yard and has a large, vicious dog that regularly escapes its fence. With fur raised, teeth bared, and hideous, red demon eyes aglow, he chases anyone who dares to set foot out of his house. Sometimes the stand-off between this beast and the animal control personnel can last nearly an hour before they can get a good, clean shot at him with the tranquilizer dart gun. Then, naturally, there's the time it takes the police to coax the gun-wielding owner out of his house and into a pair of cuffs. I guess we all have our crosses to bear.

Around 10:30 we woke up Dustin and headed for Bobby's house in Pasadena. It was a lovely, old, two-story house on a very quaint, tree-lined street. The furnishings were a cross between tasteful antiques, such as a large, gorgeous carved-wood grand piano, and primitive tribal artifacts from Africa that Bobby had attained through his safari travel agency job. On the living-room floor was a brown, bearskin rug Bobby called Vera, and from above the stairwell a huge moose head with a long strand of pearls around its neck stared ominously down on anyone ascending. "That's Pearl," Bobby informed me as he showed me upstairs to my room.

I was given Dustin's room, and he stayed in his dad's room for the night. It had been a long day of travel, excitement, introductions, disappointments, fear, relief, and sightseeing, so I went straight to bed.

Lying in the dark looking around at my unfamiliar surroundings, a child's room filled with children's posters and toys, I thought how strange life could be. That very morning I was at home in Dallas, playing fetch with my dogs, taking my daughter to her bus stop; a few hours later I was sleeping in a complete stranger's kid's bed, halfway across the country, a block from the Tournament of Roses Parade route.

On the dresser across the room was a small aquarium that cast a shimmering glow across the ceiling. Staring at the flickering patterns of light, I was vividly reminded of lying in my own bed as a boy, staring at the glow-in-the-dark chicken-bone skeleton I had made in Cub Scouts that hung from my ceiling lamp from the time I was seven until I left for college. I still feel exactly the same inside as I did then, I thought, yet I am nearly forty. I felt embarrassed as I experienced the childish pangs of homesickness and thought about my wife and kids, my own bed and bathroom. Does a person ever feel completely like a grown-up? Only eight more nights to go before I can go home to my family, I reassured myself as I drifted off to sleep.

The aquarium glugged loudly every four to seven seconds, all night long. For no reason I can think of, I slept well.

EIGHT

The Reluctant Mime

The next morning I rose early, and, not having been murdered in my sleep, met Bobby and Dustin in the kitchen for breakfast. Bobby in boxer shorts and T-shirt, Dustin in striped pajamas, and me in my Winnie the Pooh nightshirt and furry, Eeyore slippers, we chatted, drank coffee, and ate bagels as if we'd been friends for years. Dustin asked me to draw a couple of pictures for his pals at school who were fans of mine, which I gladly did. After he left for school, a couple of friends of Bobby's who were also fans of *Bizarro* came over for breakfast.

Jay and Sam were licensed massage therapists, and we all sat down in the dining room with coffee and bagels. My voice was a bit deeper than usual that morning, a little raw from the combination of a slightly sore throat that had been coming on for a day or so and the nonstop acquaintance making of the previous day.

Nonetheless, the four of us had a delightfully Californian chat about the myriad beneficial effects of rubbing different parts of the body to attain everything from chronic pain relief to a parking space at Wal-Mart. At some point the conversation turned to homeopathy and I learned that walrus dander scraped from the left, front fin of a prepubescent cow is an excellent treatment for aching feet. It was a breakfast that was teeming with what I find most endearing about California culture—the routine acceptance of anything that would be considered preposterous in the Farm Belt.

After Jay and Sam left, I went upstairs to shower and get dressed for the day's activities.

A short while later, when I had cleaned up and put on a pair of jeans, I was standing at the bathroom sink shaving. The door to the hallway was open and Bobby appeared at the top of the stairs with a cup of coffee in his hand. Leaning against the door jamb, he launched into the story of his life without any prompting whatsoever. Dustin, he informed me, was his natural son, but he'd never been married or divorced.

He and his partner of some eighteen years, Steve, had been living for more than a decade in a small Mississippi town. Everyone there knew they were gay, but, contrary to what one might expect in a small Mississippi town, no one hassled them.

At some point, Bobby had been talking to an old female friend who lived in Seattle and had recently been paid as a surrogate for an infertile couple. During the course of their conversation, she mentioned to Bobby that she'd be willing to do it again if he and Steve ever decided they wanted a child. Bobby decided that he *did* want a child, so he made the arrangements, flew up to Seattle, and impregnated her.

At this point my curiosity got the best of me and I interrupted. "Hold it. How did you impregnate her? Artificial insemination?"

"No, I just did it the regular, old-fashioned way," he said with a wily smile.

"Was it difficult?" I wondered aloud. "I mean, I would think it would be tough to do that purely for business purposes, especially with someone I was friends with."

Bobby shook his head slightly and cocked his jaw. "No, I just went up there and did it. Just like that."

"And you got her pregnant on the first try?" I said, amazed.

"Yup. First try," he boasted, fairly beaming with pride.

"It didn't bother Steve that you were actually having sex with someone else?" I queried.

"Steve didn't know," he said with a twinkle.

"He thought it was going to be artificial insemination?"

"No, he didn't know I was trying to get a kid," he explained. "I didn't tell him until after she was pregnant."

"You're kidding!" I shrieked.

"I always figure it's easier to ask for forgiveness than permission," he answered with a wicked smile.

So Dustin was born and Bobby and Steve began raising him, pretty much like any other couple in Mississippi, with one notable exception. Once again, contrary to expectation, Dustin was accepted at school and not hassled by the other children about his alternative family. In fact, it didn't really concern Dustin in the least that his family was different until he was nine years old and they moved to another state.

As the result of a business opportunity, the three of them moved to Miami, Florida. In his new school there, Dustin was harassed constantly by the other children, learning the entire spectrum of derisive terms for homosexuals in a very short time. Parents wouldn't let their kids play with him, and Bobby and Steve had a lot of explaining to do to Dustin. They immediately began looking for somewhere else to live and moved to Pasadena soon after.

In California, Dustin was once again accepted by the other children, and the entire family is living happily ever after. In comparison to the kids he now goes to school with, many of whom count entire casts of soap operas as their parents, Dustin's family is rather simple and old-fashioned.

In the short time it took me to shave, all my questions about Bobby had been answered without my even having to ask. But I wondered what had caused him to be so forthcoming and trusting. I'm not the sort of person people usually confide in easily; this was much more like something that would happen to my wife. In addition to the "Judy Garland gene," she is also in possession of the "Ann Landers gene," whereby people regularly tell her everything from their religious beliefs to their sexual preferences within minutes of having met her. I, on the other hand, will know someone for years without knowing much more about him than the way he looks. It is not uncommon for me to come home from having lunch with a longtime buddy and have my wife ask something like, "How's Rick? Is the baby sleeping through the night yet?"

Bewildered, I ask, "What baby?"

Exasperated, she indulges me, "Rick and Patty had a baby a couple of months ago, remember?"

"Who's 'Patty'?"

"Rick's *wife*, you idiot!" she flings at me in disgust. "We went to their wedding two years ago next month. I wore a floral print dress, and you wore your green sport coat with your Doctor Seuss tie. We sat in the eleventh row on the groom's side next to a red-haired woman whose husband had just lost his job at Frito-Lay and an old man who was recovering from gallbladder surgery! *Remember?*"

"Sort of," I offer feebly.

"I can't believe he didn't mention the baby even *once!* What did you talk about?"

"I don't know. Movies . . . new video games . . ."

"I can't believe you sometimes," she says for the umpteenth time.

You can see why I was surprised when Bobby began telling me the story of his life. I wondered if I might not have absorbed the scent of some truth-serum hormone from my wife, causing Bobby to spill his guts involuntarily.

Then something else occurred to me. The day before, Shane had done a similar thing by telling me the story of his girlfriend and the backfiring E-mail surveillance caper. Had I somehow attained the Ann Landers gene by osmosis? Was I turning into my wife? Would I soon be able to extract personal details about the lives of strangers at weddings?

The rest of the morning was spent driving around Los Angeles on a whirlwind tour of the local sights. I stopped to take a picture of Lucille Ball's old house in Bel Air for my eight-year-old daughter. She had, in the past few years, become a huge fan of the old *I Love Lucy* show, watching episodes on tape over and over until she could recite entire scenes, complete with Ricky's much-exaggerated Cuban accent, a trick we called upon her to perform on many a car trip. She had also become fascinated with Lucy and Desi trivia, watching documentaries about them and retelling the facts she had learned.

We also stopped by the old Grauman's Chinese Theater (which is called something else now, but who cares?), where movie stars have been leaving their prints in the cement for decades. It was a warm, sunny morning, and there was a formidable crowd of tourists milling around, taking pictures, gazing downward, measuring their hands and feet against those of various celebrities. Bobby and I split up to look around independently, and I tried to find Lucille Ball's prints so I could take another picture for my daughter. As I was wandering through the crowd, someone touched my arm and spoke to me.

"Hey, come over here. I want to show you something," he said.

I looked up with some confusion and saw that it was a middle-aged Asian man with thick, horn-rimmed glasses taped together at one corner. His shirt was vivid, shiny, lime-green polyester, and he wore tight, white bell-bottom jeans and green patent leather shoes.

"What do you want?" I asked warily.

He smiled warmly as he tugged at my arm and said, "I want to show you something."

"What do you want to show me?" I asked casually, not

ready to trust him but not inclined to run screaming through the streets for a policeman, either.

"I want to show you the prints you've been looking for." He winked and smiled knowingly.

I smiled a little, too, content to humor him for the time being. "How do you know what I'm looking for?" I asked.

He leaned closer and spoke quietly as he made a circular motion in the air with his index finger. "I know how to spot a man who's 'spinning the wheel.'"

These words struck me like a pillowcase full of auto parts, and I instantly realized this guy could be for real. "Sajak?" I said, leaning toward him and looking through his thick lenses, deep into his eyes. "Is that you?"

He chuckled a little and said, "No, my friend, I am not he. But it is he who sends me."

"Do you have a message for me?" I asked eagerly.

"I have something to show you," he said, and tugged at my arm again.

I enthusiastically followed him through the crowd to a remote corner of the densely packed plaza, eager to see what Sajak had sent him to show me. When he reached his destination, he stopped, turned around, and put one hand on my chest.

"Wait a minute, someone is already there," he said. He looked over his shoulder at a couple of tourists gazing at a set of prints on the ground. I strained to see around him to find out whose they were, but the crowd was too thick. After a moment, he lowered his hand and said, "Come on. The coast is clear."

We took a few more steps, and he motioned to the ground before him dramatically. "Behold," he said in a quiet, reverent voice.

I gazed down at the square of concrete before us and saw a pair of hand- and footprints with a signature below. I squinted to read it but could not make out the sloppy writing, now old and worn with time. "Whose is it? I can't make it out," I said.

"You can't make it out!" he snapped, a bit annoyed. "It's Garry Moore!"

"Garry Moore?" I asked, a little confused. I recognized the name but couldn't place it.

"Yes! Garry Moore! Yes!" he spat. After pausing a moment to absorb the puzzled look on my face, he could see I was still drawing a blank. "Garry Moore was the first great game-show host!" he announced. "Remember *I've Got a Secret*?"

"Of course, yes!" I exclaimed as it started to come back to me. "I used to watch that when I was a kid!" I stared at the prints again, waiting for him to say something else, to tell me why Sajak wanted me to see this. He, too, gazed toward the ground, an intense look of reverence and awe on his face.

After a few moments of silence, I asked innocently, "So what's the deal with it?"

He looked up at me incredulously, as if I had just asked if I could borrow his new Mercedes to compete in a demolition derby. *"What's the deal with it?"* he repeated. "This is hardly the time for levity!"

"I wasn't kidding. I was just wondering why Sajak wanted me to see this," I explained apologetically.

The strange man glared at me as though he had been supremely insulted. "Garry Moore is the *father* of American game-show hostery, young man. Pat Sajak wouldn't be who he is today had this great man not blazed the trail!" His tone was both paternal and condescending. He seemed disgusted with my ignorance.

I looked at the ground again for a moment, then back at him, still bewildered. Clearly exasperated, he continued his lecture.

"Nor would there be a Gene Rayburn, Wink Martindale, Monty Hall, Tom Kennedy . . ."

"Yes. I see," I said reverentially, pretending to grasp his meaning. But he seemed to be able to tell I was bluffing.

". . . or Peter Marshall or Allen Ludden or Alex Trebek or Hugh Downs!" he continued forcefully.

I tried to play along tentatively, hoping some understanding would begin to present itself. "And so Pat wanted me to see it because he was a big fan of his?" I asked timidly.

The man just stared at me through his Coke-bottle lenses

for what seemed like minutes. Receiving no response, I looked at the prints again, then at the man, then the prints.

"Is that it?" I asked again. "He just wanted me to see them?"

"Why is Sajak wasting his time with you?" he uttered bitterly, and strode off briskly through the crowd. I chased after him, still eager to know what it was that I had missed.

"What do you mean, why is he wasting his time with me?" I called out as I pushed past dozens of tourists. "Hey, I'm doing my best. I just don't get it, okay?" Without responding, he kept walking. "What am I supposed to do? How am I supposed to know what you're talking about if you don't tell me?" I pleaded to no avail. Aggravated at his enigmatic stubbornness, I finally reached my limit. I stopped and shouted after him, "So it's a slab of sidewalk with Garry Moore's signature! *Big deal!* I'm supposed to be *impressed* by that?"

At this, the little man stopped dead in his tracks and spun around. With an icy stare he lifted his arm out in front of him and pointed one bony, accusatory finger toward me. He spoke slowly and deliberately. "There are none whose wheels are so still as those who will not spin." As the words sank into the murmur of the crowded plaza, he turned and walked away.

"Thanks, that helps a lot," I called out half-heartedly.

More than a little embarrassed by the spectacle of it all, I wandered back through the crowd to find the Garry Moore prints again. Perhaps I had missed something. Perhaps the meaning of this encounter would suddenly occur to me if I studied the cement more carefully. Given the nature of my experiences with Sajak thus far, however, it was no surprise to me when I could not find them anywhere. Finally, I ran into Bobby again but said nothing to him of what had taken place, and we left.

Throughout the morning my voice had continued to descend into the irretrievable depths of hoarseness, and the few words I had shouted as I chased Sajak's disco-clad messenger had pushed it beyond the breaking point. I had the sinking feeling I would soon be rendered completely mute if I didn't do something to treat the condition immediately. We stopped at a convenience store, and I bought a bagful of over-the-counter remedies that included cough drops and bottled lemonade.

Bobby understood that it was necessary for me to conserve my voice as much as possible, so it was a quiet drive to our next destination. He had agreed to drop me off at the home of my next overnight hosts, a nuclear family residing in the suburbs of Orange County, some forty minutes away. As we drove, I thought about my encounter at Grauman's and tried to make some sense of it, but I came up empty. Was it just me, or was Sajak's guidance becoming even *more* obscure? I was feeling very tense about the morning's confrontation, but at least I wasn't as apprehensive about the next stop on my tour.

Cyndi, the matriarch of the family I was to stay with that night, had first contacted me several years earlier, inquiring about buying one of the original *Bizarro* drawings. We hit it off well during that first conversation and started something of a long-distance friendship. Her husband, Sandy, was a captain with the Los Angeles Police Department, and Cyndi began buying the original art from virtually every law-enforcement-themed cartoon I'd published. The entire family had become avid *Bizarro* fans, reading it daily in *The Orange County Register*. Cyndi and I chatted by phone a few times each year, and I was a permanent member of their Christmas-card list. The greeting-card photos showed the yearly progression of their family: Julie, the oldest daughter and her husband; Steven, their only son; and teen-aged Lindsay, their youngest.

Cyndi had mentioned more than once over the years, "If you're ever in L.A. and need a place to stay . . . ," so when I began planning the E-mail tour, I sent her a letter asking if they'd be interested in being one of my hosts. They accepted readily and became the only link in any of the cities I have visited whom I did not meet through the Internet. In spite of our phone and mail association, this visit would be our first face-to-face encounter and my first chance to speak at length to any of them other than Cyndi. As fate would have it, however, my voice was all but completely gone by the time I arrived.

As Bobby pulled up in front of their angular, *Brady Bunch*–era split-level home, Cyndi appeared at the door.

"Welcome!" she called out, smiling broadly.

"Hi!" I mouthed, a wisp of hushed air escaping soundlessly from my throat.

"He has laryngitis," Bobby informed her as we approached the front door.

We entered, unburdened ourselves of my luggage, and Bobby and Cyndi introduced themselves as I whispered and pointed to my throat apologetically.

From the kitchen, a half level below, appeared Steven, their tall, ruggedly handsome, twenty-four-year-old son who was living at home temporarily while attending the Orange County Police Academy. He was in the middle of grabbing a bite to eat before leaving for the academy and approached us, sandwich in hand, wearing gray sweat pants, tennis shoes, and a tight white T-shirt stretched taut across his broad, muscular frame. A giant black handgun was in a holster strapped around his waist.

"This is my son, Steven," Cyndi announced as we all shook hands. "He's on his way to the police academy in a few minutes."

"You eat with a *gun* on!" Bobby exclaimed abruptly, struggling to conceal a swoon as he shook Steven's hand. Steven greeted him politely and made some explanatory remark about the pistol.

I stood for a moment, cherishing this rare and priceless clash of culture as dramatically gay Bobby with earrings and coifed hair met traditionally macho cop-to-be Steven with sandwich and sidearm. It was the sort of moment only "real life" can pull off—too exaggerated to be portrayed on TV or in the movies without being accused of being preposterous or clichéd. Weeks later, after I had returned home, Bobby wrote to me of this meeting: "Hope your visit with the cop's family in Orange County went well. What was the deal with Mr. Handgun eating lunch wearing a pistol? He was pretty cute, though—I'd let him frisk me *anytime.*"

The three of them chatted for a few minutes as I looked on in silence. I whispered my thanks to Bobby for his hospitality, and he left, leaving me alone with my new hosts.

As we retired to the barstools between their kitchen and den, Cyndi prepared some hot apple cider for my throat, and we attempted to converse. The frustration of being so completely disabled in such a situation was profound. It was awkward enough to have invited myself into the homes of strangers, but to be unable to talk to them was unbearable. I thought ahead to the people I would be meeting in the days to come and began to sink into a vile depression at the thought of being rendered a pathetic mime. For the most part, the only reason people had invited me into their homes in the first place was for the chance to get to know the person behind one of their favorite cartoons. Robbed of my voice, I was also robbed of a large portion of my personality. I certainly wasn't prepared to be able to work my way across the country with funny faces, charades, and shadow puppets.

Shortly after Steven and his gun left for the academy, Cyndi's husband, Sandy, returned home from work and Lindsay from school. The Wassons are an extremely likable and friendly family and made me feel almost as though I were visiting relatives. They were relaxed, helpful, and eager to make me feel at ease about my silence predicament, but underlying the outward congeniality I sensed a feeling of disappointment in all of us. After years of abbreviated long-distance dealings, we were finally presented with a chance to get to know each other in person, only to have the opportunity snatched from our grasp at the last minute and irretrievably dropped into a deep, dark, silent crevasse.

We all did the best we could considering the circumstances

and had an enjoyable evening with a small group of friends they had invited over. We joked and exchanged stories, mine distilled down to a whispered few sentences, theirs a little longer to compensate for my lack of vocal endurance.

Through a combination of Morse code and semaphore I asked Sandy some questions about the O. J. Simpson case. The verdict had been handed down only a few weeks before, so I had not yet reached my current level of complete and total saturation. It was an interesting conversation as Sandy knew all the officers involved, including Mark Fuhrman. He was able to give me a professional's point of view of the case, which only served to further cement in my mind what most people have believed all along: Justice is blind. And sometimes deaf and dumb and numb and senseless, too.

Fortunately, the friends they had invited over for the evening were a boisterous crew that kept themselves and me howling with laughter most of the evening without my help.

The next morning my voice had recovered only marginally and I sensed that it would fade quickly once I started using it again. Sandy and Cyndi drove me downtown and dropped me off, luggage in tow, in front of the L. A. Times building, where I was to meet Nancy Tew, the editor in charge of the comics page, for lunch. I had been looking forward to speaking with Nancy for weeks and had a number of issues I wanted to discuss with her. My prospects for achieving much during this discussion were extremely poor, however, because of my recently acquired muteness. But you can't fault a guy for trying.

For some time, the *L. A. Times* had been running *Bizarro* only every other day, rotating my cartoon with another one in the same rectangle. They also did (and do) this with a number of other features as a way of offering a greater number of different comics to their readers without using any more space. It is actually a very clever solution to a problem that is facing the entire newspaper industry; the cost of newsprint is rising while subscriptions are falling. This has caused a financial crunch that has forced many papers to reduce their size and their costs and increase their ad space. When cutting costs, many papers will go first to the syndicated comics and columns, which they have to *purchase,* and cut back on the number they buy. While cutting back one's expenditures during hard economic times seems to make sense at first, to my mind it is a mistake. Of the three main components of a newspaper—news, ads, and syndicated features—the comics and columns are the only thing readers can't get somewhere else more easily, i.e., radio and television. To cut the number of comics and columns is to cut the one reason that many readers subscribe to the paper in the first place. People frequently say they only buy the paper for the comics, or for a columnist, but very few people say they only buy the paper for the news or the ads.

So the *L. A. Times*'s solution to the rising cost of newsprint was to conserve space without cutting the number of comics. It seemed a clever and admirable solution—with the exception of using *my* comic as one of the ones to be rotated, while a couple of other notably cheesy, less original cartoons (and with fewer readers, I would guess) were being printed every day. Although I had no real plan for getting to the bottom of this grievous situation and correcting it, I was hoping my lunch with Nancy Tew would be a step in the right direction. Once again, life showed me how wrong I can be.

In L.A. the comics editor is not a crusty, hard-nosed, white guy over fifty, as most editors seem to be, but a warm, intelligent, and friendly woman of undiscernible age. Originally, I was glad she was a woman as I get along with women better than men, especially *older* men. But, alas, without a voice with which to get along, it was a moot point. The majority of the lunch consisted of the tedious process of her asking me "yes" or "no" questions and me nodding and coughing. I'm sure she was thoroughly charmed.

I had had high hopes of gently persuading her that *Bizarro* had more merit than a few of the comics she was printing daily, and to give me a permanent, daily spot and maybe even pick up my Sunday panel. But by way of filling the silence with energetic chatter, she told me enough about herself and her theory of comics to leave me feeling that I was probably lucky to have any spot in the paper at all. It was my impression that while she obviously liked *Bizarro* enough to buy it, she felt my comic was often too abstruse to appeal to a wide enough audience to warrant printing it every day. She also mentioned a few of her favorite comics, and I could immediately see that our taste in cartoons was somewhat different. I quickly gave up my original objective and spent the remainder of the meeting just trying not to lose the tentative spot I had been given. I began to feel as if I were drowning in a whirlpool of my dying hopes for the meeting, and in my panic my thoughts turned again to Sajak. Desperate for some support or guidance I looked everywhere for a sign from Pat: in my salad, in my soup, in the swirling reflections of the ice cubes in our drinks. When Nancy returned to the buffet, I even picked through the remains of *her* salad looking for even a tomato seed or crouton that resembled him. There was nothing. Not a single vowel or consonant.

Even *with* my voice I don't know what I thought I would have been able to do, really. In truth, I expected my game-show guru to lead me through the darkness and light my path, giving me just the right words to say. Or perhaps he would take the situation in hand completely and inspire my editor companion to turn to me during lunch and say, "Dan, I'll be honest with you; I'm in over my head. I've lost faith in my own judgment, I'm overworked, and my boss is threatening to fire me if the comics page doesn't improve. You seem like a bright, talented guy with a kind heart. Could you redesign the entire comics section for me?"

With appropriate humility, I would agree to help and begin by placing my comic prominently on the front page, putting the handful of others I thought were good inside on page two. I would then relegate a token number of other popular but dull comics to a page hidden in the back somewhere. I would also add *Bizarro* to the Sunday comics section, replacing *Calvin and Hobbes*'s half page (the retirement of which had been announced that very day, to the sobs and moans of the entire nation). She would thank me and ask me not to tell anyone, and I would nod in compassionate understanding and slip out the back door. Months later, the sudden and incredible surge of the *L. A. Times*'s circulation would be attributed to its bold move in the area of comics, and papers all over North America would follow suit. Within a couple of years, *I'd* be the one retiring to the sobs and moans of the nation and some *other* hoarse slob would be having lunch with an editor, fantasizing about restructuring the comics page!

But Sajak did not step in and solve my problems for me; spiritual guidance rarely comes in the form of a rescuing superhero. Instead, I sat there silently trying not to burp inadvertently or spill soup all over her and get myself canceled completely. After lunch we went to her office for a few minutes while waiting for the security guard downstairs to call to notify me that my next connection had arrived to pick me up.

While we were at her desk, we discussed the forthcoming retirement of *Calvin and Hobbes* and she asked if I had any suggestions for what to replace it with in the Sunday comics section. I hoarsely whispered, *Bizarro*. She glanced up and smiled as if I were joking and proceeded to mention a few of the candidates she had been considering, along with her line of reasoning for each. This was definitely not a person who was in over her head or had lost faith in her judgment.

I shrank to the size of a Smurf doll and waited quietly for the security guard to call. When the phone finally rang, she stood up, leaned over her desk, and peered down at the fuzzy little blue gnome sitting in the middle of the huge chair and told me that my ride had arrived. I thanked her for lunch, hopped down, and waddled toward the elevators, trying not to get stepped on.

On the ride down I struggled to maintain some feeling of dignity despite the huge contrast between my goals for the meeting and its actual outcome. With more than a little bitterness I was also wondering why Sajak had abandoned me at such a crucial time during my trip. Just then, something caught my eye in the elevator's shiny, brass-button panel. I leaned forward to get a better look, and, to my great alarm, staring back at me from where my own reflection should have been was Sajak.

"What are you doing!" I gasped, clutching my chest. "You scared me to death!" I felt the elevator stop between floors.

Unimpressed, he leaned casually against the wall panel on his side of the reflection and said in a calm voice, "Sorry. How was your lunch?"

"You've got to be kidding!" I hissed and croaked. "How do you *think* my lunch was? Listen to my voice!"

"Sounds like you're getting a little laryngitis," he said sympathetically. "You'd better take it easy."

"Where were you when I needed you?" I demanded, glaring at him between the seven and five buttons.

"What happened? Why did you need me?" he asked innocently enough to convince me he really hadn't been aware of my dilemma in the past hour.

"I was *trying* to make a good impression on the cartoon editor of one of the biggest papers in the country, and I could hardly speak! Couldn't you have helped me out a little? Couldn't you have helped me plead my case?"

Pat knit his brow as he carefully considered his reply. "I don't know how much I could have helped, Dan, even if I *did* work that way. This isn't the Ozarks, you know, this is Los Angeles, California. People here don't take as readily to visions in their potato salad as they do back where you come from."

"I'm *not* from the Ozarks!" I spat back.

"Whatever," he said with a wave of his hand. "Look . . . this is *your* pilgrimage, *your* life. If anything is going to get done, *you're* going to have to do it. I'm not a witch, I can't just wiggle my nose like Samantha and have Larry Tate change his mind about firing you," he added sarcastically. "Besides, I didn't even know you were having trouble."

"Didn't *know*? Aren't you supposed to be watching me? After all, you're the one who insisted I take this journey of the soul in the first place."

"I beg your pardon! I believe that financing your book tour on the backs of your fans was *your* idea, Mr. Marketing Genius," he quipped indignantly.

"*My* idea, inspired by *your* harassment from the spirit world . . . or the fifth dimension, or *wherever* it is you live!"

Unaffected by my gibe, Pat straightened himself and replied proudly, "I live in the hearts and minds of America's game-show watchers if you must know." He paused reverently, then continued, "Besides, you obviously don't understand the first thing about the spirit world. While I am aware of your general progress and can see more of the big picture than you can, I don't just sit around on Mount Olympus all day in a toga watching your every move in the reflection of a magic pool."

"I don't expect you to hold my hand," I replied defensively. "I'd just like a little more guidance in difficult situations, okay? I'm not very good at this sort of thing."

Pat relented, saying, "The only way to get better at it is to *do* it, but I'll try to keep a closer eye on you in the future."

With a gentle shudder, the elevator started moving again as he added, "We've got to get going now. You've got someone waiting in the lobby, and there's a delivery driver on the second floor who's in a hurry to get back to his car. He's double parked."

"Wait a minute!" I cried. "I want to ask you about something!"

"Sorry, it will have to wait. We don't have time," he said impatiently.

"It's about Garry Moore!" I blurted out.

Pat's head snapped around and stared at me point-blank as the elevator jerked to a halt again. "What about Garry Moore?" he asked.

"I want to know who that guy was that you sent to show me Garry Moore's footprints in the sidewalk," I said calmly.

"You were at Grauman's today?" he inquired, obviously concerned.

"Yes, I was. And this weird little man came up to me and wanted to show me Garry Moore's footprints in the sidewalk. He said you sent him, but he wouldn't tell me *why* you wanted to show me those things or what they were supposed to mean to me. Can you shed some light on it?"

Pat smiled a bit, then explained. "First of all, I *didn't* send him, but I'm not surprised he contacted you. How did you react?"

I told Sajak how I had failed to see the point behind the strange man's efforts and how angry it had made him. Pat covered his mouth with the back of his hand and stifled a laugh.

"Ooh, I'll bet he was steamed!" he said as he continued to battle a chuckle.

"Who was he? What was the big deal?" I asked, wanting to be let in on the joke.

Pat sobered up a bit and explained. "The man you talked to *was* Garry Moore. Or the ghost of Garry Moore, rather. Every time a game-show host takes someone under his wing, Garry comes down from his throne in disguise and pesters them into recognizing him as the father of the genre. It's sort of pathetic if you ask me."

"Is he the father of the genre?"

"Yes, of course he is, that's what's pathetic about it. He's the most venerated gaming emcee of all time, yet he remains eternally insecure about his place in the industry," Pat explained.

"What's his problem?" I wondered aloud. "Most people would give their right arm to achieve the level of success he did. You'd think being *numero uno* would be enough."

"You're not taking into account the 'show-business ego,' my friend. No amount of praise is *ever* enough," Pat admitted. "Plus, I think he's a little bored. After a lifetime of parties, openings, celebrity shindigs, signing autographs, doing interviews—the afterlife is a bit of a disappointment for him."

"A disappointment? But aren't there *tons* of dead celebrities for him to schmooze with?"

"Well, you'd think so, but apparently the whole celebrity phenomenon is a human invention—it only works on Earth. In the afterlife, everybody is sort of faceless and equal. That's pretty hard for Hollywood-types like us to deal with," he lamented.

"Well, if I'd known, I would've acted impressed," I said, feeling a bit sorry for old Garry.

"Yeah, it would've made his day. He's a really nice guy, actually. Next time I see him, I'll smooth it over with him for you."

The elevator started to move again as I asked Pat one final question. "What's it like to be able to talk to dead guys?"

"It's pretty cool if you can stand the smell," he quipped.

"That's disgusting!" I shrieked.

Pat laughed mischievously. "I'm just kidding . . . spirits don't smell, you knucklehead. I'll see you later."

The doors opened on the second floor and Sajak disappeared from the button-panel reflection as the antsy delivery driver rushed in.

Pushing the events of the morning from my mind, I thought forward to the person waiting in the lobby, Sarabeth.

Sarabeth was a woman I had corresponded with many times by E-mail, long before I began making my tour arrangements, and I looked forward to meeting her. She seemed very sweet and genuinely thrilled at the prospect of meeting me, and, after my disastrous lunch with Ms. Tew, I needed a self-esteem boost in the worst way. Sarabeth had asked if she could bring along her best friend, Alyce, also a big fan, so I was ready for a relaxing afternoon of ego stroking with a couple of doting middle-aged ladies.

As the elevator doors opened onto the fairly cavernous lobby, before I even glimpsed sight of my contact I was instantly and ferociously attacked by a chemical onslaught of an intensity rarely experienced by anyone since the Gulf War.

NINE

Flirting with Kryptonite

The air was thick with a man-made floral assault that made me wonder if I had momentarily been transported from the L. A. Times building to the cosmetics department at J C Penney. My eyes burned, my throat swelled shut, and my hair became nearly straight. Across the way, perhaps thirty feet from me, I could see a woman, presumably Sarabeth, standing at the guard desk. There was no one else in the lobby; the perfume cloud had to be hers.

In preparing for my trips, one question that always came up in the E-mail correspondence was "Where do you want to eat?" I had been very careful to tell each of my hosts that the only thing I could not eat was fish. (I'm not allergic to it, I just can't stand it.) Along those lines, I also made sure to tell each of my overnight hosts that I don't smoke and am slightly allergic to cats. I can stay in a house with a cat or two, as long as I don't touch them, but I probably wouldn't do well in a house with twelve or more cats (a situation that comes up much more frequently than a reasonable person would think it should in a civilized nation). I thought I had covered all my weaknesses with these three caveats, but with the opening of the elevator doors in the L. A. Times building came the realization of one I had missed: artificial fragrances. They are my Kryptonite.

I don't mind strong fragrances of *all* kinds; I'm not one of those chemically sensitive invalids who has to live in a giant, sterile sandwich bag out in the desert. I can stand the smell of food cooking and flowers blooming and pine trees pining. I don't even mind the emanation of a cattle truck. What I can't stand, however, are *chemically created* fragrances. Not being a chemist, I don't know what it is exactly that causes my throat to swell shut, my tongue to enlarge, my eyes to water, my nasal cavities to burn, my heart to pound, my lungs to collapse, my scalp to throb, and my brain to shrivel when I smell these odorous agents. All I know is that something stinks and I can't breathe. I have only become sensitive to this in the past few years, but having become so, I have become all too aware of how many people in this country drench themselves in Eau de Old Lady several times each day. I've also noticed that people who do this to themselves are also very likely to use all kinds of other flowery chemical weapons designed to stink up the house and car, too. In a short time, their sniffers are so desensitized that, like smokers and people with litter boxes in their kitchens, they are the only ones who don't know how bad they smell. Men are just as likely as women to offend in this area, but it is my experience that the wearing of these chemical disguises is an almost exclusively American practice. In most other locations around the globe, people smell good by simply remaining clean. (Of course, in a few other places, less savory human scents are actually considered desirable, but we will leave that issue for another forum.)

There was no way that Sarabeth could have known this about me since I hadn't mentioned it (then again, how does one mention such a thing politely? "I don't like seafood, I'm a nonsmoker, I'm a little allergic to cats, and, oh yeah, you're not one of those people who wears a ton of cheap cologne, are you?"), so she had no idea that her personal bouquet was tantamount to forcing me to eat boiled catfish while holding a chain-smoking cat in my lap all afternoon.

Realizing it was too late to remedy the situation, I braced myself, resigned to enduring the odor politely in silence. What's a little lack of oxygen among friends?

Crossing the lobby with a smile, I introduced myself, retrieved my bags from the security guard, and headed outside with Sarabeth. She informed me that Alyce, the friend she had said she was bringing along, was guarding their illegally parked car. Once outside the building, I detected the density in the air increase twofold; just my luck, Alyce, too, was a member of the scent brigade. Clearly, I was doomed to an afternoon of labored breathing.

On a more positive note, Sarabeth and Alyce turned out to be just what my punctured ego had hoped for and more. They were extremely attentive and complimentary, providing precisely the atmosphere of unrestrained adoration that I needed, although they were not the doting middle-aged ladies I had pictured. True, they were forty-something schoolteachers and mothers, but both were complete knockouts who could have passed for thirty, dressed to the nines in tight sweaters and high-heeled shoes, gigantic, matching Louis the XIV curly hairdos, and dripping in jewelry. Very soon I realized that these were a couple of sexy schoolmarms who had broken free of their suburban shackles for the day and were determined to live life to its fullest—at least for one afternoon. They were up for anything, hurtling toward the fast lane, living on the edge, hellbent for leather. They had left the kids and the kitchens and the snot-nosed students and the spouses and the grocery lists behind for one frenzied, extravagant day in the city with an off-the-wall

cartoonist. A mute cartoonist with a shriveled brain who was already a little homesick and could scarcely breathe, but a cartoonist nonetheless.

Tossing my bags in the trunk, I climbed into the backseat of their car. As we discussed our options for the afternoon, I asked politely what fragrance they were wearing. Simultaneously, they answered, "Ornament by Vanna White." It was a sign from Sajak, of course. A token nod to tell me that he hadn't forsaken me, that he was still guiding me, that a person must endure hardship to achieve his goals. I was comforted and optimistic, if a little dizzy from the lack of fresh air.

After much debate about what to do, we decided to walk up and down Venice Beach and chat. I'd always been a fan of kooks and strangeness and the weather was ideal, so the activity seemed perfect. The afternoon was quite enjoyable, even if it wasn't "frenzied" or terribly "near the edge."

Venice Beach lived up to its reputation as the display case for the nation's foremost nonconformists, and I enjoyed immensely the chance to view it with two such attractive and flirtatious women. I had been happily married to the same woman for sixteen years and was on that particular afternoon still as infatuated with her as I was after our first date and had never had any thought of cheating. But I am still human and not immune to the charms of other women or the shallow pleasures of flirting. So flirt we did, all afternoon and into the evening.

Sarabeth was happily married and consequently less earnest in her advances, but Alyce was quite a bit more assertive. She had been divorced from her first husband some years earlier and had recently experienced a falling-out with her latest boyfriend, so there was nothing to inhibit her in her role as temptress. She understood that I was a very devoted family man right from the start (and even commented on how I had lavishly dedicated every one of my nine cartoon books to my wife and daughters), which may have encouraged her advances all the more since she knew I was "safe." But her flirtation became increasingly bold as the afternoon wore on. By the time she had had a couple of glasses of wine over dinner at a dark Italian restaurant, she was becoming downright overt.

Though I never seriously considered acting on the situation, I will admit that I was somewhat flattered by the prospect. I found her extremely attractive and played the game perhaps a bit more than I should have. By the time we finished dinner and moved on to the bookstore for my signing, the three of us were becoming so familiar that we must have looked like a mobile ménage à trois.

At a large dinner gathering, a guy once asked me, "What's the best thing about being a cartoonist?" Tired of answering the same questions in the same old way, I blurted out the first thing off the top of my head: "The groupies."

It got a good laugh, as we all realized how stupid it sounded; cartoonists are about the last pseudocelebrity types one would expect to have groupies. I had certainly never encountered any in my own career. But in L.A. I was meeting what could have potentially been my first. It was a terrific feeling at age thirty-seven, and I found myself drunk with the notion that a goofy little dork like me could be a sex symbol to a stranger. Only in Lala Land.

At the bookstore the crowd was larger than it had been at the previous signing but still a bit of a disappointment. The only thing more embarrassing than arriving at a deserted signing table alone is to show up with an entourage. If you're going to be decked out in ridiculous clothing (which I usually seem to be) with a pointy mustache and a fabulous babe on either arm, you'd better make damn sure there's someone waiting for you when you do. The small crowd of eight or ten people was not quite enough to justify our entrance. I was reminded of a boxer I once saw who climbed into the ring wearing a gold lamé robe, gold boots, and gold, leopard-skin trunks, only to be knocked out in the first round by a guy dressed like a real boxer.

Sarabeth and Alyce hung around the table with me for the duration of the signing, taking pictures of each other leaning over my shoulder and nuzzling my cheek while I wrote in people's books. During all of this, a dumpy and disheveled man with thick glasses stepped up to the table to have me sign his book. He was wearing a T-shirt with bold letters across the front that read IS YOUR CHURCH ATF APPROVED?, obviously referring to the Bureau of Alcohol, Tobacco and Firearms' attack on the religious compound of David Koresh and his followers in Waco, Texas, a year or so earlier. I thought it was a funny shirt and commented on it.

"Oh, I like your shirt!"

"Thanks very much," he began in a cartoonish voice reminiscent of Ratso Rizzo. He continued as he rummaged through a plastic shopping bag, "I have all your books here, Mr. Piraro, and want you to sign them all for me if you don't mind, including the new one."

I was impressed that he had been following my career. "Absolutely, no problem. I like anybody who likes me," I chattered as I began signing.

"And since you like the shirt," he continued, "let me give you something else." He searched comically through his shopping bag again, produced a computer floppy disk, and handed it to me. I attempted to read the hastily scrawled inscription on the label as I thanked him. I figured it was some comedy piece he had written about David Koresh.

When I had finished signing his books, he tucked the ungainly pile under his arm, gathered up his shopping bag, thanked me, and said good-bye. As soon as he shuffled away from the table, two security guards descended on him like California condors on a lame chipmunk, grabbed him by the arms, and began hurrying him toward the exit. Before I could process this scene, the publicity liaison for the store, a friendly but excitable woman named Sue, appeared from somewhere behind me and began frantically shouting questions at me.

"What did he give you? Where's that thing he gave you?" she barked.

I reached into the pocket of my backpack and produced the disk.

She grabbed for it frantically, shouting, "Give me that! That's got *viruses* in it, that will destroy your computer! That guy's a nut, he thinks he's David Koresh or Jesus or something!"

Just before Sue snatched it out of my hand, I read the ballpoint-pen inscription on the label: THE TRUTH ABOUT DAVID KORESH, JESUS CHRIST, AND THE ATF.

Disk clenched tightly between two fingers to avoid unnecessary contamination, she shrieked, "He comes in here all the time and bothers authors. He thinks he's reincarnated from David Koresh or something! This thing's got viruses, I guarantee! I can't let you keep this!" And she disappeared with it as suddenly as she had come. (Weeks later, the evicted customer sent me a long, rambling E-mail about how much money he regularly spent at that store, how unjust his apprehension was, and how he intended to take his considerable book-buying business to the competitor down the block from then on. I wrote back and asked him if he knew where I could get a T-shirt like his.)

At nine o'clock, the book signing was officially over and I was to say good-bye to my lovely companions for the day and meet my new host for the night. I was scheduled to be picked up at the bookstore by a freelance publicist named Thomas, who lived in Hollywood. But as the signing came to an end, he was nowhere to be seen.

Alyce and Sarabeth hung out in the store with me as I waited, wondering what could have happened to make him so late. I related how when I had called him from Dallas to tell him I wanted to accept his offer to stay the night, he had seemed unenthusiastic and a little cold.

By 9:15, we wondered if he had stood me up.

At 9:20, Alyce formally invited me to stay at her place if he didn't show. I nervously said I appreciated the offer but that I was sure he was on his way.

At 9:21, Alyce reminded me that I was more than welcome to stay with her if he didn't come soon. I thanked her again, said he was probably just stuck in traffic, and began to wonder what would happen if I were forced to accept her offer.

At 9:22, in a sultry voice remarkably like Sharon Stone's, Alyce suggested I call it a night and go home with her. Trying not to tremble visibly, I said that perhaps I should at least call Tom and see if he was home.

I rushed to a phone and called the number. It was Thomas's answering machine, into which I said, "Thomas, this is Dan Piraro, the cartoonist guy you said you'd let stay at your house tonight, and I'm at the bookstore and I hope you're on your way to pick me up because there is a very attractive woman here who's about to devour me."

At 9:24, I returned to where Sarabeth and Alyce were standing and told them I had left a message on Thomas's answering machine.

At 9:24:01, Alyce said she was sure he wasn't coming and why didn't we just throw my stuff into her car and take off.

I began to feel light-headed as the day's innocent and amusing flirtations were about to snap back like the end of a bullwhip and take out my eye. All day long I had been pretending to be a big celebrity with an irresistible way with the ladies. In truth, I'm a guy who's been married since he was barely twenty-one and has had no experience with casual sex since then. Even before I was married, I typically dated only one person at a time and didn't get terribly physical until I'd known her a while. Here, for the first time in my entire adult life, was a woman who seemed to be letting me know in no uncertain terms that she would probably sleep with me if I wanted to, after having known me only a few hours. It probably would have scared me to death even if I were single, but as a happily married father of two, it was terrifying.

If she took me home and let me stay the night in a bed of my own, no strings attached, fine. But all I could think was how awkward it would be if she got me to her place and threw herself at me full force. She looked to be in terrific shape (you don't get a body like hers past the age of twenty-two without working out a *lot*), and I wondered if I would even be *able* to defend myself. And, God forbid, what if Sarabeth wasn't as harmless and committed to her husband as she seemed? What if the two of them decided to gang up on me? How in hell would I explain to my wife that I had been molested simultaneously by two gorgeous women in Los Angeles? How does a guy maintain the look of a victim when his victimization entails every teenage boy's fantasy come true?

At 9:25 I said let's give Thomas until 9:30 at least. Alyce agreed and began tapping her foot, clicking her nails, and staring a hole through her watch. I watched anxiously as numerous people walked in and out of the store, but no Thomas.

At 9:29:59, a dark-haired young man walked into the bookstore with an inquisitive look on his face. The three of us were shoulder to shoulder near the door, staring questioningly at him. He walked past us slowly, staring back. I couldn't tell if he was looking for someone or just wondered why these three strangers were glaring at him. As he headed toward the back of the store and disappeared, I winced and Alyce let out a sigh of relief.

More people walked in and out of the door as Alyce grabbed my arm and announced, "That's it, nine-thirty! Let's go!"

Just then, the dark-haired man returned from the back of the store and asked me if I was Dan. *"YES!"* I shouted, and grabbed him by the shoulders as if he were my long-lost twin brother. "I thought you'd never get here!"

"You told me on the phone to be here at nine-thirty," he explained, a little taken aback by my enthusiasm. "I wondered if that was you when I came in, but I thought I'd go back to where the signings are to see if you were still there. When you were gone, I figured that must be you up front."

Smiling broadly, I apologized for the mix-up: "My mistake. The signing was over at nine." Alyce and Sarabeth hugged and kissed me good-bye and thanked me for a wonderful day. I thanked them for the same, for it had indeed been a most enjoyable afternoon and evening that had made me feel ten years younger (as well as fortunate to still be alive). They took a couple of last pictures of us together, then each grabbed one of the large posters announcing my signing from the easels by the door and left.

As soon as they were gone, Thomas turned to me and said hesitantly, "Am I wrong, or were they both very disappointed to see me?"

I explained the whole story to him on the way to his car.

Thomas and I went to a terrific little restaurant in Hollywood for a late-night dinner, then back to his apartment. He was dressed very smartly in a silvery-gray sport coat, black turtleneck, and black trousers. His apartment was decorated in the same color scheme, almost everything in either black, white, or gray.

At first I found him cold and somewhat remote, just as I had on the phone, and thought him a bit shallow and pretentious. His demeanor was very guarded and distant, and his apartment was almost a gay cliché of meticulous, colorless chic. Thus far, I was not enjoying this short leg of my journey very much, one of the consequences of choosing people at random, and was grateful that I was leaving for the airport early the next morning.

Within a short time, however, both of us began to loosen up, and we found ourselves engrossed in self-revelatory conversation, telling each other the great triumphs and heartbreaks of our lives, just as I had done with several of my other hosts. In this way, I found out he had been a championship figure skater, but *roller*, not ice. I told him I hadn't even known there was such a thing as competitive figure *roller* skaters, which was quite obviously a hot-button topic with him.

"That's just the problem, *no one* knows about it because it's never on TV! They only put *ice* skaters on TV!" he declared with exasperation. "That's something I'm trying to do in my business [public relations], get more roller skating competitions on television."

He then showed me a home videotape of some people skating in a recent competition. I was appropriately complimentary of their abilities, even though I didn't feel I knew enough about it to comment, but I was also immediately aware of the vast disparity between roller and ice skating. "It's very different from ice skating, isn't it?" I said tentatively.

"Yes!" he stated proudly. "We can string together a lot more complicated moves because we can glide a lot further! There's much less friction with ball bearings in wheels than with blades on ice."

I agreed politely but couldn't help but notice what I considered to be several formidable obstacles to his goal of getting this sport on national TV—the most obvious encumbrance being that roller skating is a lot *slower* than ice skating and, therefore, inherently less exciting to watch. Because of the weight of the skates, you can't jump as high, either. Also, the skates make an incredible amount of noise as the wheels clunk like bricks against the wooden floor each time the skater puts a foot down. So much so, in fact, that the noise of the skates on the tape we were watching actually drowned out the music. This could have been due to the limited technology of the home video recorder, of course, but it was very distracting nonetheless.

But what do I know? There's no sport in the world slower, clunkier, and more boring to watch than bowling, and it's been on television for years. And you've got to figure if people can watch golf and auto racing on television, they can watch anything. Roller skating is certainly more interesting than watching cars drive around in circles, and some of the accidents are nearly as good, too.

Somehow this discussion led to Thomas telling me of a personal tragedy that had touched him earlier that year. His lover of seven years, David, had died of AIDS only nine months earlier. Thomas had resumed skating after a ten-year hiatus shortly before David's death and had promised him that he would win a medal for him at the Southwest Pacific regional skating competition in July.

After David's passing, Thomas was faced with arranging a last-minute trip to Scotland, where David was from, for his funeral. Though the couple had always been welcomed and accepted by David's family there, at the funeral Thomas was openly shunned, left to face his grief alone.

Back in the States, he found himself too overcome with grief to function. Almost immediately, his skating instructor encouraged him to return to skating and make it to the competition in David's honor. Thomas followed her advice, picked himself up, and worked all the harder toward that goal. At age thirty-two, he kept his promise to David and won a bronze medal against competitors half his age and the right to compete at the national championships.

As Thomas told me this story, he produced a photocopy of an article that had run in the *L. A. Times* in a regular feature called "Local Hero." It was the sort of column that each week features a different local person who has done something particularly commendable in his or her life. But to my surprise, the article was not about Thomas but about his skating instructor, Mary, and how she had been instrumental in getting his life back on track despite his grief. "I owe every ounce of that bronze medal to Mary," Thomas was quoted as saying in the article.

He had been the one to submit her name to the paper as a possible subject. I thought it very admirable that he thought of *her* as the hero, in spite of all *he* had accomplished in the face of tragedy.

As I sat listening in the cool, dimly lit, black, white, and gray of his apartment, my original impressions of Thomas melted away. He no longer seemed shallow or pretentious but wounded and cautious. His apartment was no longer a meticulous, trendy cliché but a collection of articles chosen to reflect the preferences of the couple who lived there, now serving only as painful reminders of the missing companion and lost relationship. Photos of Thomas and David, souvenirs of their travels together, inanimate objects that used to be chairs and lamps and wall hangings now seemed to exist solely to speak of a lost future, the injustice of biological happenstance. These rooms were appropriately black and white and gray.

Somewhat to my surprise, I found myself relating my own family's loss to AIDS a few years earlier, a man named Steve. He had been my wife's and my friend since before we were married, my wife considered him her *best* friend, and he was a routine fixture in our home for many years. He was there for the birth of our children, he was there for every party and holiday, he was there when we barbecued in the backyard in the summer and when we stayed up late to watch Ed Wood movies on TV on the weekends. Our kids considered him an older brother, although he jokingly encouraged them to call him "Aunt Spiffy."

He wasted away slowly and painfully, as most with AIDS do, and died in 1991 at the age of forty-six.

Having shared our sob stories with sniffles and teary eyes, like a couple of old ladies, Thomas and I decided to call it a night. I was to sleep on a futon on the living-room floor; he retired to his bedroom. As I switched off the light and prepared to lie down, I glanced out of the large plate-glass window overlooking the street. A bus passed by the streetlight below, and on its side I could just make out a *Wheel of Fortune* advertisement. I took comfort in Pat Sajak's grinning face and thought about the second leg of my West Coast trip: San Francisco. I was to leave first thing in the morning.

TEN

Into the Jaws of Weirdness

I landed at the San Francisco Airport with a slowly improving but still pathetically weak voice. It was only the morning of day four of my nine-day trip, and I was already exhausted. I was discovering what politicians in democracies have known for centuries: It isn't easy meeting new people and being on your best behavior eighteen hours a day. I think it's even possible that this is the reason some democratic countries become dictatorships: The president is tired of having to be "on" all the time.

It also occurred to me that as exhausting as my experience had been so far, it was only a tiny sample of what a months-long political campaign must be like and that any person willing to put up with such a grueling schedule clearly isn't fit to lead. I congratulated myself on my cleverness and hoped I might one day get to use that quip on a national TV talk show, until I found out later that Will Rogers had already said it. (A similar thing had happened to me the first time I said, "I never met a dog I didn't like.")

Stepping off the plane in San Francisco, I realized that, just as in Los Angeles, I had not arranged a way to recognize my next contacts, a woman named Sue and her husband, John. So just as I had done at LAX a few days earlier, I strolled casually to the baggage claim area looking inquisitively into the faces of any likely candidates I passed. While waiting near the luggage carousel I checked to make sure my fly wasn't open, and, within a few minutes, Sue and John were able to spot me based on the picture on the back of my book.

When Sue first contacted me as a fan months earlier, she mentioned she was involved in an organization that rescues racing greyhounds after retirement and places them in homes as pets. As a lifelong dog lover, I was interested in her work and eventually agreed to design and illustrate a T-shirt for an upcoming reunion in the Bay Area of families that had adopted greyhounds. Sue was very grateful and was one of the first people to respond to my solicitation letter about my book tour.

She and John weren't equipped to put me up for the night, but they volunteered to drive me around the day I arrived. We had agreed that they would pick me up at the airport, which is on the southwest side of the bay, and drive me up to my book signing at the northwest end of the bay that afternoon, stopping along the way at my former editor's house for lunch.

When we got into the car, they said that we had plenty of time and would I mind if they drove me by their house in Berkeley to meet their dogs first. Never being one to turn down the opportunity to meet a good dog, much less three, I agreed.

On the way there we drove across the lower level of that double-decker bridge that collapsed during the last big earthquake, trapping people in their cars between the two levels like lunch meat on a sandwich. They pointed this out as we crossed on the lower level and I shuddered.

To a solid-grounded Midwest boy, it always seems a person must be more than half crazy to live under conditions where the buildings may become jiggling towers of gelatin at any

moment. When I mention this, Californians always say, in reference to my part of the country, "What about tornadoes?"
Then I say what about grass and forest fires, torrential rains,
floods, and mud slides. (A friend of mine from there once said
that living in California with its earthquakes, fires, and floods is
like living in the Old Testament.) Then they mention rednecks,
the Klan, and people with very large pickup trucks, hats, and
belt buckles. I counter with the hideous abundance of health-
food cafés and the frightening lack of institutions that sell fried
meat, not to mention the hoards of starry-eyed, would-be actors
and actresses cluttering the wait staff of every restaurant. As
you can see, this argument can go on indefinitely. I guess no
matter where you live, you choose your poison.

But perhaps even more frightening than the threat of a sudden earthquake while we traveled the lower level of the eighty-
seven miles of built-to-collapse Sandwich Bridge was the way
John drives. I should preface this by saying that John and Sue
are among the nicest and most pleasant people one would ever
want to meet, and I in no way wish to seem ungrateful for their
considerable hospitality and friendship. But John drives with a
style that I have seen before on several occasions, which I call
the "BHDD technique." It is so named because the passengers
of a car whose driver is employing this technique look like those
bobbing-head dashboard dolls.

The technique is one wherein the driver rhythmically
alternates the full force of his or her foot from the accelerator
pedal to the brake pedal constantly as long as the car is moving. Gas pedal to the floor for three seconds, brake to the floor
for three seconds, gas for three seconds, brake for three seconds, and so on.

People who drive this way often experience a much slower
rate of wear on their upholstery because they also tend to sit bolt
upright, chin out over the steering wheel, barely even touching

the seat. This benefit is outweighed, however, by the increased wear on the brake shoes and the deteriorating effects of frequent cleaning of the carpets due to the nausea of the passengers.

Apart from being a little sick to my head and stomach from the whiplash ride to John and Sue's house, I experienced one other discomfort that was not their fault. In my ongoing effort to recuperate from laryngitis, I had taken to drinking hot liquids and fruit juice almost unceasingly from morning till night, making it very difficult for me to be away from a rest room for more than a few minutes at a time. I had come to visit the men's room routinely before I left any building and again as soon as I arrived at the next. The long ride from the airport to Berkeley combined with John's dynamic style of driving was nearly a lethal combination on my bladder.

I survived in fairly dry shape, however, and enjoyed meeting their three very large and skinny dogs after I'd visited their bathroom. I made one more trip after playing briefly with the dogs, and we left, BHDD style, for our lunch date at the home of Stan Arnold, my former editor.

Stan and his family are among some of my favorite people of all time. He lives in a modest but comfortable house in Marin County and was an editor with *The San Francisco Chronicle* for many years, then later headed up its syndication company, Chronicle Features. In the course of his career, he is credited with "discovering" both Dear Abby and Gary Larson, as well as giving who knows how much support and guidance to innumerable other well-known writers and cartoonists along the way. He and his busy and outgoing wife, Jane, herself a columnist for a number of years, have raised three creative and productive daughters.

The youngest daughter is Jean, who lives a few miles away in San Quentin (the town, not the prison). After a ten-year stint in the U.S. Merchant Marine, during which she became the first female engineer ever and then the first to achieve the rank of chief engineer, she moved back to the Bay Area and took a job at Chronicle Features. There, among other duties, she replaced her father as my editor after his retirement at age seventy-one.

Jean and I became close friends over the course of the years that we worked together, and she joined us for lunch at her parents' house.

Each time I had visited San Francisco in the past, I had stayed at Stan and Jane's house, and I always looked forward to our infrequent visits with great anticipation. In recent years, however, Stan had experienced a loss of hearing that had left him to depend more and more on hearing aids and the volume and enunciation of his visitors. On this visit, with my raspy voice and greatly reduced volume, our communication attempts became comical. We sat on adjacent chairs out on the backyard patio grinning and nodding, our entire conversation relayed through Jean, who sat between us like an interpreter.

This fact, coupled with my lingering jetlag and fatigue, left our meeting much more like one between Nixon and Brezhnev than either of us would have liked—the only substantial difference being that neither of us lied or dropped veiled threats of nuclear retaliation. Even so, Stan always has something interesting to relate, and this visit was particularly rich in that regard.

The back of the Arnolds' house is lined with a number of huge plate-glass windows that face the backyard. Stan proudly pointed out a vague, ghostlike shape in the middle of one of them, which, upon closer inspection, could be seen to be the waxy, transparent imprint of a bird. According to Stan, a bird of some unknown species had flown so hard into the glass one afternoon that it left an unbelievably detailed visual image of itself on the glass. One could clearly make out the eye socket, beak, individual feathers, the ridges of the legs and feet. Even more eerie, the bird had struck the glass in the shape of a cross; wings outstretched to either side. My own neurotic religious experiences aside, I found myself feeling I was in the presence of something very special, and it immediately occurred to me that the look of the thing was uncannily similar to the famous Shroud of Turin. (Accordingly, Stan admonished me not to tell of this phenomenon lest his yard be suddenly filled with camped-out pilgrims seeking spiritual enlightenment. But in the interest of science and truth, I feel compelled to do so anyway.)

Standing on the patio with my glass of lemonade, I studied the strange, avian shrine for a good while, contemplating my place in the universe. Then my euphoria was broken by yet another of my quasi-hourly visits to the bathroom.

I enjoyed visiting with the Arnolds, as I always do, and continued to sip hot tea and lemonade all afternoon, preparing for my book-signing engagement later.

When the time came, we all went to the bookstore, which was only a couple of miles away. Unlike my two desolate experiences in Los Angeles, the bookstore in San Rafael was packed.

In front of a table and podium at the back of the store, a couple of dozen chairs were lined up, all of which were filled with people waiting to see me. More people gathered to stand around the perimeter as I arrived, and I was much heartened and very pleased to see such interest. It was particularly nice to have happen at a time when I had my adopted family with me, a chance to show off in front of Mom and Dad, as it were. The only downside was the knowledge that when a store sets up rows of chairs and a podium in front of your signing table, it indicates that they want you to speak for a time before you sign. Feeling overwhelmingly lucky and grateful to have attracted so many people, I wasn't about to disappoint them by not speaking in spite of the fragile condition of my voice. So I asked for a large pitcher of water with lots of lemons in it, went for a quick visit to the bathroom, and stepped up to the podium.

In such situations I always talk extemporaneously, as I find that if I prepare remarks I invariably sound like a novice small-town newscaster reading badly lettered cue cards. Despite my concerns about my voice, it held out fine. By now, I was gaining strength and volume, although I sounded very much like a gravelly voiced, Mafia hitman.

As usual, I spent a couple of hours at the store signing books and talking to fans, then began looking for my overnight hosts, who were to meet me at the store. They were Heather and Ray, and, unbeknownst to me, they had been there all along, waiting.

Heather was a young woman in her twenties who had written an interesting postscript to her letter offering to put me up while I was in San Francisco: "Plus, I'm a lesbian, so I'll be no threat to your wife." I admired her humor and candor and chose her fairly early on as one of my sponsors. Ray was her friend and roommate.

I had been told ahead of time that she was going to throw a party for me that night at their house in Alameda, which is on an island in San Francisco Bay, and that a photographer from *The San Francisco Chronicle* was going to be there to take pictures for a story the paper was doing about my book tour.

I greeted them happily, bid farewell and thanks to the Arnolds and John and Sue, swapped my bags from John and Sue's trunk to Ray and Heather's, visited the rest room one last time, and we took off.

By the time we left the store it was around 6:30 and getting dark. Heather and Ray had already been filled in about the problems I was having with my voice, so they told me I didn't have to talk all the way home, I could save my strength for the party. I was grateful and, still exhausted, climbed into the backseat to try to catch a nap on the way there.

As we headed down the highway, I laid my head back, closed my eyes, and thought about how great the book signing had gone and how much fun I was having, but also how tired I was from all the glad-handing. I would have given anything at that moment to have been on my way home to rest, to be with my wife and kids, but, instead, I was on my way to party at a house full of strangers on the other side of the bay. I opened my eyes briefly and asked how far it was to their house. They said about forty minutes. I glanced at my watch, closed my eyes, and fell asleep.

About thirty minutes later I woke up with an incredible urge to pee, only to find we were stuck in bumper-to-bumper traffic on the Golden Gate Bridge, less than halfway to Alameda.

Thinking I was still asleep, Ray and Heather were quietly lamenting the route they had taken, too late now to change. I sat quietly and waited to see if traffic was going to let up.

We crept along the highway at a snail's pace, the minutes passing slowly and excruciatingly. I kept thinking I should ask them to find a rest room and stop, but I knew San Francisco well enough to know that there wasn't any convenient place to stop nearby on a Sunday night. I was also a little embarrassed, having only just met these two and not having gotten a chance to get to know them at all, so I waited.

Soon we were trapped on the lower level of the Sandwich Bridge. We had been in the car for just over an hour, and I was beginning to feel pain and numbness in my lower regions. Finding a rest room was becoming imperative. My teeth and gums ached for some inexplicable reason, and I felt on the verge of losing consciousness. I knew I had to say something, even though there was nowhere to stop along the bridge. I half wished there would be an earthquake, the bridge would collapse on us, and my misery would be over. The cars crept along at a walker's pace.

"Hey, guys?" I croaked hoarsely, startling them both. "I know there's nothing we can do about it right now, but as soon as we get off this bridge I think we should find a rest room. I've been drinking liquids nonstop for days because of my throat, and I've really gotta go."

They both surveyed the road ahead, miles of red taillights reaching across the water. "Okay, I'm sorry about this traffic," Heather offered apologetically. "I don't know what's going on tonight. It's usually not like this."

After another thirty minutes or so on the bridge, we finally reached dry land again and I was honestly beginning to worry that I wouldn't make it and jokingly said so.

I was trying desperately to convey the urgency of my condition without blowing my celebrity cool. I felt like a big baby, not being able to ride in a car for more than an hour without stopping to go to the potty, and I imagined them telling their friends, "Yeah, we drove that cartoonist Dan Piraro around San Francisco one night, and he kept having to stop every few minutes to take a whiz. He must have a bladder problem or something." As much as I hated the prospect of continuing to nag them, I thought it would certainly be a lot worse if I didn't and they were able to say instead, "Yeah, I had to sell my car because that cartoonist Dan Piraro flooded the backseat and we could never get the smell out."

Ray pulled off the bridge onto a desolate urban street in Oakland, and we began looking for a bathroom. We spotted a gas station, and I shouted, "Let's try that place!" Ray pulled in.

Wriggling out of the backseat of the cramped two-door Pontiac, I jogged around the side of the building. Both restroom doors had obviously been chained and padlocked since the seventies.

I jogged back to the car and told them what I had found. "I'm gonna look around the back of the building and see if I can find a place to go," I said. They laughed sympathetically, and I disappeared around the corner.

The back of the building led onto a dimly lit, shallow vacant lot, then onto the next street. There was a group of menacing-looking men sitting around a dumpster a few dozen feet away. This was not the place.

I jogged back to the car again and jumped in. "We'll have to find another place; there's a bunch of people back there, and they didn't look too friendly." Ray sped off, now completely aware of the delicate and crucial nature of my situation. A couple of run-down, deserted blocks of low-to-no-income apartment buildings away he swerved into a generic, all-night convenience store. I raced inside.

"Do you have a rest room? It's an emergency!" I said to the small man behind the counter.

"I don' got no ress room," he replied matter-of-factly.

"C'mon, man!" I pleaded. "It's a real emergency! Give me a break!"

"I don' got no ress room," he repeated robotically as he shook his head and looked away. I literally growled at him like a dog and ran back to the car.

Heather offered her condolences, then suggested, "Look, we're only a couple of miles from the house now and nothing out here seems to be open. Why don't we just try to make it? There's not much traffic through here."

I said okay and concentrated every fiber of my being on the already trembling muscles in my groin.

As we flew through the streets at what Ray considered to be the fastest he dared go without drawing the attention of the police, we turned onto a long, straight street with eight or ten stoplights in a row. Each one was green except for the one directly in front of us. As it turned green, the next one, only a half block ahead, turned red, and so on, block after block.

Many times in my adult life I have questioned the existence of God. At that moment, I felt sure He existed, and for some reason He hated my guts.

When we had finally traversed the Valley of Lights, we turned again and I spotted a Jack in the Box restaurant. "Let's try that place!" I commanded.

"Are you sure you can't wait?" Heather reasoned. "We're only a couple of blocks from home."

"I really think we better stop!" I shouted. I felt like a jerk as I raced from the car and through the front door.

Inside, a young man was talking to a teenage girl at the counter. I flew past them, heading toward the back of the dining-room area where they presumably kept the rest rooms, but a large trash container blocked the entrance to that entire side of the building.

"Can I use your rest room, please?" I barked frantically at the girl behind the counter. "It's an emergency!"

"They closed," she said casually, without looking up.

"Look, either I use your bathroom, or I pee all over this floor right now! I'm *not* kidding!" I said, in my most authoritarian voice. Something in my eyes told her I wasn't bluffing.

"O-oka-a-ay," she sang in resignation as I burst past the trash-can barrier.

A few minutes later I strode out the front door with a million-dollar smile on my face and hopped into the car. Ray and Heather asked me what I had said to the girl, and I told them. We laughed about it the rest of the way to their house, which was, of course, just around the corner.

The party that night was a great deal of fun, especially so in light of my close brush with death by bladder rupture earlier that evening. We arrived nearly two hours later than we were expected to and had to tell and retell the story of the traffic delays and the bathroom safari.

Heather had invited twenty-five or so of her friends, mostly twenty-something-year-old lesbians, a few gay men, and her parents, Ron, a retired police officer, and Sherri, a June Cleaver–style mom.

Ron and Sherri were terribly gracious and spent most of the time in the kitchen making tiny pizzas and quiches. They were the sort of people one is more accustomed to running into at an engagement party or holiday dinner than at a mostly homosexual college beer bash. I love that about California.

The San Francisco Chronicle was planning to run an article about my book tour and had sent a photographer to the party who hung around for an hour or so snapping pictures of me as I munched chips and talked to people. "Just pretend I'm not here," she kept saying as she stuck the long black camera lens within inches of my face, the flash attachment blinding me as I stuck a glob of chips and guacamole in my mouth and talked to Bohemian-looking young people in strange haircuts, odd, ill-fitting clothes, and garish makeup. Pretending she wasn't there was like trying to ignore a live squid attached to your neck.

Out of all the pictures of interesting combinations of strangoids and freaks at the party, the photo *The Chronicle* ended up using was of me standing in the kitchen drinking a beer, an incredibly stupid, droopy-eyed look of half-consciousness on my face and my mouth full of snack food, flanked by Heather's mom reaching into the oven for quiche and her dad reaching into the microwave for a tray of pizzas.

One of the highlights of the evening, next to the street-level tour of Oakland rest rooms, was a game Heather had mentioned in her E-mail letter to entice me to stay with her. The game utilizes a nylon beach ball, and the object is to kick it around the sparsely decorated, high-ceilinged dining room in an effort to break the ugly, circa 1970s, glass and brass chandelier. Heather maintained in her original letter that thus far the chandelier had proven to be indestructible. After a couple of hours of a fairly large and aggressive group of us (most of whom were more than a little under the influence of excessive amounts of beer) slamming the ball into the light fixture repeatedly and failing to damage it in any way, I am inclined to agree with her. But I consider myself a better man for having tried.

The next morning, Heather gave me a quick tour of Alameda in Desire, her 1965 Chevy Impala, of which she is very proud. She told me later that she also refers to it as "The Chick Magnet" but confesses she hasn't had a date since she got it.

My voice was still compromised but slowly improving, and I was drinking fewer liquids all the time, so I was proudly able to endure the twenty-minute tour without a single rest stop.

Heather and I made an instant connection, the way people often do, and I sensed that we would be good friends if we lived closer. Within a very short time after meeting her, I found myself extremely fond of her, and the feeling only grew during our twenty-four hours together. She wrote to me some time after I had returned and said she had felt similarly about me.

That afternoon I was to sign books at a distant, suburban bookstore, then go all the way back into the city around 4:30 to a cocktail party being given by my next host. Ray and Heather generously volunteered to drive me all the way out to the suburbs (as long as I promised to limit my fluid intake), wait for me during the signing, then drive me all the way back into the city to my party. As payment for their kindness, I bought them a tank of gas, and they were invited to stay at the cocktail party for as long as they wanted within the standards of social acceptability; two days, for instance, would have been considered excessive.

ELEVEN

The Vanished Roommate

The suburban book signing went reasonably well considering its relative distance from civilization, and Ray, Heather, and I made good time back into the city. We had some trouble finding the home of my next host but arrived on time nonetheless. The three of us were dressed pretty casually (jeans, T-shirts, sandals, tennis shoes) and assumed we might be a little underdressed for the cocktail party. But in late-twentieth-century California nobody gets too worked up over that sort of thing. It isn't that uncommon there to go to a funeral in a swimsuit or rob a convenience store in a top hat and tuxedo.

The building Ed lived in was a small, attractive, three-story, three-dwelling apartment building in a nice neighborhood on a hilltop overlooking the bay and the city. I had chosen to accept his invitation to stay at his place based on his initial description of it and himself:

Hosting you in the Bay Area sounds like a kick. I am an avid fan, although I have not purchased any of your books (I don't buy Larson, Garfield, or Peanuts either). I am a fine outstanding member of the gay community, with a nice flat in the

Potrero Hill area with a wonderful view. My guest room is not large, and I am told the mattress is a little lumpy, but I would be honored to share my humble abode. I can give you a good cocktail party with a fun crowd, and show you a good restaurant or two (Dutch or on your publisher??).

If none of the above scares you off, please put me in the running for host.

I couldn't resist the opportunity to stay with an outstanding member of any community in a nice apartment with a wonderful view who was willing to introduce me to a fun crowd, so Ed was chosen early on in the selection process.

When we arrived, the party was already under way and I could immediately see that his sales pitch was by no means overstated. His apartment was small but lovely, with a magnificent view, and the crowd was definitely both interesting and fun. Ed had invited all of his most interesting gay friends, as well as a few token straight folks, for my benefit I was told.

The crowd was nicely dressed and seemed to be primarily well-to-do. A table in front of a window overlooking the entire city and half of the bay was ornately laid out with sumptuous hors d'oeuvres and a large, impressive centerpiece of flowers.

After a barrage of introductions, Heather, Ray, and I slinked over to the food table and talked among ourselves for the first few minutes, trying to absorb the culture shock. From Bohemian beer bash and '65 Chevy to upscale balcony cocktail party in a matter of a few hours is enough to give a person whiplash. Consequently, Heather and Ray didn't stay long, opting to make their exit after only a few minutes.

Settling into the party, I adapted quickly to the change in scenery like the traveling chameleon I had become. My voice was still very rough and weak, and I found it difficult to speak loud enough to be heard over the crowd. I had a number of interesting conversations nonetheless, and, even though at no point during the party did anyone produce a nylon beach ball or try to break anything, I enjoyed myself immensely, as I usually do when there is free food and drink.

Standing in my usual place, near the hors d'oeuvres table, I was introduced to a distinguished-looking doctor with silver hair and a nice suit. I greeted him politely and routinely, as he was the umpteenth person I had met in the past few days, when he said something that shook me awake with the force of an air horn on a Mac truck.

"I believe you used to be Richard Ernst's roommate in college," he said casually.

I stared at him, mouth agape and eyes wide, searching for words with which to respond, but none would come. If it had been a sitcom, I would have dropped my glass on the floor.

"I . . . you . . . how do you know Richard? I haven't heard his name in years!" I splurted finally.

"Well, it was sort of a coincidence, really," he explained. "I was invited to another party this evening by a good friend of mine, and I told him that I had already been invited by Ed to attend *this* party being given in your honor, and he said, 'Oh, Dan Piraro was Richard's roommate in college.' Richard is a good friend of his and was a patient of mine a few years ago. I'm an ophthalmologist."

"I can't believe it, this is such a strange coincidence! I haven't heard from Richard in more than fifteen years. After I left school, we corresponded quite a bit for a while by mail, but then he began moving around the country and sending me these cryptic letters without return addresses, and then he just disappeared. He stopped writing, and I've never heard from him since."

"Well, you probably wouldn't recognize him now," the doctor said.

"Why not?" I asked, almost afraid of the answer. (Had he been in a disfiguring accident? Had he had more plastic surgery than Michael Jackson? Had he become a woman?)

"He's all pumped up. He's a big muscle man," he said with a smile, arching his arms out to his sides.

"You're kidding! . . . When I knew him he was just a normal-sized human like me," I chuckled in disbelief. "Well, if you see him, or if you think of it the next time you talk to your friend, *please* tell him I'd love to hear from him. Have him call me or write to me."

The kind doctor agreed, and a few months later I did, in fact, receive a letter from my old college roommate. We have maintained communication since then and rekindled our friendship of years ago. This coincidental reunion has remained one of the strangest and most unexpected benefits of my travels.

The party at Ed's had started in the late afternoon and was over by seven or so. It was still early, so Ed and I walked down to a neighborhood Thai restaurant for a bite to eat. During dinner, as had become the custom of each of my road companions, Ed told me the story of his life. By this time I was beginning to expect my hosts' stories and looked forward to them with anticipation. Like great literature, each person's story was unique in its events and combinations but rich in familiar experiences and emotional consequences. The "true confessions" of my readers were becoming an addiction as strong as any soap opera or serial drama.

Not unlike Thomas, the roller-skating public relations consultant in L.A., Ed's story was one of tragedy and victory. After a lengthy and successful military career, Ed became a civilian branch chief for the Naval Engineering Division of the Maintenance and Logistics Command Pacific, U.S. Coast Guard, in San Francisco. He moved there to assume his new position in 1985 with his partner of one year, Kevin. (They later determined that both of them had unknowingly been HIV positive when they met.)

Kevin fell ill in early 1988 and died in July of the following year. Ed had no symptoms at that time and continued in his job with the Coast Guard.

By early 1994, he was feeling exhausted by midafternoon on most days and felt he was beginning to exhibit bad judgment where personnel matters were concerned. He applied for a disability retirement from the civil service, and it was approved. After receiving approval, he called a meeting of his group of twelve coworkers and told them he was leaving in two weeks on disability retirement. He also told them his disability was related to AIDS and that "in answer to your next question, yes, I'm gay." He doesn't think that his homosexuality surprised any of them, but he does believe all were surprised and upset to hear of his illness.

Ed and Kevin bought the beautiful apartment building that he was currently living in when they first moved to San Francisco, and Ed had changed very little in it since Kevin's death. At the time of our meeting, he had been HIV positive for around thirteen years but was still in fairly good health, experiencing very few symptoms, and his blood counts had remained stable. He was, however, taking about fifteen pills a day, and in his bathroom was a collection of pharmaceuticals that would have rivaled Elvis's.

What struck me most about Ed's story was his undaunted optimism in telling it. Despite the loss of his partner and his serious medical condition, he remains relaxed and cheerful, even when talking about his illness. I commented on this, and he told me he honestly believes he can make it.

"I used to believe that attitude was 30 percent of health, but now I think it's more like 70 percent," he told me. "I think diet, exercise, lots of sleep, moderation in all things, challenge but not stress—there's a big difference—and companionship are the most important facets of surviving it. I believe that with all the medical advances being made, a person can actually survive this thing."

Part of Ed's attitude includes honesty and openness, and he readily agreed to let me tell his story. For that, and for his hospitality, I am grateful.

In extreme contrast to the warm and enjoyable evening I had spent with Ed and his friends was the hellish night to come.

Upon returning to Ed's apartment, we decided we'd had enough consciousness for one day and moved to retire early. Ed showed me the small but comfy-looking guest room; a 10' x 10' space with loaded bookshelves entirely filling two walls, a desk, a closet, a love seat that folded out to a bed, and a single window.

Ed folded out the bed, after which there was no room left on the floor to stand other than a small, square space near the door. He climbed over the bed to the closet and showed me where there were more blankets and pillows if I should need them. If it got too warm or stuffy, he told me, I was welcome to open the window. I was scheduled to do a radio show the next morning at 7:30, so we agreed to set our alarms for 6:00 A.M. in order to leave by a quarter to seven. I thanked him, assured him I'd be just fine, and he went off to his room to bed.

The room was a bit warm, so I climbed across the bed and opened the window, which overlooked the quiet street two floors below, a few inches. I got into my sleeping clothes, a pair of summer-weight pajamas with a repeating pattern of ducklings splashing in rain puddles, and climbed into bed to read a bit before turning out the light.

As I read, I heard a faint but distinct buzzing sound pass by my ear. I looked up from my book and around the room, my eyes crossed to focus on the area within a few inches of my face, but I could see nothing.

A moment later, I heard the sound again, this time in my other ear, and I quickly leaned my head down and away from the sound, attempting to see the perpetrator against the white of the ceiling. I spotted the little varmint, a common mosquito, and I followed him upward through the air, standing slowly and carefully on the mattress, never taking my eyes off of him until, SMACK!, he was no more.

Satisfied that I had killed the last remaining mosquito in California so late in the year, I returned to my book, became drowsy, and turned off the light.

I fell asleep immediately, the exhaustion of the past few days pressing down on me like Rush Limbaugh in a soaking-wet flannel suit, when I was suddenly aware of the buzzing sound again.

I jerked awake, with an itching sensation on my temple like a weasel biting into my face. I slapped at it in the dark, nearly knocking myself unconscious.

In the next few minutes I heard the sound over and over as I slipped between sleep and consciousness and back again, slapping at my face, dozing off, clapping my hands together near my ear, drifting off again, covering my head with the blanket, throwing it off and gasping for air. Eventually, I realized I was going to have to get up, close the window, and try to catch the other mosquito that had gotten into the room. This I grudgingly did, very irritably and dead tired.

I turned the light back on and lay on my back on the bed, completely covered except for my left arm, which lay extended across my chest as bait. I lay there staring at my exposed arm with the patience of Marlin Perkins, waiting to be attacked once more.

Before long, I heard the telltale buzzing again and slapped at the tiny dive bomber. It took several attempts to capture and kill the other mosquito, but at long last I did and I could again return to my slumber without fear of disturbance.

No I couldn't.

No sooner had I turned out the light and dozed off than I was attacked again. Buzzing, biting, itching. In my groggy state of half sleep, I tried again to survive with my head under the blanket, but it was simply too suffocating. I then tried to sleep with just my mouth sticking out of a tiny opening, like a fish eating bugs off the surface of a pond, but within minutes a mosquito had bitten me on the lip. If I *had* been a fish, I'd have eaten it.

Furious, I jumped up and turned on the light again, determined to annihilate every last insect in the room no matter how long it took. Once more I lay still, staring at my left arm until the enemy came in for a hit, then swatting wildly at it with my right.

It took more than thirty minutes of merciless killing before I was satisfied that I had cleared the room of mosquitoes completely; there had been nearly a dozen in all.

I looked at my watch and cursed the time and the amount of sleep I had lost chasing these infuriating pests. I lay there with tiny red welts on my face and neck and a swollen lip, watching and waiting to be absolutely certain I hadn't missed any before allowing myself to fall asleep again. I could barely hold my eyes open.

Glancing at the now closed window, I saw what looked like a squadron of mosquitoes outside resting on the glass. I blinked and sat up a little to be sure of what I was seeing; they seemed to be spelling out the words "Surrender Dorothy."

Suddenly, I was aware that the window itself had come to life, the elaborate, pleated curtains around it grinning demonically and mocking me. It was instantly quite clear that this seemingly innocent architectural device was evil incarnate, a haunted orifice that had psychically beckoned me to open it, knowing full well what hungry hordes of airborne vermin were lying in wait outside it, with no screen to hinder their offensive.

I shrank away from the window in horror to the other side of the mattress and rubbed my eyes, simultaneously frightened and fascinated by this peculiar and malevolent presence. The elbow I had been propping myself up on suddenly slipped off the edge of the bed and the room jerked to brightness.

It was instantly daylight outside, and a wave of hyperreality and sunlight washed over me and told me it was morning and I had been awakened from a dream.

The travel alarm clock on the desk was bleating wildly; it was 6:00 A.M. I turned it off and touched my lip to see if it was swollen, thinking that perhaps the *entire* episode with the mosquitoes had been a dream. But the itching welt there, and several others on my face and neck, told me that at least that much of the previous night's experiences had been real. As further proof, the floor was littered with insect carcasses.

I hurried to the shower.

Ed drove me into the city and dropped me off at the radio station. As I had a few appointments downtown that day, including lunch with Bill Griffith, creator of *Zippy the Pinhead*, we agreed that I would wander around the city for the day and call Ed to come pick me up from Bill's house that afternoon.

I had been worrying about the radio show ever since I had lost my voice several days earlier, but by that morning it was strong enough to function, even though I sounded like a cross between Harvey Fierstein and Bea Arthur.

At the radio station I said nothing about the laryngitis and just went about my business meeting the two DJs and doing the show. They played a "mystery guest" sort of game in which they gave clues as to who was in the studio and the listeners called in, each getting to ask one yes or no question, then guess who I was.

"We have a guest in the studio today," they announced after a song and went on to explain the rules of the game.

"The first hint we'll give you is that you probably wouldn't recognize his face, but you've seen his work, and he makes thousands of people in the Bay Area laugh every day. We'll take the first caller now."

Somehow, after only a couple of questions, someone guessed correctly that I was a cartoonist. He then guessed, "Are you the guy who does *Calvin & Hobbes?*" (probably because Bill Watterson had been in the news announcing his retirement a few days before). This guy obviously didn't know much about Watterson, who is reportedly a complete hermit, hasn't given so much as a phone interview in ten years, and would more than likely rather catch a bowling ball thrown from a speeding truck in his mouth than be on the radio.

"No," I answered hoarsely, "Unlike that guy, I still have to work for a living."

The next caller asked, "Are you Garry Trudeau?"

"That's the guy that does *Doonesbury,* isn't it?" one of the DJs chimed in.

"No, my wife's a *lot* better looking than Jane Pauley," I croaked.

(Although my wife *is* quite beautiful, I recently met Jane and Garry at a party in New York for the twenty-fifth anniversary of *Doonesbury* [no, I'm not above name dropping], and I would like to say that they are both *terribly* nice people, not stuck up in the least, as one might expect, and as good looking as Jane is on TV, she is so cute in person you just want to take her home and put her on a shelf, which Garry sometimes does, rumor has it. Not wanting to be just another of the typical, ass-kissing, "I've-been-a-fan-of-yours-for-years-and-enjoy-your-reporting-*so*-much" sort of groupie that she had doubtless been talking to all night, I told her instead: "You know, I have *always* thought you were really cute on TV, but I gotta tell you, you are even *better* looking in person." She blushed a little and said thank you, and Garry smiled proudly and put his arm around her. "No, I mean it," I went on, not to be satisfied until I had made a complete fool of myself. "I expected you to be much *less* attractive in person. I figured that they probably use special makeup and camera tricks and latex to make you look better on TV, but you're *gorgeous!*" They probably both wanted to kill me right there on the spot [and who could blame them?], but they're just too nice—and they have very lucrative careers to think of.)

The DJs took another call, and the voice instantly sounded very familiar to me, but I couldn't quite place it. At first I was afraid it was one of my friends in the area who was going to blow my cover.

"This guy sounds like someone who's spinning the wheel," the caller said. "Could it be . . . Garry Moore?"

"Sorry!" announced one of the DJs. "Who's Garry Moore?" asked the other.

"How about Vanna White?" the caller chuckled sarcastically.

"Sorry, only one guess per caller," the DJ snapped, and punched another button.

By this time I had recognized the voice as that of the ghost of Garry Moore. I wondered if Sajak would approve of his making prank calls on his behalf.

The next call-in contestant was a woman with a knowing sound in her voice. "I think I know who this is!" she giggled. "Is it Dan Piraro?"

The DJs hit some sound-effects button that tells everyone within a five-hundred-mile radius that she was correct, and she won sixteen dollars. As it turned out, she had been at my book signing the day before and recognized my raspy voice.

After my segment of shameless self-promotion was over and I was getting up to leave, one of the DJs told me, "You have a *great* voice for radio!"

"Why thank you," I croaked graciously, still not mentioning the laryngitis.

"Yeah, you sound really cool—like a rock singer who's been on the road too long!" said the other.

I smiled confidently and wandered out of the building, making a mental note to fake a whiskey voice if ever I was on that station again so as not to disappoint anyone.

TWELVE

The Wacko's Lair

A couple of months before my trip to California, someone E-mailed me a copy of an interview with Bill Griffith. In it, he was asked one of the stock seventeen questions that cartoonists are always asked: What other comics are you a fan of? His reply was *The Fusco Brothers,* Robert Crumb, and *Bizarro.*

I was very flattered by this, as Bill is one of the icons of cartooning and one of the very few people to bridge the chasm between the underground and commercial markets successfully. I was pretty sure he lived in San Francisco, so I decided to try to arrange a visit with him while I was there. I sent a letter to him via his syndicate, King Features in New York, and asked him to get in touch with me if he was interested. A few weeks later he called.

When I told him why I was going to be in San Francisco, how I was conducting my book tour, and that I was going to be staying with fans, his reaction was priceless.

"You're very brave," he said in his sedate, almost deadpan voice. "I spend most of my time trying to *avoid* my fans."

I laughed, but understood what he meant completely. As strange as some *Bizarro* fans may be, *Zippy* fanatics make them look like Young Republicans. He went on to say that he'd be happy to have lunch with me and we could meet at his house, but he preferred I not bring anyone with me. I agreed, and we set the date.

When I left the radio station that morning, I had a few hours to kill before I was due at Griffith's. I took the elevators down to the lobby and went outside with no particular plan in mind.

After having been with a new acquaintance every minute of every day for the past week (most of whom mistook me for a celebrity), I hadn't anticipated the relief I would feel in getting away for a while until I stepped out of the building and onto the bustling streets of downtown San Francisco. Suddenly, being alone was an absolutely rapturous experience: no one to talk to, no one to entertain, no questions to answer, nowhere to be for several hours. The sky was crystal blue (somewhere above the buildings), the grass was vibrant green (in a park somewhere probably), and I could feel the earth rotating on its axis beneath my feet. Ah, the simple pleasures of anonymity. No wonder Elvis was a crackpot.

I went to Chinatown and bought my daughters some cheesy, Oriental satin pajamas (which has become a sort of tradition every time I go to San Francisco, dating all the way back to when the oldest one was a toddler; they each have quite a collection in various sizes and colors). Then I attempted to drop by the Cartoon Art Museum, primarily to see if it was really using the original art I had donated or if its staff would have to rush to get it out of the hall closet like the hideous, inscribed wall clock we got as a wedding gift from my wife's aunt and uncle.

But, alas, the surprise inspection would have to wait for another time as it was the one day of the week that the museum was closed. (Or the staff spotted me coming and, not remembering where it had stashed my artwork, turned out the lights and slapped an hours-of-operation sign on the door that listed *that* day as the only one on which the museum were closed, having one for every day of the week for just such an occasion.)

I killed the rest of the morning dodging streetcars and listening to the wacko street preachers down on Mission, then grabbed a cab and headed for Griffith's.

Bill is a very relaxed guy with a casual way about him that almost makes him seem as though he is bored with existence. (Or perhaps he was simply bored with *me*.) But he has some terrific stories to tell, as oddball artists who have known a lot of other oddball artists often do.

One such story is about one of my favorite cartoonists of all time and perhaps my single biggest influence as a cartoonist: Bill Kliban.

Most people know Kliban (if they know him at all) as the guy who did the original cat book. By the "cat book" I mean the book of cat cartoons published in the late seventies that started the cat (and dog) book craze. His cat is still one of the most popular and well-known cartoon cats (after Garfield, who isn't really a cat but a trained walrus in a cat suit that is kept heavily sedated and forced to perform against his will), and is easily recognized by its black stripes and red tennis shoes.

Kliban was a cartoonist under contract to *Playboy* magazine, where he did some wonderful work in the sixties and seventies. Legend has it that when Kliban was in his studio trying to think up gags, he would often mindlessly sketch and doodle all manner of strange characters and circumstances, entirely for himself, with no publishing venue in mind. After years of this activity, he had accumulated quite a pile of these drawings, some of which contained his now famous cats. Many of these drawings were complete nonsequiturs, but somehow they were hilarious and provocative nonetheless. Kliban assumed they were unpublishable.

Bill Griffith told me that one afternoon he was at Kliban's house visiting his wife, M. K. Brown, who is also a cartoonist of some note whose work has appeared in *The National Lampoon* and other publications. He happened to see a pile of these other drawings and loved them. He encouraged Kliban, who had underestimated their appeal, to try to get them published. Eventually, he did.

The cat book sold millions of copies and made Kliban a fortune. His other, stranger, noncat cartoons were also published in book form, have sold well, and are still in the humor sections of most bookstores today. His first such book, *Never Eat Anything Bigger Than Your Head & Other Drawings,* was my first exposure to surreal, nonsequitur humor. It was the book my roommate, Richard, showed me in 1976, during my few minutes in college. I have perused it since then as frequently as many people do their Bibles.

My afternoon with Bill Griffith was entertaining and rewarding. We talked about the injustice of an industry that keeps clever, hardworking guys like us down while often rewarding derivative, milquetoast cartoonists with riches beyond their dreams. (I spoke adamantly and slammed my fist down on the table; Bill spoke quietly, with dignity and maturity.)

We complained about the declining importance placed on drawing skills in newspaper cartoons. (I spoke loudly and with disdain, waving my arms in the air and spitting on the floor; Bill spoke softly with just a touch of sarcasm.)

In the end I think we both learned a lot. I learned that legends of American pop culture like Bill Griffith aren't necessarily intimidating and inaccessible; they can be quite friendly and hospitable. I also learned that you don't have to let the inequities of the cartoon business make you stressed and irritable, shrieking in frustration one moment, sobbing bitterly the next. Instead, you can relax, accept the system as it is, and concentrate on your craft. In the end, it is the quality of your feature that is important, not the size of its client list. (At least that's what those of us without enormous client lists tell ourselves.)

Bill learned that perhaps his fans aren't the only people he should be hiding from.

As planned, Ed picked me up at Bill's, then, later that night, dropped me off at a small bookstore on Haight Street called Booksmith, where I was to speak and sign books.

The talk and signing that night was well attended, and, as the store was in the heart of legendary Haight-Ashbury, the crowd was my most bizarre to date. It is not uncommon in that neighborhood to see any sort of person known to inhabit the earth, from transvestites to skateboarding retropunk rockers to gray-haired hippies left over from the sixties still selling marijuana-shaped, patchouli-scented candles on the street corner.

As usual, my overnighter for that evening was to meet me at the store after my signing. His name was Ken, and since I knew he lived not far from the bookstore, I wondered what sort of carnival geek from Neptune he would be. He showed up right on schedule, a couple of minutes before I was ready to leave.

To my great surprise, Ken was exceptionally common looking. He almost looked out of place in his businessman's haircut, business suit, tie, and overcoat, and he reminded me of a plain-clothes detective. I had chosen to accept his offer of lodging for that night not because he had written a particularly charming or humorous letter but by default. He was the only volunteer who lived anywhere near Haight-Ashbury, and he didn't mind driving me to the airport at 5:00 A.M. the next morning.

As we prepared to leave the store, I was accosted by an enthusiastic young man who had attended the signing and wanted me to look at and critique his own cartoon efforts, of which he had a gigantic binder full. Travel-weary and still hoarse, I politely resisted, citing a *very* early flight the next morning.

But he was not to be discouraged so easily. "Please! I drove all the way in from San Jose to see you tonight! It would mean so much to me! It will only take a minute!" he pleaded as he waved the fifteen-pound collection in front of me.

"I have a *very* early flight tomorrow, and this nice gentleman is going to drive me to the airport, so we really need to get to bed," I stated again, apologetically.

"*I* can drive you to the airport! You could look at them in the car on the way there!" he bellowed.

"I have to leave his house at *five A.M.*," I said ominously.

"I don't care! I'll be there! It means that much to me!" he insisted.

I didn't want to disappoint him, but every professional cartoonist's nemesis is the aspiring amateur who is trying to break into the business without a shred of talent. As is the case in all the creative arts, professional cartoonists are inundated with requests from amateurs asking for advice and criticism. It's no problem when the artist has some potential, and most people are happy to help an up-and-comer. But sadly, the reason most unpublished cartoonists are unpublished is because their work is without merit. You are then faced with three choices: lie and say you love their work (which does them no good), tell them the truth and crush their egos into dust (which makes you look and feel like a jerk), or fake a stroke, then run away when they go to call an ambulance (my personal favorite).

Since I had all my luggage with me, the third option seemed out of the question.

I looked at Ken to see if he minded and said, "Well, it would save you from having to get up at the crack of dawn."

"It's fine by me," Ken said with a shrug. "I don't care. Where are you coming from, San Jose?"

The two of them got together and began discussing the extremely complex directions to Ken's apartment from the southern end of the bay. It was estimated that to get to Ken's by 5:00 A.M., he would have to leave San Jose as soon as he got home that night. As I listened, I began to suspect that this zealous youngster hadn't lived in the area long. I was becoming increasingly skeptical about this kid's likelihood of showing up on time and getting me to my flight. Ken assured me that he would take me if the guy didn't show.

The youngster thanked me profusely, promised he'd be at Ken's at 5:00 A.M. sharp, and said good night. Ken and I walked a couple of blocks to his car and talked about the likelihood of ever seeing him again.

If Ken looked out of place in Haight-Ashbury by virtue of his "normalcy," his car certainly did not. It was a '79 Honda Civic (the very small, boxy, goofy, hatchback predecessor to Honda's snazzier designs of today), and it was painted primer gray. On each door was spray-painted a large, yellow diamond, like a road caution sign, with the silhouette of a rhinoceros in the center. On the front of the hood was a two-foot-tall fake rhino horn. The car itself looked as much like a rhinoceros as the old AMC Pacer looked like a pregnant toaster. It ran like one, too. In addition to the accumulative roars and rattles of nearly two decades of use and abuse, the driver's side door would pop open every forty-five seconds or so, setting off a whining buzzer and turning on the interior lights. Without pause or comment, Ken would grab the door handle, slam it shut, and keep driving.

To describe Ken as reserved would be like describing Hitler as cranky. He said very little on the way to his apartment, and what he did say was cryptic. As we drove through the old and dilapidated neighborhoods leading to his apartment I learned that he worked in an office, which explained his attire, and though he was only in his late twenties, he had already traveled around the world extensively before settling recently in San Francisco. No matter what either of us said, his facial expression never altered one molecule from a wide-eyed, stiff-jawed intensity that reminded me of a person sitting on a plane with a bomb hidden in his briefcase.

We pulled into a decrepit parking garage on a run-down side street and parked the rhino. Ken's apartment building, an old brick structure with a cathedral-sized iron-barred gate across the entrance, was across the litter-strewn street. Ken opened the gate with a key, and I schlepped my bags up the few steps to the door, then inside to the long, dimly lit hallway. His apartment was the first one on the right.

The inside was right off the cover of *Young, Financially Challenged Artist's Digest* and looked not unlike the first apartment I had some nineteen years ago. The front door opened into a small, main room at the front with windows overlooking the street; to the left was a series of rooms off a long main hallway. This main room, originally designed as a living room, had a table, a desk, some books, a lot of clothes and assorted junk, and a futon on the floor. This was Ken's room; his several roommates occupied the other rooms. Only one was home when we arrived, and I was unclear on how many others there were. Ken was not an artist, but his roommates apparently were.

At his suggestion, we dropped off my bags and walked to a local coffee shop for a late-night caffeine buzz and a chat. The café was a small, run-down storefront with a counter behind which was an appropriately goateed neo-Bohemian and some coffee-making supplies and equipment. Littering the room were a few mismatched tables and chairs, a small handful of groove-cat coffee junkies, and little else. We parked at a tiny table for two against the front windows and started talking.

The conversation was relatively bland and tense, until Ken

said something that made it suddenly much less bland and a lot more tense.

"I have a confession to make," he said evenly, staring a hole straight through my head and into the cosmos, just as he had been since I'd met him. "I've never really seen your cartoons."

Mildly confused, I took the bait. "What do you mean?"

"I mean I'm not really a big fan of your work or anything. In fact, when I invited you to stay, I didn't even know who you were. I just saw the letter you sent out on a guy's computer at work. I've never even seen your work; I just thought it might be interesting to invite you and see what happened."

He waited for my response the way Anthony Perkins waited for Janet Leigh to get into the shower.

Not wanting to show my growing sense of alarm, I bluffed casually, "Interesting. So you've never even seen my cartoons?" I smiled as though I couldn't have cared less, but, inside, my mind was running through all the possible scenarios. I had assumed in sending my solicitation letter only to those people who had written to me as fans first that I would be relatively safe from victimization. When people wrote back to me with their offers, I hadn't thought to double-check their names against my mailing list. Obviously, this was a huge and potentially fatal loophole in my screening process. I was very troubled to see how easy it had been to defeat my system.

"I was actually pretty surprised when you called and said you were coming," Ken went on with a slightly malevolent smile. "It was weird at the bookstore watching people make a big fuss over you, because to me, you were just another random guy."

Just another random victim, you mean.

"Well, to tell you the truth, I actually prefer it this way," I lied through my teeth. "I've gotten kind of sick of fans fussing over me all the time—like that guy tonight with the comics he wanted me to look at."

"Yeah, he was weird," Ken said.

You should talk.

"Well, you managed to slip right past my screening system,

but at least you admit it," I coughed. "Now I know where I stand with you."

"Yes," Ken said with a smile, the first significant change in his expression all evening, "which will make my plans for you all the more interesting to carry out."

I chuckled suavely, like a bad actor in a Noël Coward play. "Your *plans* for me, eh?"

"That's right."

"And what might they be?" I asked indifferently, up to my eyebrows in a good, old-fashioned game of chicken. I was determined not to display my panic before I had determined what he was up to.

"Part of the fun is waiting to find out," he clucked through his now Grinch-like smile.

I weighed my options: I could stick it out, take my chances, and hope that he was just kidding, or I could run screaming out of the café and down the street, hoping to retrieve my luggage later with a police escort. I was leaning toward the running and screaming plan until I remembered that one of Jeffrey Dahmer's victims got away and ran screaming down the street, only to be ignored and quickly recaptured. I looked out the window at the various ne'er-do-wells roaming the street and thought it didn't look like the kind of neighborhood where people were standing ready to rush to the aid of someone running and screaming like a maniac. One thought kept racing through my mind: "Where the hell is Pat Sajak when you need him?"

I had little choice but to stay put and hope for the best.

A while later, Ken admitted he was just kidding about victimizing me. He really *hadn't* seen my work before he saw my letter on a coworker's computer, and he *did* invite me to stay just for the hell of it, that much was true. But the nefarious *plans* part had been a joke. I wanted to believe him and had few other options, so I swallowed my fear and went back to his apartment for the night. But joke or not, dangerous or simply quirky, any way I looked at it, this guy was a wacko.

Back at his place, moments after settling in for the night in his futon under the front windows, Ken having disappeared into the back of the apartment to sleep elsewhere, I realized my error. I was indeed to be victimized that night.

I turned out the light and immediately noticed a surprising lack of darkness. Just outside the window was a halogen street lamp, which lit up the room like a Las Vegas sidewalk.

But light wasn't all that was streaming through the windows; I could clearly hear the earth-thudding sound of rap music coming from a boom box in the very near vicinity. Suddenly, I heard the sound of someone running down the entire length of the hall outside wearing what sounded like large, loose, wooden shoes, then flying full-speed through the huge iron gate, letting it crash shut behind him with bone-jarring force.

The boom box out on the sidewalk was soon joined by another, playing completely different rap music, which didn't seem to bother either owner. I could now hear voices outside, shouting in an attempt to be heard over the music.

A few moments later, the wooden-shoed person hurried back into the building, letting the iron gate crash behind him again, and ran the full length of the hall in the opposite direction. This performance was repeated several more times over the next hour or so, like a Dutch relay race, before I finally became desensitized by the cacophony and fell asleep.

I awoke only once more during the night, when one of Ken's roommates came home in the wee hours of the morning, opening the door and wheeling in a ten-speed bike, gears clicking loudly, and leaning it against the wall a few feet from my bed.

I had set my alarm the night before for 4:00 A.M. I figured that would be enough time to take a shower and get dressed, gather my things together, and be watching out the window for my ride a few minutes before five.

When the alarm went off, I dragged myself out of bed and into the turn-of-the-century shower, exhausted after so little sleep but exhilarated still to be alive after having spent the night in the same building with Ken the Wacko and who knows who else. At about 4:15, while I was still in the hot, steamy comfort of the shower, I could just make out the sounds of a commotion out in the hall. For a moment I wondered if Ken really had been waiting for me to get into the shower like Janet Leigh.

My enthusiastic would-be cartoonist/rabid fan had arrived forty-five minutes early to be sure he wouldn't be late. (I should have known.) Instead of waiting quietly outside for me to come out, he had come pounding on the door to make sure he had the right place.

One of Ken's artist roommates, a guy named Joe, had answered the door. Joining them in Ken's room, which doubled as entry hall and bike storage for the small dwelling, I gently chastised my overzealous driver and apologized to Joe, who was very gracious and said he didn't mind at all and that he suffered from insomnia and wasn't asleep anyway. Soon, Ken joined us, and the three of them sat around the room gabbing while I got dressed, packed up, and ready to go.

On the way to the airport, I leafed through the giant collection of cartoons my new friend had brought and gave a running commentary of advice and encouragement. Much to my surprise and relief, the work was actually good, in spite of the fact that the drawings were a little rough and unprofessional, which he freely admitted. I was relieved to be able to tell him honestly that with a little more work on his drawings, I thought he could make it as a professional cartoonist. He came into the airport with me and continued to exuberantly extract increasingly more specific and detailed advice out of me, never ceasing until I walked down the tunnel to the plane. For a moment, I worried that he might actually buy a ticket and come along for the ride.

In the final assessment, I'd have to say he was a pretty good guy with a lot of talent and twice as much enthusiasm. With the right breaks, he could be eating up newspaper space very soon with his own syndicated feature, passing me and my moderate career as if I were standing still, replacing *Bizarro* in dozens of markets, winning awards, and making money hand over fist.

If he does, I might be having lunch with another bitter cartoonist sometime in the future, complaining about the business and trashing our colleagues as usual, and I'll be able to say of him, "Yeah, that guy once woke up an entire neighborhood at four in the morning to find out what I thought of his cartoons. I should've thrown his whole book out the window of the car while I had the chance."

The Dim Reaper

My spirits soared as I flew into Portland. I'd had three successful appearances in San Francisco, survived a night of
high weirdness, taken a much-needed nap on the plane, and the
view of the mountains outside my window was breathtaking.
Though I wasn't going home for three more days, I knew I
could relax somewhat with the family I was staying with in
Oregon.

I was greeted at the airport gate by Karen and her two-
year-old son, Sam. They were happy to see me, and we chattered excitedly as we moved through the airport. A few feet
away from the gate, a woman walked up to me and said something everyone longs to hear from the time he's a little kid
dreaming of fame and fortune: "Excuse me, but are you Dan
Piraro?"

"Why yes, I am," I replied calmly. "How did you know?"

The woman held up a newspaper with my picture in it. "I
saw the article about your book tour in this morning's *Chronicle*,"
she explained, holding it out toward me. "Would you mind
autographing it for me?"

I was light-headed and giddy with pride, as pure, two-hundred-proof ego juice coursed through my veins.

It was pure coincidence, of course, that the article *The San Francisco Chronicle* had planned about my book tour happened to run that morning, and a woman on my flight happened to see it, happened to be a fan of mine, and happened to recognize me in the Portland Airport. But it could not have happened at a better time.

Karen, the woman who met me when I got off the plane, was my older sister, and appearing successful in front of relatives is always infinitely more satisfying than anything else. My sister would now think I was much more "happening" than I really was. To further enhance my illusion of cool, we were headed to a TV station where I was to appear on a local talk show. I almost felt like a real celebrity.

My three-day visit with my sister and her family was fun and relaxing. Less than two years apart in age, we were pretty close as children but had seen very little of each other in the past few years since her move to Oregon. I had only seen her son once since his birth, and he knew me only by his parents' references to the cartoons in the paper. They had shown him my cartoons many times and explained that these were Uncle Dan's cartoons. Accordingly, he had come to refer to me as "Uncle Cartoon."

As it was midweek, my brother-in-law, Chuck, had to work, so by day, Karen and Sam and I were on our own. Having been raised in the blandness of the flatlands, I have always been awe-stricken by dramatic landscapes, and so I was in paradise as we hit a few of the area's more scenic locations. Two of my favorites were huge bumps of ground that Oregonians call "mountains" and a great deal of water that locals claim goes all the way to China. This they arrogantly refer to as "the" ocean, even though I saw ones just like it in both Los Angeles and San Francisco.

My sister seemed proud of it, though, so I didn't say anything about the other two.

Without slighting the scenery and coastlines of California, which are gloriously beautiful, I find the Oregon coast particularly inspiring. The water crashing against the jagged rocks and dramatic cliffs coupled with the frequently dark and brooding skies always reminds me of the paradoxical nature of life: beauty and danger, glory and pain, ecstasy and agony. Standing on a rocky outcrop watching the powerful strokes of the waves crash against the land and letting my eyes follow the millions of swells and crests out to sea, disappearing into seeming infinity, it is easy for me to sense the presence of a higher power.

Back home in Dallas, standing on a cement outcrop near the expressway, watching waves of gasoline-powered vehicles throbbing against the pavement, letting my eyes follow the millions of headlights and antennae as they disappear into seeming infinity, or the next overpass, it is a little bit more difficult. Sometimes you just have to get out of Gotham City to be able to see the Bat Signal in the sky.

At night, all four of us went to my book signings, which were reasonably well attended considering the fact that the Portland newspaper, *The Oregonian*, had stopped publishing my cartoon some months earlier because of what it termed a "poor showing in a reader survey." (This was an example of a paper letting the 2 percent or so of the elderly readership that fills out a comics survey dictate the comics page for the entire community. The generous turnout at my signings in spite of my cancellation and the fact that my own sister, who reads the comics every day, never even *saw* the survey are fair indications of how inaccurate surveys can be.)

The night before I returned home, I sat in the living room with my nephew. My brother-in-law had gone to bed early; my sister was in the kitchen on the phone. Being more or less brain-dead after nine days on the road, I stared blankly at the TV, channel surfing. Sam was very intellectual for a two-year-old, and preferred instead to scan the dozens of children's books he had memorized word for word.

I resisted stopping on any one program long enough to be exposed to a plot line or an idea that might make me think and just kept hitting the channel button with a slow, steady rhythm. Wishing to avoid intellectual stimulation of any kind, I wanted nothing more than to kill the next couple of hours till bedtime painlessly, before returning home the next morning. I watched the images flash onto the screen at one-second intervals, barely long enough to be identified by my brain before being replaced by the next, completely unrelated image. It was almost identical to watching music videos on MTV.

A preacher; some monkeys; a weather map; a cop car; dancing detergent; a happy, beautiful, blond woman talking about feminine hygiene; the Bundy family; an evangelist crying; a Jetsons cartoon; an Asian soap opera; the war in Bosnia; Charles Grodin; a college basketball game; a happy, beautiful, blond woman driving a fast car on a wet street; Jim Lehrer; beer . . .

Suddenly, an image crossed the screen that threw my finger into spasms as I tried frantically to stop the mindless succession of pictures and return to the appropriate channel. The image was a wall of glittering rectangles, some blank, some with letters of the alphabet. There was an infinitely glamorous woman, a goddess of sorts, standing at the ready, gliding across the floor to turn a blank rectangle around, then returning to her post. The woman was attired in a dazzling gown of dozens of folds and pleats of silky fabric, like curtains at a funeral parlor.

She was Vanna White, and the show was *Wheel of Fortune*.

Transfixed, I stared as Pat Sajak appeared on the screen. Why had he chosen to contact me now? I wasn't in need. I wasn't succumbing to a panic attack or being stalked by a wide-eyed, modern-day Gomez Addams in a coffee shop. I even had my voice back. My trials, for the time being, were over, and I was heading home, where I could relax, vegetate, and hide from the world for as long as I needed. Home, where I could embrace my family, catch up on my work, use my own bathroom, develop my film. The last thing I needed now was guidance from a meddling game-show host/spiritual mentor. Especially one who was conspicuously missing every time I *really* needed him. Maybe he was just popping in to apologize for leaving me alone with Ken.

I watched in silence as Pat routinely and professionally officiated the game, blatantly ignoring my presence. Suddenly, the camera moved to a close-up of one of the contestants, a rotund, big-haired woman with sparkle-framed glasses who was attempting to solve the puzzle.

"You can never go home," she said slowly and carefully.

"You can never go home," my nephew mimicked absentmindedly, without looking up from his books.

The music swelled, the crowd applauded thunderously, and Sajak congratulated the portly contestant as Vanna moved to center stage and turned over the remaining letters to reveal the phrase: YOU CAN NEVER GO HOME.

Without thinking, I sat bolt upright and shouted, "What the hell is *that* supposed to mean?"

My sister poked her head into the room. "What?" she asked with the phone still cradled under her jaw.

"Nothing," I said sheepishly, waving her back into the kitchen.

I watched intently as Sajak went about the business of the show, still ignoring me. Every now and then he would cast a smug, knowing look at me, then return his attention to the drooling contestants.

Crouching on the floor in front of the TV, my face close to the screen, I said quietly but firmly, "I hope that's not meant for *me*, Sajak." He still ignored me, so I waited until he was in a close-up shot and spoke directly into his ear, my lips nearly touching the screen.

"That wasn't meant for *me*, was it, Pat?"

Still no response.

He had come to the end of the segment and was breaking for a commercial: "We'll be back for round two, right after this."

The screen went black for a second, but, instead of fading into a commercial, in the center of the shiny, gray-green glass Pat's disembodied head appeared.

"Don't interrupt me while I'm working, Piraro!" he scolded.

"What do you mean? I was just asking if that puzzle was meant for me! Besides, I didn't contact you—*you* contacted me! I was just surfing and minding my own business! This isn't even your time slot!" I shot back defensively.

"You're very irritable all of a sudden, Dan. Maybe you don't *need* my help anymore," he threatened.

"What help? You ignore me for days on end, then make a cameo appearance in an elevator to tell me I have to do all the work myself. Now you seem to be insinuating that I can't go home yet," I argued. "I've been away for a long time, and I'm tired and I want to go home!"

"I'm not telling you anything that isn't true."

"Now what's *that* supposed to mean?" I snapped.

"The meaning will become clear in time," he said cryptically.

"Why can't you come out and say what you mean!" I barked, becoming more angry by the second.

My sister popped her head back into the room. "Are you guys okay?" she asked with one eyebrow skeptically cocked.

I broke character and smiled. "I'm just playing with Sam."

"Okay. I'll be off the phone in a minute." She smiled and disappeared back into the kitchen.

"I've got to go," I said quickly.

"Wait!" he commanded. "Watch the next game. It's important."

The screen immediately returned to the final frame of a commercial for tub and tile cleaner. In a flash, the show faded back in and Pat was starting the next game. Once again, the puzzle was a popular phrase. As the contestants guessed the letters one by one, I soon had what I thought was the solution, but I didn't know 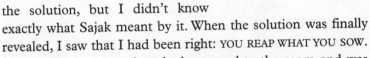 exactly what Sajak meant by it. When the solution was finally revealed, I saw that I had been right: YOU REAP WHAT YOU SOW.

By this time, my sister had returned to the room and was sitting next to me, so I didn't dare try to contact Pat.

"Why are you watching this dumb show?" she teased.

"I like it," I uttered begrudgingly. "And it's good for Sam. He can learn to read by guessing the letters."

"He's not even paying attention," she scoffed. "He's reading books."

"Well, I like it," I insisted, still wondering what Pat was getting at.

When the next set of commercials came on, my sister left the room again and Pat came back to the screen.

"Do you get it now?" he said impatiently.

"Get what? 'YOU CAN NEVER GO HOME.' 'YOU REAP WHAT YOU SOW.' I'm supposed to keep traveling forever and never go home and in the end it will pay off?" I hissed in a frenzy.

"You have a lot more cities to visit, don't you?" he asked.

"I'll go back out on the road after I've had time to recuperate. I need to go home and spend time with my family," I argued.

"Home isn't always where you think it is," he droned mysteriously.

Now I was really getting miffed. "What in hell are you talking about *now*, Sajak? If you get any more mysterious you're going to need a turban and a crystal ball! I might as well be trying to answer the riddle of the sphinx, for crying out loud!"

"The answers will be all too clear soon enough," he persisted. "How much time are you going to spend at home before you leave again?"

"I haven't decided; the schedule hasn't been finalized yet. I just need some time to decompress a little and catch up on my cartoon deadlines."

"How *much* time?" he nagged.

"I don't *know* how much time!" I snapped, feeling like a teenager trying to fend off a meddling parent. "And why are you bugging me now? Where were you when I *needed* you—like when that creepy guy in San Francisco was threatening to send me home in sandwich bags?"

"That guy was just joking. You were never in any real danger."

"I didn't know that at the time!" I protested. "He scared me to death!"

Pat shrugged it off. "A little fright never hurt anyone . . . besides, I told you, that's not what I'm here for."

"Then what *are* you here for?" I demanded accusingly.

Sajak's eyes narrowed as he was visibly losing patience with me. "I'm not here to jump in and slay people with a flaming sword every time you get your butt in a crack! You're a big boy, and I'm not your guardian angel!" Pat glared at me and took a deep breath. I'd never seen him get angry before, and it was a formidable sight. It looked as though his hair might begin smoldering. Then he took a deep breath, lowered his voice, and continued, calmly, almost compassionately, "I'm here to guide you, if you will let me. But *you* have to do the work. I can only point the way, nothing more."

I felt my defensive posture melting away as I began to sense the wisdom of what he was saying, and that he really cared about me. True, I was tired and the road had been long and hard, but I had to admit that it had been very gratifying and that I never would have even begun such a project were it not for Pat's inspiration. I was making progress, but I still hadn't found what I had set out to discover way back in that gutter in Monte Carlo when he had first come to me. I knew I needed Sajak's wisdom and guidance if I was ever going to hope to be able to put my life and career into perspective.

"All right, I give in, I'm sorry. I've learned a lot these past couple weeks, and I shouldn't be such an ingrate. I actually owe a lot to you."

Pat was touched by my honesty. "I knew I hadn't bet on the wrong pony. You're going make something of yourself yet."

I laughed a little, then teased back, "Okay, Pat, I'd like to buy a vowel. What do I do next?"

"Go home and tend to your deadlines and your family," he instructed quietly, taking on the persona of a kung fu master advising his protégé. "Meditate on what you have learned, the people you have met, your place in their lives and theirs in yours. And, most important, watch me on *Wheel of Fortune* weekdays at six-thirty on channel eight for further instructions."

"But six-thirty is when *The Simpsons* comes on!" I protested respectfully. "My kids will *never* let me change the channel! Besides, it's the only show I ever watch!"

Pat's face sank; clearly he was hurt by my admission. I couldn't bear to see the disappointment in his eyes.

"I'll watch," I assured him. "My kids will love it."

He kept his chin high and stared unblinkingly at me and said, "When it is time, you will find yourself on the road again." He began to fade and was gone.

FOURTEEN

Hanging with the Sloths

The plane was crowded and hot as I boarded and found my seat. It was late February and it was cold outside, but the air in the coach section was warm and thick and still. The flight was oversold, and by the time I had arrived at the ticket counter, all but the middle seats had already been assigned. I sat with my elbows glued to my sides, the passengers on either side of me already hogging the armrests by the time I sat down.

As people continued to pour into the plane in a steady stream, I began to wonder where they were going to sit and what the maximum capacity of the airplane was. It was a long way to Miami from Dallas; could the fuselage (and I) stand the strain and keep from bursting apart at the seams?

The woman to my left, in the aisle seat, had a two-year-old on her lap (or, rather, squirming and writhing *above* her lap). Across the aisle sat her husband, an impatient three-year-old to his left and a wailing infant in his arms. Their faces were as blank as those of zombies as they endeavored to weather the onslaught of ear-piercing screams and plug the trio of gaping mouths with pacifiers or bottles. The parents looked as though the life had been beaten out of them, and I wondered why any rational couple would saddle themselves with so many children so close in age. Are they devoid of a central nervous system, or do they just not know where they're coming from?

People were still streaming in through the door as if this were the last flight off an island marked as a nuclear test site. As all the seats were occupied, passengers were now sitting on other passengers' laps. An elderly man sat on mine. I complained, but my voice was muffled by the back of his heavy wool coat.

The traffic in the aisle stopped moving as the plane was full to capacity and beyond. There were no more laps to sit on, so those in the aisle grabbed hold of the straps hanging from the ceiling. There were people blocking the door, and it couldn't be closed. The flight attendants volunteered to get off so the hatch could be secured, but that would leave no one to explain the seat belts and oxygen masks.

The engines groaned ominously as we pulled slowly away from the gate.

Two and a half months had lapsed since my trip to California and Oregon. I found myself on my way to Florida, with Christmas, New Year's, and Valentine's Day behind me and a flurry of trips ahead. I had been working hard, enjoying my family, and watching *Wheel of Fortune* religiously.

And, just as Pat had predicted, I had found myself on the road again.

The arrangements for the trips were wholly unmiraculous. People wrote to me on the Internet, I wrote back. Hosts were chosen, dates were designated, flights and book signings were scheduled, tickets were mailed. Then problems came up and overnight hosts had to cancel or postpone, others had to be found, flights and book signings had to be changed. Tickets were re-issued, letters were sent and answered, calls were made. By this point, the tour had snowballed to the point where I was up to my neck in details and obligations and beginning to feel I had bitten off more than I could chew. This time around, I was exhausted before I ever left town.

Sajak stayed completely out of the process. He never acknowledged me during any of the two and a half months of shows I watched, and, as far as I could discern, he never dropped so much as a single hint in any of the puzzle solutions. I searched every episode for some shred of guidance, but found none. I wondered week after week why he had insisted on my watching every night and finally came upon what I thought must be the answer the night before I left town. It was in the solution to the final puzzle: THERE'S NO BUSINESS LIKE SHOW BUSINESS.

The performer's ego—I should have known. If he was going to help me, he wanted me at least to watch his show. It was what he was proud of, what he did best. I suppose I can't blame him.

I was going to Florida under unusual circumstances, even for me. Sometime in January, a lieutenant colonel in the Marine Corps had written to me and said that he'd seen an article about my book tour and wondered if I'd be willing to come to Tampa to sign books at a pub, of which he was a part owner. I wrote back telling him that I would love to, but that it didn't make much sense to try to sell books in a city where my cartoon had never appeared in the newspaper. Many people would never even have heard of *Bizarro*. He said he understood, but thought it might be fun anyway; the pub was always crowded with regulars, and he thought that with a little promotion on his part, he could sell some books. In addition, I could use the plane ticket he was sending me to lay over in Miami for a day and do a signing there (where I had been in the paper for about a year). I agreed, the arrangements were made, and on a chilly day in February I happily left Dallas for a few days in a tropical climate.

I was to stop first in Miami, where I would hang out and stay with a group of oceanographers and marine research scientists from the University of Miami who had written to me a year earlier about a panel I'd drawn called "Comic for the Humor-Challenged."

They asked me to join a support group they had started called SLOTH, an acronym for Sarcasm Lost on the Humor-Challenged. As the name implies, the membership consisted of people who are irritated by the occasional, witless android one meets in the course of a normal day, walking among us disguised as a human but giving himself away by an utter lack of a sense of humor and complete inability to identify sarcasm in casual conversation. I immediately knew just what they were talking about: that common phenomenon experienced by anyone who attempts to interject humor into a casual conversation with a store clerk or a stranger on a bus, only to be met by a stony stare. It is the sort of experience that inevitably makes the "jokester" feel like a complete idiot for even having tried to lighten up a routine daily encounter.

One example offered was that of a member of SLOTH who was on a crowded flight with a particularly fussy baby a few rows behind him. As the flight wore on and the baby continued to cry, he and the passenger beside him began to chat quietly about the annoyance. Some minutes into the conversation, the other passenger started into a sentence assessing the situation, then paused as he searched for just the right word: "The problem with a child like that is that they just have no . . ." Quickly, just for grins, the SLOTH member offered, "money?"

Utterly missing the joke and without even acknowledging the attempt, the man said, "No . . . discipline."

Not only did the SLOTH member feel insulted by the man's seeming presumption that he really thought the baby's problem was that he had no money, he was also appalled that a grown man could think that an infant on a plane could be "disciplined" into silence. Sometimes the humor-challenged aren't just dull, they're scary.

I accepted membership in SLOTH, as my motto in life is never to turn down a chance to be a part of a club that would have me as a member, and I was sent a T-shirt with the official SLOTH logo on the front, a black circle with a picture of a sloth in the center, hanging upside down from a branch with a wooden crutch propping it up from beneath.

Nearly a year later, when I wrote to my list of E-mail addresses in Miami looking for a driver and a place to stay, two of SLOTH's founding members, Dan and Kevin, answered immediately. They gladly volunteered to pick me up at the airport and run me around town, but, regrettably, neither had room to put me up for the night. Besides them, there was only one other person who responded to my plea, and all he wanted to do was take me to dinner.

I waited until very close to my departure date, but there were still no offers to put me up. Meanwhile, my publicist had arranged for me to be featured on a hip local entertainment magazine show, so I *had* to find a reader to stay with since that was the whole focus of the story. I swallowed my pride and wrote to my fellow SLOTH members.

"Are you *sure* one of you guys couldn't find room for me?" I wrote. "I can sleep on a couch or the floor. I don't mind, really."

Both founding members (there are only about five members in total) were appalled that Miamians hadn't been more hospitable, so they discussed it and decided that I would stay at Kevin's. Kevin also reluctantly agreed to let the TV show film my segment at his house. He was somewhat familiar with the program in question and, being a very genuine, down-to-earth intellectual scientist type, obviously detested it and its pretentious "hipness," but he consented politely, realizing the value of such publicity to my book sales.

With my accommodations problem resolved I felt better, but I was discouraged by the lack of response from my readers. I had gotten a lot of positive mail from Miami, so I knew people there liked my comics, but for some reason they were not interested in helping me out. Who would have thought that the citizens of Miami would be more skeptical than those of Los Angeles? I was also a little apprehensive about the SLOTHs. I had begun to get a picture of them as a bunch of vindictive eggheads who had been ridiculed and spurned by their peers all their lives and whose only purpose in life was to exact their revenge on society by using their superior intellects to sling sarcastic barbs at passersby, then deride their responses, whatever they might be. But it was only for one night, so, once again, I figured I could stand anything for that long.

Kevin met me at the airport and took me to a terrific local restaurant for lunch, where Dan and a couple of other SLOTHs were waiting.

I was extremely pleased to find out that, once again, my apprehensions were completely wrong. They were eggheads all right, all of them with masters degrees in science or better, but all were very friendly, likable, and polite and not vindictive in the least. Their sarcastic barbs were reserved only for the most pompous and humorless boobs, and we got along very well, as their humor sensibilities were delightfully similar to mine.

Kevin was a very intelligent, warm, and soft-spoken man of around forty, who is much too tall (a lot taller than I), with thick, short, bristly red hair and a long, bushy red beard. Dan was more the size of a normal human being (only slightly taller than I), also very warm and intelligent but less soft-spoken, with black hair and small, round wire-framed glasses. Even though he is in his twenties, Dan is one of those guys with a big, thick clump of hair and a boyish quality to his face that makes him look much more like a twelve-year-old genius child.

At my request they told fascinating stories of their many voyages around the world on scientific vessels, and I listened intently, slipping into a private fantasy of myself working on the deck of a ship off the coast of Sri Lanka with the bright blue of the Indian Ocean contrasting against my tattered white pants, rolled up to the knee, and my skin, dark brown and sun-baked, as I pull strange, complicated, scientific contraptions dangling at the ends of long ropes from the depths of the sea and record the readings of the many dials and gauges.

At their request I told stories of how I get up every morning at 6:00 A.M. and stare at a blank piece of paper over coffee and Wheat Chex, trying to think up a cartoon. They, in turn, slipped into private fantasies of themselves working on the deck of a ship off the coast of Sri Lanka with the bright blue of the Indian Ocean contrasting against their tattered white pants, rolled up to the knee, and their skin, dark brown and sun-baked, as they pull strange, complicated, scientific contraptions dangling at the ends of long ropes from the depths of the sea and record the readings of the many dials and gauges.

Dan was working on his Ph.D. and had only to complete his dissertation. I asked what it was about, and he casually answered that he was studying the production and removal of methyl bromide in the oceans by using a technique called gas chromatography/mass spectrometry. I told him I just happened to have written a paper in high school on the very same thing, and I'd be willing to sell it to him for a nominal fee if he needed it to help him with his dissertation. He politely declined my offer, seemingly determined to do the work himself. Kids sure have changed since I was in school.

At the table there was one empty place setting. I asked

about it, and Dan explained that they had invited humor columnist Dave Barry, who lives in Miami, to join us for lunch, but didn't expect him to show up.

Sometime ago they had gone to one of his readings at a local bookstore and approached him afterward with a SLOTH T-shirt and an invitation to join. He accepted the shirt and nodded politely, but they hadn't heard from him since. They figured this would be a good time to invite him to a meeting since all five members would be there, including the one out-of-towner—me.

Kevin added that a woman claiming to be Barry's assistant had called the day before to say that he wouldn't be able to make it to lunch because he was out of town. The SLOTHs cheered this news and considered it a triumph that they had gotten an *official* refusal. I cheered as well, but, out of a juvenile sense of competition, I wondered if I, too, should have refused their invitation, that showing up for lunch with these guys somehow made me seem less important and successful than Dave Barry. But then I remembered that I am, in fact, much less important and successful than Dave Barry and that I had absolutely no better place to be and was actually having a great time. And even though Dave Barry was doubtless having a much *better* time wherever he was at that moment (by virtue of his greater importance and success), I was still glad I had come. Having won that argument with myself in a matter of only a few seconds, I reflected on what a wonderful thing mental health really is.

After lunch we were all to return to Kevin's house to meet the film crew from the hip local TV show. We waited at Kevin's for the TV crew for nearly an hour after they were scheduled to arrive, then decided to call the station and see what had become of them. The receptionist who answered the phone had a lot of difficulty finding anyone who knew anything about me or the crew, but eventually she located someone who told us they had canceled the shoot because the camera guy hadn't shown up for work. Someone had called my publicist in Kansas City that morning and left a message on her voice mail. As fate would have it, however, my publicist was out of town and hadn't picked up her messages.

I wasn't the least bit surprised by this lack of professionalism, as it's the sort of thing I'd come to expect from local TV shows, especially the hip ones. In fact, I have come to believe that with both organizations and individuals, the hipness quotient is frequently inversely proportionate to the level of dependability. That is to say, the more hip, the less responsible. In Dallas, a local *Regis and Kathie Lee* clone talk show had called me after seeing an article about my mooch tour and said the hosts would simply *love* to have me on and their producer was very excited about it and would call me back "in a few minutes" to schedule a date—I never heard from anyone again.

So it didn't surprise me that the Miami show canceled because one guy didn't show up for work, but I was disappointed that I was losing the publicity. I'd called *The Miami Herald* the week before about doing a little story of some sort about my appearance and someone had sounded interested but in the end decided for some reason that my visit to Miami was best kept a secret.

It all added up to one thing: If no one knows you're in town, you're pretty much destined to have a lonely book signing. One positive aspect of this was that coming to this realization early in the day allowed me to get my crying over with long before I reached the store. The SLOTH members were very understanding and patient about this and waited politely outside the bathroom door, only knocking a few times to ask if I was *sure* I was all right.

The waterworks being dispensed with, I spent the rest of the afternoon with Kevin touring the research facility where he worked, meeting all the other friendly brainiacs that work there, viewing the hundreds of tanks of sea slugs that are bred there for research, and looking at strange, handmade, scientific contraptions that people dangle into the ocean to check for scientific stuff (if I may use the technical term).

As incredibly dry as all that sounds, I actually had a great time. I've always had a natural interest in science, even though

I have no formal education in the field (come to think of it, I have no formal education in any field). I also rather enjoy the company of scientific, intellectual nerd types, not only because I find their research and discoveries fascinating but because they make me feel very butch. Even though I am a small guy, it is easy for me to imagine that even if I couldn't beat them at *Jeopardy*, I could probably kick their asses.

Late that afternoon, Kevin handed me off downtown to the reader who had volunteered to take me to dinner. His name was Al, he worked for an advertising firm, and he whisked me to South Miami Beach for dinner at a sidewalk café. He assured me that even though the restaurant was at the opposite end of town from the bookstore, we would have plenty of time to eat and get back by seven.

He was half right. We had plenty of time to eat, but getting back to the store by seven proved to be an impossibility, no matter how fast or recklessly he drove.

As soon as we had paid the check, we leapt over the café's railing, sprinted the four blocks to the car, and careened through the streets at blinding speed in Al's two-seater sports car, all the way across town and right up to the door of the store. In spite of my repeated admission that it didn't matter what time I got to the store since no one knew I was in town and there would be no one waiting for me, Al did his best to make good on his promise. I arrived about twenty minutes after the hour, and, just as predicted, no one was waiting. Even the store personnel seemed surprised to see me, except for the store publicist guy who had set up the appearance. Apparently, he's pretty good at keeping a secret, too. One thing I learned during my brief stay, Miamians are a tight-lipped bunch.

The signing went about as I had expected, as I sold only a few books to a handful of walk-bys who had no idea I'd be there but happened to be *Bizarro* fans. One such sale was to a young boy of about twelve who spotted me as he walked through the front door and was, judging by the look on his face, thoroughly blown away at the sight of me.

"I don't believe it!" he gushed, out-of-breath and wide-eyed.

"I was just walking in and I looked up and saw the sign and I said to my dad, 'That's him! That's the guy I was just talking about!' I don't believe it! You're my favorite cartoonist!"

It seems this kid had written to me on E-mail the day before I left Dallas but didn't mention where he lived. Consequently, when I wrote back, I didn't tell him I'd be in Miami the next day.

He had just read my response that very evening and, walking into the bookstore a few blocks from where he lived, had been telling his dad how he had written to his favorite cartoonist and I'd actually written back. Then presto; there I was right in front of him.

It was a funny coincidence of the sort that adults are more or less used to, giving birth to expressions like "It's a small world." But the kid went on and on about it and seemed genuinely rattled by shock, unable to grasp the situation and file it in a logical slot in his brain. I kidded around with him for a while and signed a book for him, including a fairly elaborate drawing. Finally, he and his dad left, and, as they walked out the front door, the kid was still staring at the book in his hands, wagging his head in disbelief.

I have wondered since if the experience had any sort of weird effect on him, perhaps causing him to be obsessed with the Internet, writing letters to celebrities of all sorts twenty hours a day, rarely sleeping, skipping school, trying desperately to make them appear before him.

The rest of the time I spent talking to the SLOTHs and the handful of their friends who had come by the store. It was a pleasant-enough evening, even though I didn't sell a lot of books. At nine o'clock, we caravaned to Kevin and his wife Leslie's house for a few more hours of merrymaking.

Breakfast the next morning had a dreamlike quality about it. Even though it was mid-February, the three of us sat around the table in shorts and T-shirts, the windows open, drinking the juice from oranges picked from Kevin and Leslie's own tree that very morning, eating deliciously sweet, homegrown grapefruits and bread Leslie had baked the day before. Out the back windows, their small yard looked like a scene from *Gilligan's Island* with lush greenery and huge palm trees dripping with moisture and glistening in the early morning sun.

There is something intoxicating about the tropics in winter. They lure you in with a sensuous warmth and beauty that makes you want to leave the brown and bitter cold of your home and settle in beneath the welcoming fronds of a giant palm. You feel you could throw away your shoes and long pants and sweaters and coats and live in a hut on the beach: no heating bills, no snow shovel, no electric blankets or rubber boots. Just warm, tropical breezes and delicious, fresh fruit.

But then summer comes. Your clothes are drenched with sweat before you're finished getting dressed after your shower, the third one of the day. You step outside and your eyeballs sizzle in their sockets like spit on a hot engine. The upholstery in your car has become liquefied and the plastic of your steering wheel is dripping like candle wax onto your thighs, burning holes into your flesh. The humidity is such that you need only to take a deep breath to quench your thirst. The intoxication of the tropics has turned into a hangover that won't go away until Christmas.

Kevin and I dropped Leslie off at work and went on to the airport. In saying good-bye, I told him they were welcome at my house any time, and I meant it. The group that sponsored me in Miami were intelligent, kind, witty, well educated, well traveled, open-minded (and I could probably kick their asses). What's not to like? I added them to the list of remarkably wonderful people I was meeting almost everywhere I went. As much as I hated to admit it, I was having difficulty maintaining my normally cynical and pessimistic attitude toward Homo sapiens.

FIFTEEN

Salvador Presley & the Persistence of Graceland

As I left Miami and headed for Tampa, I found it difficult to maintain my normally cynical and pessimistic attitude toward Homo sapiens, but not impossible.

City after city, I dreaded meeting the next host, yet each time I was pleasantly surprised by what I'd found. (Even in the case of Ken the Wacko I was pleasantly surprised he wasn't really going to kill me.) A brighter person would have long ago learned his lesson and realized that most people are pretty good folks once you give them a chance and get to know them. It's ridiculous to go through life expecting the worst. But some people have to run full-speed into the tree of knowledge without a helmet before they learn certain things, and in this case I was one of those people. Even though I had been proven wrong in almost every case, I couldn't help but wonder if Tampa would be the exception to the rule. My sponsor there was the marine lieutenant colonel who was part owner of an English-style darts pub with a couple of other people, including the son of the late British actor Robert Morley.

That was about all I knew about Rick, and the images that

little bit of information conjured up were none too attractive: big, burly, conservative, macho, intolerant, narrow-minded, regarding blind conformity as a virtue. (Come to think of it, that was a fair description of Sister Mary Pterodactyl.) Since I was old enough to know what the military was, I have assumed I would be exactly the sort of person that would annoy a career military guy beyond his limits. This, I thought, was my best chance so far of getting stuck with a narrow-minded, right-wing, hard-drinking, corn-cob-up-the-butt jackass. A real man's man. And I had precious little hope of feeling even the least bit butch around a guy like that.

You guessed it, I was wrong again.

Colonel Rick was a small, almost elfish man (about my size) in his forties with a disarming, boyish grin and an "anything goes" attitude toward life. He was quite the ladies' man by all appearances, but remained unmarried. He lived in a comfortable house with a swimming pool, four barbecue grills in the backyard (he seems to forget he already has some and keeps buying new ones), and a pool table on the back porch.

His best friends were a couple of fellow bachelors that lived in the area: Dale, a computer whiz and old marine buddy with the same lust for good living, and Doc, a cool guy with a big boat.

Rick couldn't have been further from my imagined stereotype, and I realized instantly that the only person who was being narrow-minded was me. He works for some kind of computer company and travels all over the world, virtually weekly, giving seminars and speeches about computers. When he's at home in Tampa, he hangs out at his pub.

Rick, Doc, and Dale picked me up at the airport and took me back to Rick's house to get settled and change clothes. We were joined by Rick's attractive, twenty-something-year-old girlfriend, Connie, and then we piled back into the car, grabbed some submarine sandwiches, and headed out to spend the afternoon on Doc's boat.

I don't know much about boats, but I think Doc's is a pretty good one. It was about the size and shape of the S.S. *Minnow* (to continue my *Gilligan's Island* references theme) and was what I would call a "cabin cruiser." (I don't know if that's technically correct, but it had a "cabin" and it "cruised.") It was an older boat, all made of brown wood and brass fittings, not one of those modern, white and blue fiberglass jobs they make nowadays. There was a main room with a table, a few chairs, some cabinets, a small refrigerator, and a portable TV, then a bedroom in the bow with a tiny bathroom and shower. Up on top of everything was a big deck with an awning over it.

From the uppermost deck, Doc steered the boat as the rest of us sat around in plastic lawn chairs and drank beer. We cruised out a ways into Tampa Bay and anchored, shooting the breeze and joking around like old friends. Of course, three of them *were* old friends, but they made me feel as if I was, too, and that was the good part about it.

That evening we went to Rick's pub, Mad Dogs and Englishmen, where they set me up at a big table on the front patio with stacks upon stacks of my books. Between Rick and me, we connived just about every person who happened through the pub that night into buying a book or twelve, but we still had plenty left over by the time we called it quits and went home around 10:00 P.M. I shudder to think how many customers Rick might have permanently lost that night by forcing me and my books on them. I have since heard that for weeks after, it wasn't uncommon for the pub to receive numerous phone calls each night from people asking if there were any special events or guests that evening. It wouldn't surprise me to find there was a landfill outside of town filled with *Bizarro* books.

By the time we left, I had signed, gabbed, and partied for four solid hours, a new record. I was exhausted.

The next morning we were up bright and early and Rick had another sizable stack of my books for me to autograph as gifts for his millions of friends. In the end I signed more books in Tampa, where I am virtually unknown, than in any other single city.

My flight home wasn't until afternoon, so Rick and I decided to take in the Salvador Dalí Museum, which was just

across the bay in St. Petersburg. This two-hour side trip was a
turning point in my book tour—and my life.

Since earliest childhood, my self-image has always been
that I am an artist. I cannot remember a time when I wanted to
be anything else (except for the brief phases every young boy
passes through during which he wants to be a cowboy, fireman,
astronaut, or cocktail waitress).

When I was a teenager, Salvador Dalí was my favorite artist
and I studied and emulated his work diligently. I even sent a
letter and some photos of my work to him when I was about
eighteen to see if I might be able to meet him or apprentice
under him. I received no response.

As an adult, I found it difficult (make that impossible) to
support myself by selling paintings, so I fairly quickly fell into
commercial illustration, drawing pictures for advertisements.
Unhappy with the stressful, uncreative, back-stabbing world of
advertising, I immediately began looking for another way to
make a living as an artist—a compromise of some kind. Cartooning became that compromise.

While syndicated cartooning is essentially a commercial
venture and doesn't allow the no-holds-barred creative license
that fine art does, I am still able to be creative, exercise my own
judgment in most cases, and be my own boss. I have always felt
extremely fortunate to have been able to land a position in such
a competitive and desirable field, but there remained within me
a conflict between the two functions: commercial breadwinner
(cartoonist) and tortured painter (artiste).

The cartoonist within me is concerned with keeping
Bizarro fresh, improving the quality of the work, making the
best business deals, saving for retirement, and sending the kids
to college. He scoffs at so-called fine art as a frivolous luxury to
be indulged in only when there are no "real" deadlines to meet.
The artiste in me, on the other hand, has a passion for "true"

art, that which comes boiling up from the subconscious with no care or concern for the rules or desires of the outside world. He wants to live in a garret, subsist on what little food he can beg or steal, paint constantly, and dream of his work hanging in a museum sometime after his (hopefully dramatic) death. He resents the cartoon business and sees it as an obstacle to truly meaningful expression.

In spite of this ongoing, inner struggle, I have managed throughout my career to keep both of these personalities happy over the years, but because of the extra strain the planning and execution of the Mooch Tour had put on my already hectic schedule, I had found it necessary to ignore the artiste in me for many consecutive months. By the time I got to the Dalí Museum in Florida, it had been over a year since I had touched a painting. The artiste was deeply buried, but losing patience.

I had heard from several people over the years that the Dalí Museum was very impressive, so I was thrilled to have the chance to go. I expected to enjoy it, but its effect on me was much greater than I anticipated.

In person, Dalí's paintings are a visual and spiritual feast. The museum has an enormous collection of his work, the largest in the world, and many of his most famous images are there. Some are remarkably small, the size of a piece of notebook paper or smaller. Many are much larger than I would have imagined, perhaps fifteen feet wide and two stories tall.

His imagination and vision combined with his technical mastery were inspiring beyond words. I was filled with the desire to create art again and felt that I must paint soon or die. The cartoonist walked into the museum, but two hours later he was bound and gagged and locked in the janitor's closet and the artiste walked out.

The only thing that kept me grounded on planet Earth during this near out-of-body experience was my mustache.

In the year before this visit, I had grown a mustache and a small, pointy beard on my chin. They were disconnected, so could not be called a goatee really. I think the proper term is "Vandyke" (so named because of the resemblance to Dick Van Dyke's brother, Jerry, after he'd been drinking chocolate milk). Most people just said I looked like the devil.

I'd never worn facial hair before this because my wife disliked it, but I started to grow it in this case just for kicks one day when I was mad at her, not meaning to keep it for very long. As the ends of the mustache got longer, however, they began to curl upward, and very soon I realized that with a little manipulation, I could have a little Salvador Dalí look going. This appealed to me a great deal, partly because I had always liked his art and his mustache and partly because I have this inexplicable compulsion to make myself look foolish.

So the ends of the mustache got longer and longer and I lacquered them up with mustache wax and hair mousse to make them stick up in points. I trimmed the little beard part to a point and, with my long, bushy, corkscrew hair, I looked amazingly like one of the Three Musketeers. Before long, the entire effect was so dramatic that even my wife agreed that it would be a shame to shave it off, at least until the end of my book tour. I was thus coifed when I toured the museum.

By that time, I'd been wearing this strange thing for many months and had become blasé about it, but only a few minutes after I arrived, I began to feel conspicuous. It suddenly occurred to me that I was *at* the Salvador Dalí Museum *wearing* a Salvador Dalí mustache. People would undoubtedly think I was some loser whose entire identity was wrapped up in being as much like Dalí as possible. I was suddenly stricken with the image of those goobers who spend the better portion of their adult lives dressed like Elvis, peering through the gates of Graceland.

I walked around with my hand over my mouth as if deep in thought, hoping no one would notice me. It was a Monday morning, after all, so the place wasn't too crowded; I was probably making a big deal out of nothing, I assured myself. Then a bus load of school kids arrived.

They weren't *just* school kids, either; they were *junior high* kids—the human species' most socially insensitive age group.

I skirted from one room to another, keeping my back to them as much as possible, but it is a relatively small building with a lot of open spaces and there are only so many places to hide. It wasn't long before a few of them spotted me, and began to giggle and point and whisper. Soon, a formidable group of them were following me around, trying to get a glimpse of the idiot with the goofy mustache.

I was holding my hand over my mouth with my shoulders hunched up around my ears, shuffling quickly from room to room with a crowd of teenagers following close behind. I walked faster, they walked faster. We were nearly doing that flailing walk/run thing you do at the swimming pool when you're a kid so the lifeguard won't call you down for running. Hunched over and paranoid as I was, I must have looked like Richard Nixon trying to escape a pack of rabid reporters. As I fled, I half considered bending the points of my mustache down and shoving them into my mouth to hide them, but the thought disgusted me and it was too late anyway.

Eventually, the curious students' chaperone caught up with them and scolded them for separating from the rest of the group. She told them to leave the pathetic little man alone and then herded them back to their flock. They wouldn't have Dan Piraro to kick around anymore.

Undaunted by my brush with the ego-crushing teens from Hell, I was still on a spiritual high when we got ready to leave. Rick enjoyed the museum, too, and we both loaded up with cool Dalí junk from the gift shop. I got a hat, some coasters, a bathing suit, a coffee mug, and a refrigerator magnet; Rick got some big beach towels, a watch, a pack of playing cards, some socks, a Frisbee, and a screen saver. In the old days, spiritual experiences rarely came with souvenirs. Thank God for capitalism.

On the flight back home, I could think of nothing but painting. I began planning my next project and did a few preliminary sketches in my notebook. I would use my wife as the central character, as I nearly always did, and I couldn't wait to get started.

SIXTEEN

Nutbag Envy
& Illegal Handbags

The artiste was still dominating my personality as I prepared to leave for Raleigh-Durham and Atlanta a week later.

I had endured an exhausting week of answering E-mail, making arrangements, and trying to catch up on cartoon deadlines before I left so I wouldn't be too far behind when I got back. By this time I was beginning to get tired of the whole thing from top to bottom, and all I really wanted to do was stay home and paint. But there simply wasn't any time, and I could see that there wasn't going to be until the rest of my tour was over. I had taken on this behemoth willingly and was committed to seeing it through. I was just going to have to put off the artiste until it was over. But that was several weeks and endless bombardments of trivial scheduling details away.

As I struggled with these issues, I was in a state of constant irritability and beginning to regret my decision to embark on the whole tour. I was beginning, too, to doubt Pat Sajak.

The night before I left for North Carolina, I watched *Wheel of Fortune* as usual. But this time it seemed different somehow. Instead of finding hidden jewels of wisdom, the puzzle solutions were empty and shallow, and Pat seemed pallid and impotent. Inside my head, the artiste was hard at work trying to get me to blow off the tour and use my spare time to paint.

Sajak must have sensed I was losing faith because during one of the commercial breaks he appeared in a Nike commercial.

"Hey, what's up?" he asked casually as he stepped into the foreground, dodging careening athletes.

"Nothing," I said blankly.

"You look like you just lost your best friend."

"No, I'm fine. Just tired," I lied.

"Going out on the road again tomorrow?" he asked cheerfully.

"Yeah. Raleigh."

"That's beautiful country around there. I think you'll really like it," he encouraged. "The people are very nice, too. You'll have a lot of fun."

"I don't really care," I replied despondently. "I just want to get it over with." I was laying it on thick, hoping to spur Pat into helping me in some way or giving me a quick-fix solution to my problems.

Typical of him, he didn't fall for it. Instead, he replied paternally, "You're not going to learn much with *that* attitude, young man."

"What am I supposed to be learning anyway?" I blurted sarcastically. "I keep forgetting."

"About yourself, your career, your fans, the world. You're the one who had hit the skids and wanted to put things back in perspective," he scolded. "Or have you already forgotten the gutters of Monte Carlo?"

I lost my temper. "Yeah, well, I've been traipsing all over the country for months now at the beck and call of every comics fan with a modem and I don't feel any closer to nirvana!" I ranted. "I'd like to have a life of my *own* again, Pat! I mean, how long does this have to go on? How much perspective does one guy need?" I was immediately embarrassed by my childish outburst but felt unable to go back.

Just then a basketball from the Nike commercial hit Pat in the head. He barely even flinched, just closed his eyes for a second then continued to glare at me.

"So why don't you quit?" he said with a stiff jaw.

"I just might!" I snapped back. "You know, I was watching *The Price Is Right* this morning, and Bob Barker didn't try to send me on any stupid pilgrimage!"

Pat's eyes flashed, he took a deep breath, then he spoke quietly and authoritatively. "No, I'm quite sure he didn't. I suspect he didn't try to send you *anywhere*. In fact, I'm certain he ignored you completely."

"And what's wrong with that?" I challenged him. "Isn't that what a game-show host is *supposed* to do? Emcee the game and mind his own business?"

Pat stared at me without blinking. The seconds passed in silence as if time had frozen.

Finally, he spoke. "Is that what you want? You want to merely watch the game and not play it?"

I could see the pain in his eyes, but it was too late to back down. "Maybe so," I said quietly. "Maybe I just wasn't cut out to spin the wheel, Pat."

I could feel the bond between us being stressed to the breaking point. It was terrifying to turn my back on the guidance I had come to depend on, and I felt ashamed, but the die had been cast.

Neither of us spoke for a few seconds, then Pat managed to choke out a few final words.

"Fine, then . . . I'll step out of the picture for now. The wheel is already spinning anyway." His tone was chilling and distant. His face was suddenly isolated and glowing transparently on the screen like the Wizard of Oz's. He spoke ominously, "If you'll excuse me, I've got a game show to run." Then his face drained of all color and faded away. He was gone. I angrily punched the power button and shut off the TV.

As the screen went dark, I felt a strange, simultaneous rush of relief and sorrow. The artiste was thrilled that I was free of the book tour, but the cartoonist, recently buried and repressed in my subconscious though he was, registered a sense of grief. I was also filled with doubt about the decisions I had made and wondered what Sajak had meant by "The wheel is already spinning anyway." Was he implying that the answers I sought in my life were within me all along, like the Scarecrow, the Tin Woodman, and the Cowardly Lion? Was that the reason for the cheesy Wizard of Oz impression in his final moments? Or was he just trying to bug me?

Feeling an anxiety attack welling up inside me, I quickly ran through a list of other game-show hosts I might be able to call on for help: Monty Hall, Wink Martindale, Alex Trebek. ("The answer is: 'the city where you'll meet your grisly demise at the hands of a psycho.' [Buzz.] Dan?" "Raleigh, North Carolina, Alex?" "I'm sorry, Dan, the correct question is '*What is* Raleigh, North Carolina?' I'm afraid you lose.") But it was clearly no use; Sajak had come to me of his own accord, and I hadn't the slightest idea how to conjure up another emcee—I was going to have to come up with my own answers and choose which doors and curtains I would look behind on my own from here on out. And heaven help me if I picked the wrong ones.

Meanwhile, my psyche was the scene of a raging battle between the cartoonist and the artiste. One wanted me to go to Raleigh; the other wanted me to scrap the whole project and stay home and paint. With only a few hours till my next flight, I wrestled over my options for the next morning's trip and came to the decision that I would, in fact, have to force myself to go through with it. It would be simply unconscionable to cancel at this late date, no matter how upset I was. A lot of people had made plans around me, and it was my duty to fulfill my obligations. Plus, my various neuroses aside, I'm not a quitter. My cartoonist self had won the battle, but my artiste self was far from dead.

I was afraid that in such a schizoid state I might behave badly toward my readers when I visited North Carolina. I was anxious and restless, and I feared it would take all my self-control to maintain a happy face during the next four days.

Soon after I arrived in Raleigh, however, I realized my worries were in vain. From start to finish, my entire visit was so thoroughly wonderful that even the disagreeable artiste was won over.

My sponsors there were Val and Lee, a delightful couple in their late thirties who went beyond the call of duty to make my visit with them a success.

They lived in a beautiful and cozy house filled with beagles, Japanese art, sculptures, plants, and stained-glass doors and windows. They had no children but seemingly plenty of money and frequent flyer miles and had, consequently, traveled virtually all over the world.

Lee was raised in North Carolina and speaks Japanese fluently (something not *all* the locals can do, I found out). He had lived and worked extensively in Japan and still traveled there regularly. Val was a computer artist by trade and was responsible for much of the sculpture and stained-glass pieces in their house. She was also, as I discovered firsthand, an excellent amateur publicist.

Val first approached me on the Internet after having seen my solicitation letter secondhand at work (just like Ken the Wacko from San Francisco, but, fortunately, the similarity ends there). She offered not only to fly me to Raleigh-Durham and put me up at their house but to set up my book signings and even arrange local radio and newspaper coverage. I accepted her travel offer immediately and cleared the other arrangements with my publicist. Being overworked as all publicists tend to be, she jumped at the offer: "Sure! If she wants to set that stuff up, let her!"

Within twenty-four hours, Val had confirmed two book signings, one in Raleigh, one in Durham, had sent press kits to several of the local papers, had personally contacted radio stations, and had posted details of my appearances on several computer bulletin boards that served the large computer company she and Lee worked for as well as a number of the many universities in the area. In the blink of an eye, she sent me an itinerary that rivaled that of any other city I had visited. (I was extremely impressed and wondered if she would also send out a team of special agents to scout and secure each location before I arrived and run alongside my motorcade with sunglasses, earphone, and sidearm as we made our way through town.)

By the time I arrived on Friday night, the two major papers in the area had done stories on my visit and local awareness was very high. That night, after picking me up at the airport, Val and Lee took me to a local nightspot to hear a blues band and have a few beers.

The band was good, but the main attraction by far was a woman of around forty who was dancing in front of the stage, dressed in a seventies Stevie Nix handkerchief sort of outfit. Sensing a Kodak moment in the making, the crowd moved back a bit and made room for her as she wriggled around and waved her limbs through the air slowly and comically, pausing abruptly every few seconds to point at a member of the audience, smile broadly, wink, nod, shake her head, and otherwise gesture to them as if they were having a private, telepathic conversation. (I have no doubt that *she* was convinced that is exactly what she was doing.) Then she'd toss her head back dramatically and begin wriggling again. At first the band was pleased to see someone "getting into their music," but soon I could sense their annoyance as the wiggly woman began to steal the show.

Spontaneous and unscheduled nutbags like this are always my favorite attraction anywhere I go. Authentic weirdness is always so much more entertaining than anything planned. I only wish you could publish a tour guide of that sort of thing, but by definition these sorts of people and events defy prediction. And, of course, half the fun of such an occurrence is the element of surprise. One never knows when or where a nutbag might show up and begin an unscheduled performance.

When one begins to perform, I typically find myself standing among a crowd of others, watching, smirking, giggling nervously, sometimes making fun. But as I analyze my fascination with this sort of oddball, I find that chief among my emotions is envy. In truth, I would *love* to be so liberated from the confines of social mores and so-called normal behavior that I could enjoy each moment without inhibition; the way a small child can sit in a park and sing the theme song to *The Brady Bunch* without noticing who is taking notice. I guess I'm just a nutbag wannabe at heart.

The next afternoon Val, Lee, and I had a nice little lunch at their house with a handful of their neighborhood friends, then we left for the book signings. Primarily due to Val's advance publicity efforts, both bookstores were packed to the walls and subsequently sold every *Bizarro* book they had ordered. One store completely sold out before I even got there. A number of people said they had scoured the city and found my books at other locations, and several people waited in line just to get pieces of paper signed because they were unable to find one of my books anywhere in town. It was the sort of fuss I was not accustomed to having made over me but would love the chance to get used to.

The Regulator bookstore in Durham was a small, privately owned, and very hip shop the owner of which had, according to Val and Lee, been almost single-handedly responsible for revitalizing the entire neighborhood. The area had been abandoned to stray dogs and FOR LEASE signs until The Regulator opened up a few years ago, but it was now chock-full of groovy gift shops, coffeehouses, and other artsy, college-student hangouts.

After my signing, Johnny, the likable, ex-flower-child-of-the-sixties-turned-responsible-father-of-two-girls owner of the store, presented me with a bizarre, folk-art contraption of bamboo and tin that, when mounted on a pole outside, becomes a wind-mill/wind chime thing with a bobbing farmer and nodding cow. It's the sort of thing that first makes you wonder what it is, then makes you wonder how you ever lived without it. It was the gift of a shop owner a few doors down who was a big fan of my work but who couldn't come to the book signing because she had to spend the afternoon selling bizarre, folk-art contraptions of bamboo and tin. When my signing was over, I walked down to her store, thanked her, and gave her a free copy of my book, which I autographed. (After I got home, I mounted the contraption on a pole in my backyard, where it spins and clinks and bobs to this day. I have heard she has done the same with my book.)

An hour later, the Quail Ridge Bookstore in Raleigh was also packed to capacity when I arrived. As the owner, a sweet, white-haired, older woman, led me through the shoulder-to-shoulder crowd, a well-dressed but visibly nervous woman approached me with a rectangular brown paper bag in her hand.

"Mr. Piraro?" she blurted as she reached into the bag.

Chasing away images of Jack Ruby shooting Lee Harvey Oswald, I greeted her politely.

"Could I talk to you for just one moment, please?" she asked nervously.

I stopped and listened as she began to stammer anxiously through her story.

"I work for Mary Kay Cosmetics, and Mary Kay frequently tells a story of when she was a young woman in sales, and there was a sales contest and the first prize was an alligator handbag . . ." She produced from the brown sack a newspaper clipping of one of my cartoons, matted in Mary Kay pink, as she continued.

"And she wanted that alligator handbag so bad, so she worked very, very hard and sold as much as she could. And when the contest was over, she had won, but in the meantime, they had outlawed alligator handbags, and so they had to switch the prize at the last minute. And so what she won was a fish light of some sort."

I interrupted her at this point. "A fish light?" I said, with eyes narrowed. "What's a fish light?"

"I don't know, really. I think it's some sort of a light you use to catch fish or something. But anyway," she continued, undaunted by my stupidity (ask a foolish question . . .), "she won a fish light instead of the alligator handbag, and she still has that fish light in her office to this very day!"

"Well, I'll be darned," I managed to say.

"So I was wondering if you would just sign this cartoon for her. I'm going to give it to her at the next sales seminar, and I think she'll really get a kick out of it!"

So I signed the cartoon—how could I resist after such a compelling and obviously true story? I knew it was a true story because Mary Kay is a saleswoman first and foremost, and salespeople *never* lie, especially not for the purposes of motivating other people to make money for them.

The signing at Quail Ridge went very much as the first one had: long lines, books sold out, people empty-handed after having searched all over town for a book. It was enough to make me wonder if I had stepped momentarily into someone else's life. Maybe Garth Brooks or Dr. Ruth Westheimer.

After it was over, still giddy from the attention, Val and Lee dragged me to a local Bohemian eatery where seventeen of their closest friends met us for dinner. All of them were friendly, energetic, interesting folks who were only too glad to have been on the short list of invitees. Val and Lee must have a metric boatload of friends, I thought to myself. I'm not sure I know seventeen people who would come to my funeral, much less meet me at a restaurant for dinner to help entertain an out-of-town guest if I asked them. These people must have been living a nonstop party.

One of their more interesting friends was Jenny, a left-wing freelance political activist/photographer who hangs out with the radical right and documents what they're up to. She's attended everything from Blitzkrieg Buchanan rallies to Ku Klux Klan clambakes. Most of the time she is undercover (by "undercover" I don't mean that she shuffles around inside a fake tree trunk with a camera hidden in a knothole but that she uses an alias and pretends to be sympathetic to the right-winger's cause while photographing them), and several times her identity and political leanings have been discovered and she has been bodily expelled with little regard for formality or manners. Her photos have appeared in *Rolling Stone* and *The Village Voice*, among other publications.

She followed me around for the weekend snapping pictures fairly steadily, presumably for different reasons than when she's photographing the Klan. (Come to think of it, she *was* pretty sympathetic to my cause.)

Having consciously patterned most of my life after Sean Penn, I admittedly found it difficult to resist the urge to beat her up and smash her camera on the pavement. But in the end I was glad I did not. The pictures were great, and I grew to be quite fond of her. One of the pictures she took of me hangs in a prominent place on a wall of my home, a testament to how much I liked it because I detest displaying pictures of myself in my own house. I am already all too painfully aware of how I look and don't need to be reminded. Anyone else who has any business being in my home probably is, too.

I left Raleigh-Durham much as I had left many other cities on my tour: with new friends and a renewed appreciation for the process of meeting new people. If only I'd known there were so many cool people in the world, I wouldn't have wasted all those years being shy and cynical. I reflected on the falling-out I had had with Sajak before I left home and felt foolish. Sure, I was tired of traveling so much and my life was incredibly hectic at the moment, but I hadn't been away from home for more than a few days at a time and surely the renewed perspective on life that I had gained from the experience was worth a little extra effort and inconvenience for a few months. I contemplated apologizing to Pat and asking him to continue to mentor me, but I had no idea how to contact him. Perhaps he would sense my change of heart and contact me.

But even when things are going as well as they did in North Carolina, there is a recurring desire that fills me at various intervals in my life and with various degrees of strength to quit cartooning completely. This urge first came over me a few minutes after I had signed my original syndication contract back in 1985 and has been a regular feature of my psyche ever since.

It is, I think, an inevitable result of the relentless pressure to be brilliant that a joke-a-day schedule creates. When I am signing books and meeting my readers, the urge becomes even greater and at times can bear down on me with the weight of a full-sized, recently fed mountain gorilla in an oil-soaked leisure suit. And, oddly enough, the feeling is as likely to come over me at a successful signing as at a dud.

If the store is packed and scores of adoring fans are slathering me with compliments (a situation that occurs fairly infrequently and one that you would think would bolster my confidence rather than erode it), I begin to feel a heightened sense of responsibility to please them in the future. How can I possibly continue to consistently entertain these people with fresh, new, and clever ideas? Would it not be better to quit while I am still appreciated by my readers than to continue indefinitely and become a tired parody of my earlier self?

The trend in all areas of American pop consumerism tends to be to perceive entertainers to be fading in quality rather than improving with practice. I wish I had a nickel for every time I've heard someone say of Larson, Trudeau, or Watterson, "He was never as good after his sabbatical." These are the thoughts that overwhelm me each time someone says, "I love your stuff, please don't retire like (whoever)."

But in the end people must learn to trust their own instincts and form their own opinion about their work, resisting the temptation to worry about what the public might think. If *I* still think my work is good and I'm proud of what I'm creating, that should be enough. One thought that I hold on to to give me confidence about my future as a cartoonist is that some features never fade. Who could dispute the fact that *Family Circus,* for instance, is every bit as good today as it ever was? I rest my case.

But as hard as I try to keep up my confidence, the occasional negative comment from a reader is always difficult to deal with. During one of my trips, an overnight host told me at dinner, "I don't know if I suddenly became hyperaware or what, but ever since you said you were coming to stay with me, I haven't found your work as funny." As he said it, our waiter appeared with our food and the flow of the conversation was redirected. He never explained exactly what he meant, and I didn't pursue it. I shrugged it off at the time, realizing intellectually that his perception may indeed have been altered by my impending arrival, that one person's opinion can hardly be taken as a national consensus, and that no one can please everyone *all* the time. But it was little comfort.

My well-meaning host seemed utterly unaware of what effect his comment had had on me, and I didn't let on. But the part of me that dreads every deadline like the next onset of flu, and scrambles daily and desperately through every wrinkle and fold of my brain looking for any shred of microscopic evidence that there are enough ideas left in there to carry me through the next week, much less the next several years of my contract, was hemorrhaging uncontrollably.

In *his* mind, he was only casually mentioning an odd phenomenon, which he had attributed to his own perception (although it was still a pretty weird thing to say under the circumstances, no matter how you look at it). But to my paranoid, insecure, eager-to-please other self that wants every cartoon I write to go down in the annals of humor, cherished by every English-speaking citizen of Earth for all time (second only to the invention of the TV remote control), such a comment is a fatal blow. He might just as well have said, "You have just unwittingly swallowed a fatal dose of poison, Mr. Bond, and you will die a gruesome and painful death in exactly seventeen and one half minutes, but not before you get to watch your attractive companion become my bride."

SEVENTEEN

Pop-Tarts Spiraling Toward Earth

I flew on to Atlanta the next morning for a Sunday afternoon signing. I was to stay with an old school chum of mine from Byrd Junior High School in Tulsa, Oklahoma.

John had written to me a year or so earlier after seeing my cartoon in *The Atlanta Constitution*, asking if I remembered him. I did, though as kids we had moved in slightly different social circles, and we struck up an ongoing E-mail relationship. John was a very clever guy and was fond of sending me a cartoon idea from time to time. Even though I almost never use anyone else's ideas, many of his were very good and one seemed just right, so I relented. I later gave him the original art for it, which he had hanging in his home when I arrived.

During our visit we spent a lot of time talking about the people we'd gone to school with. Though John ran with what I had always considered to be a relatively tough group of kids in junior high, he later went on to become a producer for CNN. His first marriage ended quite tragically when his wife literally ran off with his best friend, and he later married a woman with a very lucrative career of her own and settled down to a very quiet life in the suburbs as a house husband with two small children, backyard barbecues, and a minivan.

John's relaxed lifestyle proved to be a nice change of pace from the rigorous activities of the preceding days, and, after the wife and sons had gone to bed, the two of us sat up late (nearly ten o'clock!) reminiscing about old times like a couple of Civil War veterans.

One of our reminiscences was centered around watching a videotape of an old TV show we used to watch in Tulsa in the early seventies. It was called *Mazeppa Pompazoidi's Uncanny Film Festival and Camp Meeting*, and it was broadcast live from a local station on Saturday nights around midnight. It was an example of a fairly common genre of the time in which a local actor dressed in some strange costume or other would do a little schtick to introduce some corny B movie, then appear before and after each commercial break for some more schtick.

Tulsa's version, however, was hosted by a young Gailard Sartain, who later became a successful character actor in Hollywood. He was a regular member of the *Hee Haw* cast for years and played the Big Bopper in *The Buddy Holly Story*, as well as a number of other supporting roles in major films. A regular guest on *Mazeppa* and one of Sartain's best friends at the time was Gary Busey. Sartain was Mazeppa, and Busey always played a character called Teddy Jack Eddy. In those days this program was watched religiously by everyone with any hopes of ever being cool, and both John and I admitted that Sartain and Busey's strange, improvisational humor had had a profound and warping influence on our young minds.

One trick we both remembered learning from this show was to fill your mouth with cigarette smoke, then blow a soap bubble with one of those little plastic wands with a hoop in the end, thus filling the bubble with smoke. As the bubble floats away, filled with a quivering, white haze, you then shoot it in midair with a staple gun, leaving a momentary puff of smoke, which dissipates quickly into nothingness. It was an activity I entertained people with for many years until I quit smoking in

1987. It was fun, but probably not worth lung cancer or emphysema. Few tricks are, I've found.

Around ten o'clock, John announced that he was going upstairs to bed but that I was welcome to stay up as long as I wanted and watch TV or whatever. I thought this might be a good time to try to contact Sajak, so as soon as John had gone upstairs, I began searching through the *TV Guide*. *Wheel of Fortune* wasn't on at that time of night, so I just started surfing the channels, hoping that Sajak would detect my signals on the airwaves (or whatever it is he does) and make an appearance.

Cruising slowly through the regular cable channels a couple of times (pausing only briefly to watch Pamela Anderson on *Baywatch* running down the beach in slow motion) yielded no sign of Sajak. After a while, I switched to the B side of the cable, where the local access, infomercials, and shopping channels are. As I did so, I came across an elaborate and glitzy Mexican game show on a Spanish-language channel. It certainly wasn't *Wheel of Fortune*, but it was at least in the neighborhood. Having seen nothing else that seemed remotely connected, I decided I might as well try to make contact. I slinked quietly across the room and knelt before the television screen. Because I was in a strange house doing something I did not want to be caught doing, I felt remarkably like a burglar. I looked around the room, listened for any sound of movement upstairs, then placed my face close to the screen.

"Pat . . ." I whispered. "Pat Sajak . . . are you there?"

There was no response, but I figured I would keep trying for a few more minutes. "Who knows, maybe game shows are all psychically connected," I thought.

"Pat Sajak . . . come in, Pat Sajak," I tried a little louder. "Dan to Pat, Dan to Pat. Come in, Pat." I couldn't resist the obvious joke.

Kneeling on the floor before the TV for a couple more minutes, I continued to call his name firmly but quietly, with my mouth nearly against the glass. I could feel the static electricity of the screen attracting my bushy hair. I began adding to my monologue, speculating that if Pat could hear me, maybe he was waiting for me to apologize for our last conversation.

"Pat, I'm sorry for what I said," I whispered. "I was being selfish and ungrateful. I've changed my mind about the book tour, and I want to continue it. I value your wisdom and guidance, and I'd like you to show me the way." As I said this, I suddenly felt a presence in the room. I turned my head to the right, my hair disengaging from the screen's surface with a barrage of tiny crackles, and looked straight into the face of John's three-year-old son, standing only a few inches away.

"Whatcha watching?" he asked innocently.

Panicked, I scrambled for some logical explanation for what I'd been doing. Finding none, I winged it: "I was just saying my prayers before I turned off the TV and went to bed." He stared at me blankly and said nothing. I shut off the TV and stood up.

"Well, that's it, all done. Time to go to bed," I said cheerfully. "Do you want a glass of water or something before you go back to bed?"

"I want a Pop-Tart," he said matter-of-factly.

I wasn't quite sure what to say, so I asked, "Does your daddy let you have Pop-Tarts in the middle of the night?"

"Always," came the tiny man's reply.

"Well," I said, thinking that perhaps it was the fastest and quietest way to get him back upstairs, "show me where they are and I'll get you one, but then you've got to get back in bed."

"You have some in your backpack," he announced blandly.

He was right. I did have a box of blueberry Pop-Tarts in my backpack, but I was shocked that this little fellow had snooped around enough to know that. Nonetheless, I went to my backpack in the next room and retrieved a Pop-Tart for him. He thanked me, took a bite of it, and headed up the stairs. I hoped that by the time John found the crumbs, I would be long gone and no one would even think to put me on the list of suspects. Suddenly, I felt worse than a burglar; I felt like the Grinch when he was caught by Cindy Lou Who.

At my book-signing event in Atlanta, I was reunited with Walt, another old friend from my junior high days in Tulsa. I didn't recognize him when he approached me in the store, as he, like me, had long ago rid himself of a massive Afro.

Even though he was a year younger, back in our school days Walt was something of a hero of mine. He played drums, had extremely "cool" (liberal) parents, and, no matter how much heat he was under from the ruthless authorities at our school, kept a knowing smile on his face. He always seemed to perceive life as one big joke that was about to get a lot funnier.

He was as white as a Caucasian comes, with freckles and bright-red curly hair. By the eighth grade, a full two years before my parents finally cracked and let me grow my hair longer than a boot-camp private's, Walt already had a gigantic Afro, as big an Afro as any I've ever seen on any person of any race, in any era. He was a very well liked, clever, and mischievous kid who, much to the chagrin of our suburban school's extremely conservative faculty, managed to get elected student council president (with a little help from me as his campaign poster artist, and, to remind me, he brought one of the posters, which he had saved all these years, to the bookstore with him). Later that year he was impeached (by the faculty) over some kind of misunderstanding that, according to rumor, involved a party in the middle of the night held in a Volkswagen van that had been driven into the gym coach's office. The full story of Walt's political derailment will have to wait for another time, but he proudly announced that, to his knowledge, he is the only student council officer to have ever been forcibly removed from office at Byrd Junior High School.

Ironically, when I spoke with Walt in Atlanta he was wearing his hair as short as a boot-camp private. But he was still smiling as though he knew something the rest of us didn't.

Even though the Raleigh-Durham/Atlanta leg of my tour had gone better than any other and I was really beginning to enjoy the people I was meeting and even look forward to each trip, I became increasingly aware of a long-growing sense of discontent of another kind.

I couldn't describe exactly what was wrong. Everything seemed to be going well, the trips were mostly successful, I was meeting a lot of very interesting people and conquering my fear of strangers. But something was very wrong somehow. Back at home, I had been spending most of my time feeling inexplicably stressed and depressed. I was frequently irritable and felt a current of anger flowing just below the surface of my skin. The slightest provocation would set me off on a rant, not toward anything in particular, but toward the world.

I supposed it might be the stress of the tour, but by this time most of the arrangements had been made and I had only to execute the trips themselves, which was getting to be the fun part. But even though I was mostly over my fear of traveling and having a terrific time almost everywhere I went, I still had a strong sense that I should be at home. I wondered if I had been spending *too much* time away, but considering that I worked at home, saw my wife all day, was there when the kids came home from school and spent every evening with them, I figured that even with the three- or four-day trips every couple of weeks, I still saw more of my family than the average person who works in an office.

My wife suggested I go back to therapy, something I had done briefly in my mid-twenties to deal with depression, but I resisted because I was simply too busy with the tour. That, too, would have to wait until it was over. I was clearly becoming a slave to my career.

I continued, however, to search my consciousness, looking for the reason I was dissatisfied. I thought at first of the artiste/

cartoonist thing, that I'd been ignoring my fine art for so long that it was bubbling to the surface like a malevolent acid. But that didn't quite seem to hit the mark, either. I then vascillated between blaming it on the strain the road trips were putting on my other responsibilities, causing me to feel forever overworked and rushed, and pure chemical imbalance. Maybe I just needed an antidepressant. (About that time, nearly every member of every branch of my family had gone on antidepressants, it seemed, and I had come to refer jokingly to them as the "Prozac Army.")

But I figured that whatever the problem was, surely it could wait a few more weeks to be dealt with. I still had Cleveland, Pittsburgh, and Houston ahead of me, and I promised myself that even though I had offers from other cities, as soon as the last scheduled trip was over, I was hanging up my suitcase for a good long time and taking a fresh look at my life. Who knows, maybe after that I would become a cowboy, fireman, astronaut, or cocktail waitress.

Meanwhile, I spent my days working feverishly to catch up on my deadlines so I could leave town, and, as my wife was gone every evening at play rehearsals in those days, my nights were spent taking care of and hanging out with the kids until bedtime, then hitting the Internet to answer E-mail and arrange the remaining details of the final trips. In spite of my periodic attempts to reconcile with Sajak, he remained truant.

Cleveland and Pittsburgh were a strange mixture of pleasure and pain. In these cities I met some of the most interesting people yet and felt very enriched by the experience, but I was still nagged by the constant feeling that I should be at home. I found myself wonderfully entertained and content one moment, then brutally homesick and racked with anxiety the next.

Resolved to finish what I had started, however, I stuck it out and made the best of it, determined to enjoy myself wherever I was and whomever I was with.

In Cleveland I stayed with David and Holly. David was a wonderfully relaxed and friendly man of around forty, whose peaceful demeanor was partly due to his dedication to some sort of yoga that I will never be able to remember the name of as long as I live. I mean no disrespect toward it; it is clearly very important to him and gives him an enviable sense of serenity and well-being. But when I asked him what kind of yoga it was, his answer sounded as if he were trying to get something sticky off his tongue. Thinking I may have heard him wrong, I asked again, but the answer was just as unintelligible to me.

For a moment I suspected he might have been having a seizure, and, thinking back to my Cub Scout training, I grabbed a stick and shoved it between his teeth. This is always a bold move if you're not absolutely certain that a person is, in fact, having a seizure, and it can be downright foolhardy. But, luckily for me, in keeping with his pacifist philosophy, he not only resisted punching me in the face but left the stick in his mouth for the remainder of the evening for fear of offending me.

But I still didn't get the name of the yoga he practices (or maybe he was telling me the name of the guru he follows). Even when he wrote it down for me later, the letters swirled around the page and defied my abilities of comprehension. It finally became clear to me that I simply have way too much Western cement in my head, and I vowed to remedy this situation in the near future.

Holly, his life mate, was a college student and bookstore employee. They seemed to have a wonderful relationship with each other and the same admirable sense of calm and peace between them as they did individually. I envied their overall sense of well-being and contentment. It particularly stood out in contrast with my own sense of inner turmoil. I made a mental note to look into some of that for myself as soon as my tour was over.

I was originally scheduled to stay in Cleveland with a lawyer named John who had contacted me months earlier with offers of a plane ticket and a spare bedroom. After much E-mail wrangling over a period of many weeks, John was still tentative about whether or not the visit would be okay with his wife. He finally appeared to get approval from her; then we wrangled a bit more until we nailed down a date that was convenient for both of us.

After the reservations were made and I had the tickets in hand, only a week before the trip, John suddenly wrote back and said he'd still like to take me out for dinner, but would I mind finding another place to stay? His wife was, in his words, "uncomfortable having a stranger in the house with the children."

I was admittedly flabbergasted by this, wondering why anyone would suspect a nationally published, semicelebrity cartoonist to travel across the country, conniving his way into his readers' homes so he could molest their children. It seemed a peculiar thing to worry about, but then I remembered all the rumors and press about the Michael Jackson child molestation lawsuit and supposed I couldn't blame her. (I couldn't help but also wonder if one of my readers *were* to accuse me of misconduct while I was staying in his or her home and I were to flee the country as Jackson did, if I could then expect a visit from Elizabeth Taylor or Brooke Shields. Probably the best I could hope for would be Gailard Sartain in his old Mazeppa outfit and maybe Junior Samples from *Hee Haw*.)

Lawyer John and his wife did take me out to dinner at a fabulously exquisite and expensive place in downtown Cleveland. David and Holly came along as well, and the five of us had a perfectly lovely time. In spite of her unusual misgivings about my staying at their house, John's wife turned out to be a very nice woman and only accused me of misconduct a couple of times during the entire evening. One involved an incident with my foot under the table, but I maintain to this day that I never took my shoe off, so I never *technically* even touched her.

When David and Holly and I returned home that night, David showed me to his daughters' room, where I would be staying. David had been divorced for a couple of years and had a joint custody deal worked out with his ex-wife wherein their two young daughters would stay with him one week, then their mother the next. Fortunately for us all, that week the girls were away, so I had the room to myself and David didn't have to worry about trusting me in the house with the kids.

The room I stayed in was small and cozy and had a pair of twin beds, pink, lace curtains, a number of Disney posters on the walls, and assorted books and toys. In a couple of spots around the room were small pictures of the guru whom David follows, a woman with a red dot on her forehead, a pillbox-looking hat, Nehru jacket, glasses, and a peaceful half smile on her face. (As I think about it now, that smile was not unlike Walt's "life is a big joke" smile back in junior high, but this woman didn't look like the "good times van" type.) These pictures appeared in numerous places around David's house and even in his car.

Before we turned in, David told me that I could get up the next morning at any time I wished and make myself breakfast from whatever I could find in the kitchen. He cautioned me that if I got up too early I might find him sitting on the floor of the hallway meditating, but just to ignore him and go about my business. He assured me I wouldn't bother him.

I had my choice of which bed I would sleep in, the one with the 101 Dalmatians sheets or the one with a Barney the Dinosaur motif. Like most rational adults, I would rather examine a stray rottweiler for hemorrhoids than have anything whatsoever to do with Barney the Dinosaur, so I slept in the Dalmatians bed. (I cannot ascertain whether or not there were in fact 101 of them on the sheets, as I fell asleep counting them.)

The next morning I rose at what I thought was a reasonable hour, but not too early, and ventured toward the kitchen. I was met in the hallway by David coming the other direction, walking stark naked with the Sunday paper under one arm and a cup of coffee in his hand.

"Good morning," he said pleasantly with that same guru/Walt smile. "There's coffee in the kitchen. Help yourself."

He was obviously utterly unconcerned about his state of undress, so I didn't concern myself with it, either. I just figured if God had meant for us not to get caught naked in the hallway on a Sunday morning, He would have created us with a way to get coffee without having to walk to the kitchen.

Being an avid believer that when in Rome, one should do as the Romans do, I, too, removed my clothing and went about my morning routine in the nude. David and Holly seemed appreciative of my efforts to fit in, though it seemed to wear thin on them around late afternoon, when it came close to time to leave for the bookstore for my signing, so I got dressed again.

After the book signing, I made the short flight to Pittsburgh in a private plane.

In response to my original plane-ticket solicitation letter to fans in Cleveland, one of my readers, Denny, had written that if I could get to Cleveland, he could fly me to Pittsburgh in his private plane, a four-seat Piper Arrow. I was intrigued by his offer, but wary of his skills and experience. I wrote back and asked him his qualifications and what the odds were that I would become an integral part of a cornfield somewhere like Buddy Holly had. He told me some stuff about *his* flying experience versus the inexperienced young kid that was flying Holly's plane when it went down, so I decided to go for it.

The small airport where we were to meet was quite a ways out in the suburbs of the *opposite* side of Cleveland from where my signing was, and, with the absence of an adequate mass transit system on Sundays, as of late that afternoon I still had no way of getting there. Fortunately, a delightful young college student named Roula, whom I had met at the book signing, volunteered to drive me. Not wanting her to go completely uncompensated for such a drive, I offered her my eldest child in return. Her generous nature prohibited her from accepting, however, so we agreed instead that I would give her one of my cartoon originals.

We drove across town in her rattletrap college-student car (I was unable to identify the make, but, based on the rusted remains of some lettering on the passenger-side door, I guessed it might have once been an ambulance or pizza-delivery car in either Russia or Indonesia), and she pointed out various land-marks along the way such as the neighborhood where she grew up and the Greek Orthodox church she attended with her family. Of course, I had heard of both of these places all my life and was thrilled finally to get a chance to see them in person. They almost didn't seem real.

When we arrived at the airport, Denny was waiting for us at the appointed place, and, as we greeted each other and I made introductions, he asked Roula if she wanted to join us on the flight. Being unattached and at that age where spontaneity is exciting and natural (as opposed to the age *I'm* at now where spontaneity of almost any kind is threatening and disruptive and seems dangerously akin to mutiny), she readily accepted.

As it happened, Denny *was* fully capable of getting me to Pittsburgh safely, missing every cornfield we passed with professionalism and ease. Among other life-threatening obstacles that he missed were the control tower, trees, power lines, numerous small buildings, and all of downtown Pittsburgh. I was particularly impressed with his piloting skills when he allowed me to take the controls for a short time so I could see what it was like to fly a plane.

He first briefly explained to me which controls were for up/down, left/right, pitch/yaw (whatever the hell *that* is), rock/roll, squat/burp, and a number of other functions I didn't even know planes could perform. Then he let go of his steering wheel deal (technical pilot jargon for the thing you use to steer) and handed her over to me via the little matching steering wheel deal on my side of the cockpit (technical pilot jargon for a place where cockfights are held).

Planes are much more difficult to control than I would have imagined. In a car you mostly just have go/stop and right/left, which I have come to master with almost unerring accuracy, hitting the wrong pedal at a critical moment only a handful of times over the past twenty years of driving. But in addition to these four functions, planes have a multitude of other capabilities, which I discovered almost immediately. Some of these include "spiraling toward the earth," "looping and screaming" (actually, I think the screaming was Roula and Denny), and "tumbling end over end while emitting thick, black smoke."

After letting me put his plane through its paces for only a brief, few moments, Denny clamored back into his seat to take the controls and I set about the task of reviving Roula, who had inexplicably passed out.

Overall, the short flight to Pittsburgh was a blast despite the unfortunate absence of airsickness bags and the deafening noise of the engine (which was remarkably reminiscent of the sound of my first car, a 1960s Volkswagen, as it left the road at top speed one sunny afternoon and plowed through the elaborately landscaped flowers and hedges of a Tulsa city park).

When we got to Pittsburgh, we buzzed a low, lazy, circle around downtown. I wondered aloud if it would be possible to spit into Three Rivers Stadium and stuck my head out the window, but Denny screamed something unintelligible over the roar of the engines and pulled me back inside before I could see if I'd hit my mark. A few minutes later we landed at a small airport, where my next hosts were waiting in the pilot lounge.

The plan was for Denny and Roula to go out to eat dinner with the next hosts and me, then return to Cleveland afterward. Still a bit shaken from some of my spontaneous air acrobatics, eating wasn't exactly the first thing on Denny and Roula's minds, but they seemed ecstatic to be on terra firma once again, leaping from the airplane and kissing the ground with the enthusiasm of returning POWs.

EIGHTEEN

Hallway of Tears, Stairway of Wuv

y first overnight hosts in P'burgh (as some people call it, particularly those who are too lazy to type "itts") were Al and Pat, a quirky couple about my age. In spite of the way it sounds from their names, and in contrast to so many of my hosts in California, Al and Pat were a heterosexual couple. They joke that people frequently confuse them for a gay couple because of their names, and many people cannot remember which is which. In the interest of complete journalistic candor, I have to admit that I am a member of the latter group. I can't remember if Pat is the woman—short for Patricia or Patina or something—and Al is the man—short for Alvin or Allen or Albert—or if Pat is the man—short for Patrick or Patruccio—and Al is the woman—short for Allison or Alvinia or Alfredette. Whatever their names, they were yet two more examples of people with whom I hit it off instantly.

As we stood in the pilot's lounge of the small, private airport and I made the introductions between Al and Pat and Denny and Roula, I could see that once again fate had made for unusual dinner company.

There was Roula, an open-minded, intelligent, and good-natured college student; Denny, a conservative suburbanite around forty years of age with a dry but slightly corny sense of humor; me, whom you already know much too much about; and Pat and Al, who clearly had been marching to a different and category-defying drummer for a good, long time.

Al and Pat were as strange and unique a couple as one is likely to meet this side of a 1950s beatnik coffeehouse. Pat (or was it Al?) was well over ten feet tall, and no part of his body was any bigger around than the average drinking glass, except for his head, which bore the face of a fourteen-year-old boy even though Pat (or Al) was in his mid-thirties. As near as I could tell from ground level, he had small, round, wire-frame glasses and thick, short, brown hair that stood nearly straight up despite apparent attempts to comb it down. When I first saw him, I thought he rather resembled underground cartoonist icon Robert Crumb, which is not a fate one would wish on his worst enemy and which I mean only figuratively. He was actually substantially less scary-looking than Robert Crumb (as is nearly everyone else in the world, come to think of it).

Al (or maybe Pat) was a short, attractive, dark-haired woman with Woody Allen-style, black, horn-rimmed glasses and a semipermanent smirk on her face that would lead you to believe she knows something no one else has noticed yet. (Hers is a slightly more malevolent smile than the guru/Walt style.) They were each wearing loud, vintage, Hawaiian shirts. "Vintage" is the operative word here, for *everything* about their life is vintage, with the exception of themselves and the food they eat.

The five of us went outside into the bitterly cold, snow-covered parking lot and began to negotiate how we would get to the restaurant in Al and Pat's 1960s, sea-foam-green pickup truck with a short camper shell on the back. Taking the logical and time-honored approach of decent people everywhere, it was decided that we three men would ride up front in the heated cab and the two women would ride in the frigid truck bed. The female half of Al and Pat, let's just call her Al, opened up the camper door and tailgate to reveal a large, overstuffed chair, circa 1940, in the back of the truck. She graciously offered it to Roula, then climbed in and squatted on the metal of the truck bed next to it. We slammed the doors shut on them, then we three guys piled into the cab.

As soon as the male half of Pat and Al, let's call him Pat, pulled out of the parking lot, Denny and I began to discuss where we should go to eat. Of course, neither of us being Pittsburghians, it was a mostly aimless and nonproductive conversation. Pat, who had barely said a word since we'd met, opting instead to let his wife do all the talking, sat silently behind the wheel. Finally, I brazenly asked him, "So where are we headed for dinner? Is there anywhere good around here?"

Without waiting to hear Pat's suggestion, Denny piped up with his own: "Is there a Denny's around here somewhere? They're usually pretty good." I passed on the obvious joke.

I could tell by looking at Al and Pat that they were die-hard urbanites who hadn't been to a mall or a franchise restaurant since they were young enough to be forced by their parents to eat their broccoli, so I was looking forward to Pat's response to Denny's "Denny's" suggestion.

But instead, Pat drove on through the snow silently, staring blankly into the wintry night ahead. Denny and I waited nervously, wondering why this guy was ignoring us, exchanging quick glances with each other, then over at Pat. After what seemed like minutes, he turned to us slowly, with a Jack Nicholson–like look of borderline insanity on his face, and hissed abruptly, "Now that the womenfolk can't hear us I got something to say to you two." He paused dramatically, then barked, "DON'T GET ANY IDEAS ABOUT MY WIFE!"

Denny and I froze in disbelief for a second, then I burst out laughing. I figured he was either kidding or we were as good as dead anyway, so I might as well go out smiling. Fortunately, Pat, too, started to smile and Denny followed nervously a moment later.

Pat then dropped the facade and became a normal person (as normal as Pat could muster, anyway) and went on to explain that he'd been planning to do that for weeks. After contemplating the obvious fears and dangers of traveling around the country staying with strangers as I had been, he thought it might be funny if he pretended to be a psycho. Having worried about just that sort of confrontation (and coming mighty close in San Francisco with Ken the Wacko), I agreed that it was funny, as long as he was *sure* he was pretending.

The ice being thus broken, we discussed where we should eat, and, since we were not in Pat and Al's usual part of town and I had assumed correctly that they hadn't been in the suburbs in ages, Pat had no suggestions. So we decided to look for a place inside a big shopping mall. After we parked, we carried the women into the building, thawed them out until they could walk on their own, and set out in search of a delicious heap of steaming mall food. We ended up at a franchise burger joint called Fatty's Grill.

To the suburban teenagers who ran the place, we must have looked like a family reunion from outer space: a college girl, a bushy-haired, silly-mustached guy in a leather jacket, two people in Hawaiian shirts, glasses, and faded jeans, and a guy who looked as if he owned a chain of one-hour photomats (which he did). The conversation at dinner was as scattered as our backgrounds with Roula representing the liberal left, Denny the conservative right, Al and Pat the cynical and unpredictable "kook" factor, and me fueling the fire with an occasional incendiary remark like "Surely no one *really* believes that Nixon was guilty of any wrongdoing in that Watergate thing." Culture clashing has long been one of my favorite spectator sports.

Afterward, we put the womenfolk back into the truck's cryogenics chamber and returned Roula and Denny to the airport. After we saw them off, Al and Pat took me back to their place.

As quirky as I thought Al and Pat were in person, I was still not fully prepared for the sight that greeted me when I walked through the front door of their three-story Victorian house.

When they bought their huge house, it was what most people would call a "fixer-upper." All of the walls needed painting, and many were stripped of their wallpaper and peeled down to their mottled, splotchy original surface. But Al and Pat's idea of "fixing up" a house is to cover every square inch of wall and floor space (and ceiling, when gravity permits) with neat junk. Every single one of their ten-plus rooms was chock-full of old and weird stuff of virtually every description: games, books, records, mannequins, glasses, lamps, furniture, clothing, handbags, shoes, knickknacks, and doodads of all kinds. Their home is nearly identical to a resale shop and every bit as much fun to explore.

What amounted to their "living room" had a boomerang-shaped coffee table, several unusually shaped chairs from the fifties and sixties, a huge, metal hair dryer that resembles a space helmet from an old black and white sci-fi film, a hula-girl lamp, a trapezoidal picture frame around a black velvet painting of a matador, a lime-green, patent leather overnight bag with a huge "smiley face" on it, and a string of multicolored party lights shaped like the giant heads on Easter Island. And that describes less than a tenth of what else was in that room.

Al writes a "zine" (which is trade lingo for a small, home-produced, special-interest newsletter magazine thingy) about secondhand shopping called *ThriftSCORE*. Between her and Pat, they know pretty much all there is to know about this vast and interesting field and have filled their huge house with the spoils of their thousands of shopping odysseys. And the strangest thing of all is that they never *sell* anything—they only *collect*.

The room I stayed in was upstairs and had two bay windows, an enormous bookshelf full of cheesy detective novels that covered an entire wall, a 1950s-era sleeper sofa, the famous red swimsuit Farrah Fawcett poster from the seventies on a wall, and about a million other things.

The narrow hallway outside my door was perhaps my favorite element in the house. Only a few feet wide, but probably twelve feet high, the walls were blanketed with dozens of the well-known big-eyed Keane paintings: sad little boys and girls, puppies, kittens, and clowns, all with huge, pathetic, watery eyes the size of bowling balls. At the stairs at the end of the hall was a landing with a huge stained glass window, the ledge of which was lined with many different versions of the ubiquitous plastic gift statues from the 1970s of a cute little character with its arms outstretched and a placard at the bottom reading, I WUV YOU *THIS* MUCH.

This is a prime example of the thematic way in which Al and Pat decorate; after you've made your way through the Hall of Tears, you are cheered by the cute little "wuvving" statues on the stairs. It's an experience few people are ever able to forget and one that I personally rank in emotional intensity alongside the day my first daughter was born.

Apart from their marvelously and cleverly cluttered home, Al and Pat themselves are joyously cynical and fun-loving. In both of them a wicked and brutal sense of sarcasm lurks beneath a confidently relaxed and cool exterior. Once again, in a remarkably short period of time I felt as though we had known each other for years. The fact that they love my cartoons didn't hurt my opinion of them, either, though in keeping with their cool and cynical demeanor, they refrained from common "fan language" and went out of their way not to appear to be "kissing up" to me in any way. We stayed up quite late that night, in true slumber-party fashion, and had a great time just babbling about whatever came to mind.

The next morning, Pat was away at work (apparently no longer concerned I might get "ideas" about his wife) and Al took me sightseeing around Pittsburgh. Al doesn't drive, but she's incredibly adept at taking the bus almost anywhere she wants to go, so that's how we traveled. Even though Pat had assured me his psychotically jealous husband routine of the

night before had been a joke, I must admit that I found myself
watching my words and actions very closely around Al. In spite
of being on guard, the day we spent wandering around the city
was relaxing and entertaining.

At the risk of alienating most of Pittsburgh's population, let
me say that this is one *beautiful* city. But this is not a fact that
most Pittsburgonecians want to publicize, apparently.

According to the locals, up until recent decades, when the
steel mills shut down, the city deserved its reputation as a dirty,
smoky, gritty industrial town. But now that the smoke has
cleared and some renovation has occurred, it is among the most
charming and attractive communities I've ever visited.

The city cascades around, over, and across innumerable
hills and cliffs, with thousands of architecturally diverse bridges
connecting the bluffs and hillsides (every Pittsburghoid seems
to have a different number memorized: "You know, Pittsburgh
has over seven thousand bridges." "There are ninety-two thousand bridges in Pittsburgh." "We have more bridges than any
other sixteen countries combined: nearly eleven hundred.")

The streets are winding, the architecture is quaint, and the
people are friendly, unpretentious, and proud of their blue-collar
heritage. But each time I complimented the city, one or more
locals would reply quickly and vehemently with "Yeah, I know,
but don't tell anyone. It'll ruin it!" The fear is that if the truth is
known, tens of thousands of nomadic, opportunistic Americans
will flock to Pittsburgh from all over the country and turn the
place into an expensive, overcrowded, miserable metropolis.

Not wishing to be thrashed by these proud, blue-collar
folks, I readily swore my allegiance to the city's cherished secret.
But now that I am safely hidden away in my own expensive,
overcrowded, miserable metropolis deep in the heart of Texas, I
suddenly feel sadistically inclined to blow it for my more fortunate friends in Pittsburgh. I'm sorry, but I guess I'm just one of

those vindictive, small-minded creeps who can't stand the thought that someone else is having more fun than I am.

So spread the word, America: Forget Seattle, Pittsburgh is the land of milk and honey! There's gold in the streets! Real estate is cheap! Food prices are rock-bottom! Crime is non-existent! The weather is 75° and sunny all year round! The dogs don't bite! The children are clean and fresh-smelling! Cable TV is free! Full-body massages are half price! There are no bugs, diseases, lawyers, or Elvis impersonators!

Sorry, Pittsburgholians.

My bus trip with Al took us downtown, where we puttered around in the subzero weather looking at bridges and notable buildings, then met Pat for lunch. I was shocked by what I saw as he walked into the restaurant: Crazy, kooky, offbeat, wild-man Pat was wearing a gray three-piece suit with his thick, unruly tuft of spiky hair successfully combed down with what I guessed must have been either industrial-strength petroleum jelly or floor wax. He looked like a real business guy.

I asked him what had happened to the Bohemian hipster I had met the night before, and he explained to me that although he used to work as management for a nationally known rap group he was now selling corporate real estate. The suit was simply part of the game. He was a little embarrassed to be seen this way but had obviously come to grips with it long ago. Truly, here was a man leading a double life.

My time with Al and Pat flew by rather quickly, even though I still felt an underlying current of anxiousness to get home. Under different circumstances I would have loved to have stayed a few more days with them, picking through the millions of unusual objects in their house and experiencing the intense emotions of the "Hall of Tears" and "Landing of Wuv" again and again. But that afternoon my next host was scheduled to pick me up at Al and Pat's house, take me to dinner with a couple of his friends, then drive me to my book signing that night.

He lived only a few blocks away, in a three-story Victorian house that at one time was probably quite similar to Pat and Al's. But over the decades the two areas had taken radically different paths and the difference in neighborhoods and residents was now quite pronounced. Once again, the cultural whiplash when he arrived to pick me up was enough to yank the teeth right out of my head.

Fred was a conservative, deeply religious, middle-aged computer/math whiz who headed up a prestigious consortium at a major university that designed and maintained a sophisticated computer operating system. He lived in a luxurious home in a prestigious neighborhood with his wife, and together they had several grown children.

When he stepped into the entryway of Pat and Al's house, the look on his face was probably similar to what mine must have been the night before. As stoic as Fred was, even he couldn't keep the amazement off his face.

I introduced Al and myself, then we spent a few minutes in small talk, mostly about Al and Pat's unique decor. As I watched them relate uncomfortably to each other, I was reminded of any one of a number of situations depicted on the classic TV show *Dragnet*, in which a member of the rigid establishment (usually Sergeant Friday) meets a member of the drug-crazed counterculture (usually someone in a Beatle wig, granny glasses, turtleneck, and vest named something like "Blueboy").

As I disappeared through the door with my bags and said good-bye to Al, she had that knowing smirk on her face that I had come to know (but *not* have ideas about) so well. But this time it seemed to be saying "I'm glad it's you and not me."

Fred was a very pleasant man of obviously above-average intelligence and education. He talked at some length about the computer system he had designed, and I nodded and grunted nebulously as I always do when people mistake me for a computer geek. Because I publish an E-mail address in my comics and arranged my entire book tour via the Internet, Fred assumed, as many people do, that I know something about computers. The truth is that "how to use E-mail" is *all* I know about computers. I haven't even the slightest idea what model mine is, how many megagrams of byte it has, if its overdrive is soft or hard, or anything else that people commonly ask me. I can't even get to the web from my home because I've never been able to figure out how to unload (or is it download?) the special program thing that you need to view it. In fact, I generally find that computers are harder to operate than a plane is to fly, and we all know how *that* turned out. About the only difference between the two so far is that I have yet to make black smoke pour out of my computer. But give me time, I'm still young.

Fred was quite reserved and had no discernible eccentricities of any kind, and in this way he varied from most of the people who had volunteered to sponsor me. Accordingly, we did nothing out of the ordinary during my twenty-four-hour stay with him: went to dinner with a couple of his friends and neighbors, to my book signing at a suburban mall, to his office at the university to show me a little of what his computer system did (I just grunted and nodded again, but I think I got away with it), then to the university museum.

His single greatest interest in life, besides the Methodist Church and computers, was Go, an ancient Chinese game of strategy involving small black or white pebbles on a graphed playing board. A version of it is marketed in America under the name "Othello." The rules of Go are few and simple to learn but the game itself is nearly impossible to master. ("Minutes to learn, a lifetime to master," Fred told me, is an ancient quote traditionally used in reference to this game. It is an adage I had heard before but had always assumed referred to sex.) Fred has been practicing nearly every day for decades and has become quite good at it (Go, that is, not sex) and has a dining room full of trophies and awards to show for it. (He has two daughters to show for the other and a wife who is still with him, so I'm assuming he's proficient at that as well.)

I enjoyed Fred's company and particularly appreciated the fact that I was being forced by necessity to acquaint myself with the sort of person whom I would more than likely never have had occasion to meet were it not for this tour. I don't normally have the opportunity to spend much time with older, smart, rich guys—I mean men of his age, education, and social standing—and I find it good to be reminded that everyone has something in common, something to offer or share.

But all the while I was thinking of home.

On returning to Dallas, I thought I had never been so glad to see my home and family in all my life. My elation and relief at having come to the virtual end of my tour was palpable. I reveled in the warm weather, the kids, the dogs, the companionship of my wife. I had a renewed appreciation for the things I normally take for granted.

During this oasis, I tried once again to grasp the origin of my frequent depression and dissatisfaction, wondering if I could understand and analyze it better while I was feeling good about things. But the mystery was still inaccessible. The unqualified joy of being home lasted only a few days, my initial exhilaration began to slip away, and I sensed myself falling back into the abyss. I was no nearer to discovering the root of my discontent than I ever had been and began to suspect again that it might be a chemical imbalance. Maybe the Prozac Army was right: I needed to be antidepressed to enjoy life.

But try as I did to control my depression mentally, within a few days I was unable to contain it and I became overwhelmed with a sense of despair. I simply couldn't understand what was wrong. The pressure of the tour was off; I had but one trip left to take, some three weeks later, but it was only a simple overnighter to Houston and I didn't anticipate it being any real difficulty to arrange and pull off. My career was going well, my family was healthy and happy, there simply seemed no reason for the dread I felt inside, yet I could not escape it.

A week later I went outside to feed my two outdoor dogs and discovered that Frank, my oldest and my favorite, had died in his sleep. He had had a number of minor health problems of all sorts in recent years and was nearly completely blind, but my vet had assured me that none of these conditions were life-threatening. The day before, he had been completely normal and playful and loving, just as he'd always been.

I took his death harder than I thought I would. I was immediately overwhelmed with grief and sobbed uncontrollably. My wife was a great comfort, as she knew how much Frank had always meant to me and had, in fact, given him to me as a puppy when we were first married. It was very hard to say good-bye.

I wondered if Frank's death was the reason I had had the feelings of discontent and anxiety in recent months. I had often heard stories of dogs who are dying but somehow hang on to life by a thread until their master comes home, then wave their paw in the air slowly and dramatically, whisper a few meaningful words into their master's ear like "I have a confession to make; that smell in the den was because I peed behind the couch," then pass away quietly. Perhaps I had been experiencing some similar psychic phenomenon. Perhaps Frank had been sending me telepathic messages to return home before he bought the big one. As difficult as it was, maybe his death would be the end of my emotional distress.

As much as I missed Frank, I recovered quickly, taking only a couple of days off from writing cartoons and comforting myself with the fact that I had only lost a dog, thankful that no greater loss had occurred. I also wondered, as all people who have to create humor on an unrelenting schedule do, how a person could still be funny in the face of real, long-term, life-changing tragedy.

A week later, I received news at the other end of the spectrum. I was notified by mail that I had been nominated for the National Cartoonists Society's award for best panel cartoon feature of the year. I was elated. It was the first year I had ever submitted anything to the society for consideration and my first such nomination. The award was to be given a couple of months later at a black tie banquet at the annual convention in New York. I couldn't wait to go and immediately began telling myself that it didn't matter if I won, the nomination was the real honor (all the while secretly hoping with all my heart that I *would* win and that I could restrain myself from chucking a beer bottle at the podium if I didn't). Along with this excitement, however, came the same old invisible dread.

I spent only a few hours rejoicing in my accomplishment before I began allowing myself to ignore the positive and indulge myself in depression and anger once again. I was ashamed, but felt powerless to resist. Obviously, my problem had had nothing to do with Frank's death, and I fumed as I asked myself the same question over and over: "What is wrong with me?"

In the next week came an answer I would be nearly unable to endure.

Boom

I t was an average weekday night, only a few days before I was to leave for my final trip, which was to Houston. I attended my wife's latest play and was once again moved and astonished by her performance.

The play, like so many of the productions she had been in, dealt with the bitterly unhappy and hopelessly complex lives of the members of a dysfunctional family. There was the requisite amount of fighting, yelling, abuse, betrayal, alcoholism, soul-searching, adultery, pain, and sacrifice, reaching a climax in which the characters fall to their knees in surrender and beg the forgiveness of the loved ones they have wronged. Then, of course, all is forgiven and the cycle begins again, repositioning the characters for a replay of their agony at some unknown date in the future, and the curtain closes. Actors *love* that kind of stuff.

It had been a difficult play for my wife to do, however. In many ways, the plot and characters reminded her so much of her own impossibly troubled family and childhood that it became quite painful for her to perform. But actors love this, too, and draw great strength of portrayal from their own misery. In fact, most of the ones I have met through her have constructed an elaborate personal hell of shattered romances and destroyed relationships for themselves to wallow, then revel in, wearing the scars of these self-inflicted wounds like badges of courage.

My wife has, at times, worn the scars of her own Tennessee Williamsesque family like a medal of honor and openly attributes much of her acting skills to the suffering she endured at their hands. But this play struck extremely close to home, and she was increasingly more uncomfortable with what it was doing to her inside. She felt, however, that if she could make it through, it might be a form of therapy and could help her exorcise some of the painful memories of her own past. I hoped so, too.

This aspect was evident in her performance, as she portrayed her character with uncanny accuracy and depth. While the other performers in the play ranged from marginal to amateurish, no audience member escaped the performance without being thoroughly convinced of her pain. Her abilities in drama seemed boundless, and I was very proud of her.

Afterward, I congratulated her affectionately backstage, complimented the other actors, told her I'd see her at home in a little while, and left.

I didn't realize it then, but that moment backstage would be the last affectionate conversation we would ever have. Though my book tour was nearly over, the Internet was about to take my life in yet another dramatic direction.

Driving home that night I was punching buttons on the radio when I suddenly heard the familiar voice of Pat Sajak breaking into the middle of a Nirvana song. His tone was notably somber.

"The wheel is slowing down, Dan."

"Pat! Long time no talk!" I shouted enthusiastically. "I thought you'd abandoned me for good!"

He continued bleakly, "No one is ever abandoned for good.

It was merely time to step back and let the wheel land where it may."

"Why so gloomy, Pat? You sound like your show was cancelled," I kidded him.

He was tolerant but clearly in no mood for levity. "There isn't much time, Dan. I just came to say that we will no longer speak in this manner."

My mood began to moderate to his more solemn attitude, and I became concerned. "What's going on? Are you going away?"

"You are at a crossroads, and it will be necessary for you to travel alone from here on in. You might say it's time to solve the puzzle," he said.

"What kind of crossroads? Where has the wheel landed?" I asked.

He was silent for a moment, then added carefully, "It hasn't stopped spinning completely yet, but when you've been watching the wheel as long as I have, you can tell where it's going to land."

I was beginning to panic. "Where? Where is the wheel going to land?" I demanded.

"I can't tell you that, Dan, you'll know soon enough. But I just want you to remember that you don't need me to guide you anymore. You already have all the letters you need to solve the puzzle."

As usual, I was beginning to lose patience with his corny and enigmatic advice. "What do you mean, 'all the letters I need'? I can't even see the board from here, how can I solve the puzzle?"

Unshaken, he continued in a dour voice, "Inside you is a voice that tells you who you are and what you should do. Listen to it."

"You're beginning to sound like Jiminy Cricket, Sajak," I said sarcastically.

"I prefer Obi-Wan Kenobi," he answered.

"Do I at least get a parting gift?" I asked, tongue in cheek. "A home version of *Wheel of Fortune*, perhaps?"

"Just solve the puzzle, Dan," he said. And he was gone.

I drove home in silence, wondering what Sajak had meant and fearing the possibilities. I didn't have to wonder long.

My wife walked through the door an hour later, and I was waiting for her with some papers in my hand. It was nearly midnight, the children were asleep, the house was dark.

I held out the pages for her to see by the light of the porch lamp coming through the window, and her face sank as she read them with silent recognition.

What I had handed her was a series of love letters between her and one of the actors in the play I had just seen, with whom she had been romantically involved for some time and with whom she had been communicating via her private E-mail account.

When I arrived home after her play that night, I went to answer my own E-mail and found a message on the screen alerting me that a document that had been ordered printed earlier had not been completed. The computer asked if I wanted to complete the printing, and I said yes. Out came the letters.

I later found out that she had, in fact, ordered the letters to be printed out early that morning and had gotten the printed copies a few minutes later. Through some strange glitch in cyberspace, the computer decided to repeat the process when I got home that night. Perhaps it was Sajak.

In this way, without any advance warning, no siren or bell or word of caution, our marriage silently exploded and my life as I had known it ended irrevocably.

Sixteen years of memories, passion, and companionship flew through the air in tiny fragments, like a slow-motion special-effects blast with the sound turned off. We talked into the night through our tears, riddled with shrapnel, bleeding from a thousand tiny holes. My pain was eclipsed only by my disbelief; there had been no hints, no mention of discontent, no interruption in our relationship. As far as I had been aware, we had never had a serious problem in our marriage. I just never saw trouble coming. I honestly believed for a few minutes that I would suddenly wake up and it would have all been a dark and terrible dream.

The next several hours would bring unceasing discussion through strained voices of anger, rejection, denial, betrayal, disbelief, pity, and, ultimately, profound pain. I hurt so bad it scared me. (A psychologist later told me, "You feel like hell because this *is* hell.") No wonder Sajak wanted me to do this alone.

With the seemingly sudden and complete evaporation of my marriage went my life. Every hope I had had for the future, every dream I had dared to allow myself, dissolved and poured through my fingers like a melting ice sculpture. The more I tried to hang on to the dream, the faster it disintegrated. I suggested we put it behind us and see a marriage counselor, but she was not interested. She just wanted to leave and be someone else.

She had meant all the world to me, and, at one time not so long ago, she had said I meant all the world to her. Now it had disappeared like a mirage in the time it took my computer to print out a few pages of type.

The last trip scheduled on my tour was Houston, and I was to leave in three days. I canceled the trip the next morning and sank into a dark and painful place for a long time. At first, it seemed I would never come out.

Canine Logic

A s I write this I am sitting nude in the lotus position atop a sixteen-foot-tall mound of earth in the middle of my backyard garden with a peaceful smile on my face. The air is fresh and warm, the sun is shining down like an impossibly huge ball of flaming gas in outer space, and my entire body is completely shaved. Birds are singing like feathered fiddlers in the trees as bugs dance their little hillbilly jigs across the tender petals of spring's new growth. It has been nearly a year since the end of my book tour and my marriage, and as far as I can see in my little kingdom all is right with the world.

But getting here was no easy journey. The past ten months were simultaneously the most brutal and enlightening of my life. But as is often the case with intense personal battles, once they were over it seems the ground gained was worth the pain experienced along the way. Not unlike potty training a toddler.

The first few weeks after my wife moved out were unbearably lonely, and since I worked at home (and, of course, *lived* at home) it seemed I was forever kicking around in the emptiness of my house, like the world's largest solitary confinement cell. It was summer, so my two daughters were around quite a bit, but they had their own activities and friends, and I certainly couldn't expect them to comfort me. In many ways, it was even harder on me when they were home because I felt it unwise to display my misery fully in front of them. When they were around, I strained to seem at least a little "okay." When they were gone, I let go.

It became an hourly challenge to overcome my grief and find ways to distract myself. It was especially difficult on the occasions when my wife would take the kids for a couple of days and I was *completely* alone. At these times my thoughts would ricochet in a hundred directions at once as I tried desperately to figure out what had happened to my life and my marriage. Nothing seemed to make sense anymore, and I asked myself over and over who my wife had really been all those years. Either she had never been the person I'd thought she was, or somewhere along the line she had changed drastically. Whatever the case, she neglected to let me in on the secret. In her defense, however, she claimed *she* didn't know who she was or what she was doing, either. We both nearly choked on the cliché, but all she could say before she left was that she needed to "find herself."

Being a groovy, New Age, nineties kind of guy, I've always felt that it is every person's right to find herself by looking wherever she deems appropriate. But it seemed to me that when a person decides to embark on such a search, some kind of notification to her spouse of sixteen years and father of her children would be only common courtesy. At the very least a Post-It note on the refrigerator—"Am 'finding myself' in the arms of someone else tonight. Don't wait up"—might have been in order.

Sadly, a lot of people seem to have lost themselves these days. You can scarcely walk down the street anymore without being knocked down by the hordes of people milling around looking for themselves. Perhaps a kind of pop-psychology Pied Piper will come along one day and lead all of them into a public rest room somewhere, point at the mirrors, and say, "Look. *There* you are." Then they'll all say, "Ah-h-h. I was here all along," and they'll comb their hair, freshen their makeup, and go home to live happily ever after.

In my own way, my book tour had been *my* effort to find myself. Pat Sajak had been my Pied Piper, and the divorce had been my mirror. But did that mean *Bizarro* had been the rest room and my fans had been the paper towels? And would we all just fix our hair and makeup and go home, or would there be refreshments and time to make a phone call? If Pat was my Pied Piper, who was my Fairy Godmother? Would I get my cartoons finished in time to go to the ball?

As this sort of convoluted reasoning became a daily routine, I was left feeling on most days that if I spent one more minute alone with my thoughts my head would expode like a hamster in a microwave. I knew I had to get out of the house more often and be with other people. Desperate for relief, I fell into the habit of cruising around my house peering out the windows in hope of catching a neighbor in the yard to ambush for company. Particularly helpful during this phase were my next-door neighbors, Katie and Bo.

Katie was an ex-lawyer who had proudly quit the practice to become a housewife and could frequently be caught in the yard gardening or in her garage working on any one of her dozens of ongoing home-improvement projects. She and I became very close friends over the course of a few months, and I spent countless hours on her porch or in her sun room whining and crying about my miserable life. She patted me on the back, handed me Kleenex, and counseled me with the patience of a saint and the expertise of Freud himself.

On weekends she and Bo would invite me over to drink beer and eat barbecue on their patio. (Bo is locally known as the "Smokemaster General" and can do things with fire, smoke, and pork that remain a mystery in the scientific community even to this day.) I hung out at their house so much that they began to refer to me as Howard Borden, the ubiquitous neighbor from the old *Bob Newhart Show*.

But as kind and long-suffering as they were, everyone reaches a saturation point (especially when it comes to someone *else's* misery), and on more than one occasion I had to resort to trickery to get them to answer their door. A number of times I appeared on their doorstep in a dress and wig from my daughter's dress-up closet so that they would not be able to recognize me through the peephole. This started numerous unflattering rumors about me around the neighborhood, but I was too self-absorbed to care. The most desperate example of deception I employed was fashioning a dog costume out of carpet scraps from my garage and scratching on their backdoor late at night. I'm not proud of this behavior, but I was beside myself at the time and lacking any self-restraint. (Like people who are covered in tattoos and body piercings, I think of this less as a sign of illness and more as a cry for help.)

The important thing is that I have recognized my problem and worked through it. Now when I want to visit Bo and Katie, I almost always call first and ask if I can come over, and I've even gotten to the point where I usually tell them who I am and use my real voice.

Other lifesavers for me during those early dark days were my best friend, Bart, and his wife, Audria. I hung out at their apartment so much in the first few weeks of my singlehood that their landlord required an additional pet deposit. I offered to reimburse them, but they wouldn't hear of it. (That's just the kind of friends they are.) Bart had been working toward a master's degree in theology and had seriously considered becoming an Episcopal priest a few years earlier, so his abilities in the field of "feigning genuine interest in the rantings of a self-pitying drunk long after midnight" were well above average.

Audria's expertise tended to lie more in the area of verbally running down my ex-wife (they'd always had a mutual dislike for each other) and trying to "get me laid." Between the two of them, it was pretty much a full-service broken-heart repair program.

After only a couple of months of mollycoddling me, however, Bart, who is a notorious brainiac, received an incredible, once-in-a-lifetime offer from a prestigious university back east to pursue his Ph.D. in religious studies at its expense. In spite of my pleading, he selfishly accepted it. Our relationship was thus relegated to long-distance phone calls and an occasional brief visit, and their friendship ended up costing me even more than my shrink. I persisted, however, partly because they're great guys and terrific friends and partly because they let me call them anytime of the day or night and my therapist was available only during business hours.

When I couldn't get hold of three-dimensional people, I often corresponded via E-mail with the friends I'd made around the country during my book tour. Now it was my turn to play "True Confessions," as they had with me during my visit. I cried on their cyberspace shoulders, and many of them offered sympathy, advice, and counseling at length and I found great comfort in their words. (Even Ken the Wacko offered his help—"I'd be happy to take care of your problem with your ex-wife for you; to me she's just another person" but I graciously declined.) Several people offered stories of their own failed marriages (if they hadn't already told me), and most of them ended up happily with much healthier and more enjoyable second marriages. A number offered to let me come back and stay with them again if I needed to get away, and a few even called me on the phone now and then to see how I was doing. I consider many of them to be permanent members of my circle of friends and have expressed to them my eagerness to return these acts of kindness if ever they need me.

But in addition to dealing with the emotional agony of the demise of my marriage and the abrupt end to my cherished family life, one of my greatest fears had suddenly come screaming to the forefront: Since my livelihood depends on an uninterrupted stream of humorous ideas, how could I function in the midst of life-changing grief?

As I've said, this is something all cartoonists worry about—except those not writing their own material; I think one can fairly easily still *buy* gags while in grief—and I was justifiably terrified. My children's and my financial well-being depended entirely on my ability to make my relentless cartoon deadlines without pause. Due to my ex's financial ineptitude, I had no savings to fall back on and a formidable amount of debt in the form of a house, two cars, and several engorged, high-interest credit cards. So I needed the income badly.

Bizarro was my only way of bringing in a decent paycheck, but I couldn't imagine feeling less funny or more miserable. Sitting down to write cartoons in this state was a lot like trying to entertain a roomful of six-year-olds at a birthday party while suffering from a bad case of the flu. I suddenly regretted having ever chosen this career, and, for the first time in my life, I actually envied *accountants*. I had hit rock bottom.

To give you a better idea of what I was facing, go get a pencil and paper right now and take the Syndicated Humor Challenge.

First, write a fresh, completely original joke (twenty-five words or less, please), then illustrate it in a whimsical manner. Next, do the same thing each day for one full month, without missing a single day. Now continue that pace over a decade or more, 365 days a year (366 on leap years, no cheating). Now experience an unexpected grave and painful personal tragedy, which brings you daily to the brink of a complete spiritual, emotional, and psychological breakdown. (For this step, you may need the assistance of a traitorous loved one.) Now try to keep up your comedy-writing schedule without missing a single day while every fiber of your being is crying out for you to drive your car through the front wall of your ex-spouse's place of employment, armed to the teeth with an arsenal of semi-automatic weapons, shoot anything that moves, and then turn the gun on yourself. Now figure up your score.

I'm not implying that I ever *actually* considered doing anything quite so drastic; I'm only trying to illustrate how difficult it was to be funny while consumed with grief, confusion, self-doubt, fear, and anger. When thoughts of that sort occurred to me, I immediately realized the horrible injustice of taking human lives at random in response to one's own emotional pain and also that it would be relatively impossible to make my cartoon deadlines after shooting myself. Thus assuaged, I remained at my drawing table and just kept hitting myself with a large mallet until I thought of something funny.

But, still, nothing took my mind off my unhappiness, no matter what I did to distract myself. My brain replayed the events of the past sixteen years with the relentless repetition of *I Love Lucy* reruns, looking for patterns, signs, hints, reasons why this had happened. I tried everything to interrupt the current, but my mind wouldn't let it go and always found a way to relate any activity to the divorce: traveling ("if the plane goes down and I die, *then* she'll be sorry"); skydiving ("if my parachute doesn't open and I land on *her*, it would kill two birds with one stone"); going to action movies ("if I were Arnold Schwarzenegger I could squeeze her new boyfriend's head into the size of a tennis ball").

On the rare occasions when I did sleep, I still couldn't stop thinking about the divorce. I would invariably wake from fitful dreams after only a few hours of rest. How I managed to continue to write cartoons during this time I honestly cannot say, but, judging by the uninterrupted stream of pictographs with my name on them that appeared in the paper each morning, somehow I did.

Some of the ways in which I coped during the early healing process did work fairly well, though. I read a number of self-help books (or "personal growth" books as they are now sometimes called), which were remarkably useful. But not the "feel good" kind of books that try to convince you that "everyone is precious and wonderful exactly the way they are, so take a deep breath, relax, cherish every drop of dew on every blade of grass, and rejoice in your 'you-ness.'" (Actually, I did read one or two like that, but I found it relatively impossible to even *find* my "me-ness," much less rejoice in it.)

More useful were the books written with a stronger emphasis on the clinical psychology of marriage, divorce, anger, and grief. One of the most helpful dealt with controlling your anger toward your ex. It had a lengthy but poignant title: *Don't Kill Your Ex-Wife or Your Next Wife Might Be a Convict Named Bubba*. In this book, the author contends that a person in my situation is most definitely going to experience a lot of anger for a good, long time but that there are positive and negative ways to channel that anger. An example follows:

POSITIVE USE OF ANGER: *Buy yourself a new watch, then throw the watch your ex-wife gave you for your anniversary over a cliff.*

NEGATIVE USE: *Watch the look on your ex-wife's face as you throw her new boyfriend over a cliff on your anniversary.*

I followed the "positive" example from the book, despite my inclination to follow the other. Given the absence of cliffs in North-Central Texas, however, I threw the watch my wife had given me across a shopping-mall parking lot instead. I chose this course of action over its negative alternative not only because I knew it was the right thing to do but because I doubted I could throw her boyfriend far enough across a parking lot to do any real damage.

But even with these helpful examples, it still takes a great deal of time, effort, and discipline to overcome the depression and anger that is the inevitable result of having your guts ripped out by the person you trust most in the world. For those of you who have not had this pleasure, I can tell you that it is an indescribably painful and relentless torture that I can only liken to one other experience in my life: the time my third-grade teacher, a very jovial nun whom all the kids adored, finally snapped and tried to sell our entire class to a glue factory during a field trip. She was arrested before the deal was finalized, fortunately, but it took many of us years of intensive therapy to get over it. And none of us ever ate paste again. As difficult as that ordeal was to process, I think my divorce was even harder.

Perhaps even more helpful than the books I read was a divorce support group I began attending once a week. The meetings typically consisted of between five and twenty-five people at various stages of the process sitting around in a circle, taking turns telling their stories and describing their feelings. There was no "clinical expert" in attendance, and no advice was given. Each person just talked about his or her own situation and listened to others do the same. Very quickly I began to see where I was in the process, how much progress I had made, how far I had to go. I became good friends with a lot of people there and learned a great deal that helped me navigate the valley of darkness more successfully. I found the group to be both nurturing and educational.

I also became hooked like a soap opera junkie on the stories of everyone's private lives. I couldn't wait to get to group each week to find out if Mr. Erwin had gotten his car back after it was stolen by his exotic dancer girlfriend, Gretchen, or if Leona had mailed any more dead fish to her ex-husband's lover's office.

After a few months, someone in the group noticed a divorce reference in a *Bizarro* cartoon spoken by a character who resembled me, put two and two together, and asked me if I was a cartoonist. In this way, the rest of the group found out and began reading *Bizarro* each morning to see if I was venting my spleen. I found it very therapeutic to express some of my feelings in the cartoon, and, though I never used real names or caricatures, my close friends and the people in the group recognized the targets. Many of them admitted to being envious that I had such a terrific vehicle with which to express myself.

I had no idea if my ex-wife was reading my cartoons, but as she'd read very few of them in the final few years of our marriage, I assumed she was not. But on the day that the following cartoon ran, I got a startling phone call in my studio.

It was my ex-wife, whom I hadn't spoken to in several months, and she spoke sharply and authoritatively, never taking a breath. "I saw your cartoon this morning, Dan, and I just want to say I hope the *rest* of the country finds our divorce as f——ing funny as you do!" And she hung up.

Though I'd been drawing such cartoons entirely for my own benefit and honestly didn't care if she saw them or not, I

will admit that this phone call absolutely made my day. I told my friends at the divorce group that night about the call and the room broke out in applause. For a few minutes, to a small group of wounded souls, I became a folk hero.

Several weeks later, while brainstorming ideas, I designed a cartoon full of hidden messages deriding the man my wife had been involved with when we split up. It wasn't a particularly brilliant cartoon, but it was clever enough to print and, to everyone but the parties involved, the true meaning would be completely missed. To my ex-wife, her boyfriend, and a handful of our friends, however, the meaning would be blatant. But in my attempt to maintain the moral high ground, I resisted publishing the cartoon for many weeks. My attitude had been for some time that any contact with these people, no matter how incidental or justified, was beneath me. Weak and vindictive mortal that I am, however, I eventually gave in to the temptation and published it anyway. Not entirely coincidentally, I scheduled it to run on my ex-wife's birthday.

That evening the phone rang again with a familiarly ominous tone. But this time it was my ex-wife's best friend and quasipartner in the theater business. She, too, spoke sharply and authoritatively, rarely taking a breath, but her speech was a bit longer. "Dan, I saw your cartoon today, and I called to say I think you are a complete, f——ing a——hole! One day you're going to regret having tortured the mother of your children with these stupid, f——ing cartoons! I used to be on your side, but not any more. I think you've become a complete, f——ing a——hole! That's all I have to say." And she hung up.

I might have told her that most men would be greatly relieved to find out that the only consequence of running around with a married woman was a slightly pointed cartoon on the funny pages, but I didn't have time. I might also have pointed out the irony of her assertion that a few comics about divorce somehow constituted unjust retribution for adultery and dissolution of a marriage, but what the heck. It wouldn't have made any difference, and I enjoyed the call nonetheless.

The retelling of this story was also very well received at my divorce group.

As I struggled through each day of the summer trying to keep from falling into a dark pit of despair, trying to make sense of the past, and trying just to make it till bedtime without committing a felony, I often wondered about the exact nature of Sajak's role in all of this.

Just as he had said it would be, I had not heard from him since our conversation on the car radio that fateful night my life exploded. Had he known all along what I was headed for? And if so, had he caused it or merely guided me through the inevitable? In the distant future, would I look back on his contribution to my life as beneficial or deleterious?

These and a truckload of other questions were swimming through my overworked brain one morning when the phone in my studio rang.

"Hello," I said robotically.

"Is Dan Piraro in, please?" a pleasant voice inquired. Such pleasantness before lunch is usually indicative of someone wanting to sell me the Sears Auto Plan or MCI whining about why I had just switched to Sprint or vice versa.

"This is he," I uttered blandly.

"Hold for Bob Barker, please," said the voice politely.

For a few seconds the cranks and pulleys in my brain froze. *Bob Barker? The* Bob Barker? Can this really be happening? Have I become some sort of cult figure among the game-show-host crowd in Hollywood? My mind was reeling.

A man's voice came on the line: "Mr. Piraro?"

"Yes . . ."

"This is Bob Barker. May I call you Dan?" he asked cheerfully.

The voice was unmistakable, and I could almost see his snow-white mound of hair and debonair smile as I answered enthusiastically, "Sure, call me whatever you like!" I was thrilled to be talking to such an estimable member of the game-show community after so many months on the "outs" with Sajak. I'd been watching Bob since he hosted *Truth or Consequences* way back in the fifties. He was an icon of game-show hostery—a real hall of famer! "If Sajak knew Barker was calling me, he'd be so proud!" I thought.

"Say, I was talking to somebody the other day," he continued, "and he told me you'd mentioned me in a book you're writing."

"Well, yes, as a matter of fact I have," I replied. "But nobody's read it yet. Who were you talking to that knew about the book?" I was a bit dazed by all the excitement.

"Actually, it was an old friend of yours—Pat Sajak."

I should have known. They probably run into each other all the time at one of those trendy Hollywood nightclubs that the

game-show crowd hangs out in like The Daily Double on
Wilshire Boulevard or Dick's Lightning Round on Rodeo
Drive. (You may remember Dick's as the place where former
spokesmodel Veronica Spradler, from the 1950s show *You've
Got Some Nerve*, died of asphyxiation from her own hair spray
in the ladies' room at a New Year's Eve party in 1994.)

"Ah, yes. How *is* Pat?" I tried to sound casually professional, but I was secretly thrilled that my name had come up in
such sterling company and dying to know what Pat had said
about me.

"Oh, Pat's doing great, Dan," Bob answered jovially. "He
was telling me all about your crazy book tour last year and I
thought it sounded really fascinating."

"Well, yes, it was very interesting, to say the least. I had a
lot of fun with it," I vamped. "The book I'm writing is about
that tour, as a matter of fact."

"Yes, that's what Pat was saying," he replied. "That's really
the reason for my call. I was wondering if you'd be interested
in coming on my show and promoting your book after it's published."

"Wow, really? Promote my book on *The Price Is Right*?" I
yammered excitedly. "I'd love to!" I was confused as to how you
could promote a book on a game show, so I asked gingerly,
"What did you have in mind, exactly?"

"Well . . ." he paused a moment, as if he himself hadn't
completely figured that out yet, "I thought we could maybe do
something like put you and a couple thousand copies of your
book behind Door Number Two, for instance. It would be sort
of like one of the gag prizes."

Apart from being a little offended at the prospect of being
a *gag* prize, it immediately occurred to me that *The Price Is
Right* didn't *have* numbered doors. I became suspicious.

"What do you mean 'Door Number Two'? That was from
the old *Let's Make a Deal* show, wasn't it?" I asked slyly.

He seemed surprised. "It was? . . . Well, of course it was, I
know that, but we were thinking of reviving the idea for *our*
show," he explained nervously.

"Pardon me for saying so, Mr. Barker, but I've always admired you as a leader in the game-show industry, almost more than Garry Moore even. It just doesn't sound like you to appropriate an idea from another show instead of coming up with something innovative of your own. In fact, are you sure it's even legal?"

"Well, no, but my law guys are looking into buying the copyright on that idea so we can use it," he sputtered and coughed nervously.

Law guys? Who in the world uses a term like "law guys"? By this time I was sure I was being scammed, but I hadn't yet figured out by whom. Something seemed awfully familiar about that cough, though, and my brain was feverishly scanning its files trying to identify it. And the cough sounded not only familiar, but almost inhuman. In fact, it sounded a bit more like a *bark* than a cough. And it was a bark I was certain I'd heard before. I decided to test my theory.

"Well, Mr. *Bark*er," I continued casually, "I think the whole thing sounds like a wonderful idea and I'd love to talk to you at length about it sometime soon, but right now I'm afraid I've got to go. It's time to take my dog outside to . . . *play ball.*"

"*Okay, bye!*" he shouted enthusiastically and dropped the receiver on the floor.

As I recoiled from the nearly deafening sound of the phone bouncing around the floor, all seven pounds of my papillon, Steve, came racing into my studio with a ball in his mouth and his ridiculous plume of a tail wagging at the speed of light. (A papillon is a toy spaniel with big eyes, huge ears, and long, wispy hair that looks very much like a Chihuahua in a prom dress.)

"What are *you* doing here, Steve? It's not time to go out yet," I said innocently.

His voice was muffled by the ball in his mouth: "I fod I hud you say id was dime do blay baw."

"Oh, you thought you heard me say it was time to play ball?" I asked sarcastically. "Is that what you thought you heard . . . *Mr. Barker?*"

Steve's mouth fell open, and the ball dropped to the floor, rolling into a corner. He stared wide-eyed for a moment, then spoke. "How did you know?"

"Oh, come on, Steve, do you think I'm an idiot? 'Law guys'? 'Door Number Two'?"

"Yeah, I had a feeling I'd stepped in it with that *Let's Make a Deal* thing. I always get those game shows confused—they all look alike to me," he explained. "Still . . . the Bob Barker impression was pretty good though, huh?"

"It was excellent. I gotta hand it to you, you're one talented spaniel." (Papillons are a breed well known for their mimicry skills.) "You had me completely fooled for a while there. But I want to ask you—why did you do it?" I inquired.

"I wanted to cheer you up. You've been so down the past few months, and you haven't heard from Sajak in so long, I just thought it might be nice for you to get some good news," he explained compassionately.

I knew he was only trying to help, so I wasn't angry. I chose my words carefully and spoke softly. (With dogs, the *way* you say something is frequently more important than *what* you say.)

"It was very kind of you to want to help me, Steve," I began. His tail wagged, and I rubbed him behind the ears as I continued. "But you see, something is really only good news if it's *true*. The news itself might make me happy, but then when I find out it isn't really true, I feel disappointed again. Like if I told you there was a cat trapped on the porch with its butt stuck in a flowerpot. You'd be excited at the prospect but disappointed to find it wasn't true. Do you understand?"

"I understand. I'm sorry," he said with sincerity. "So I guess you're still feeling down?"

"Actually, I'm feeling better all the time, Steve." I smiled and tousled the fur on his head affectionately. "But the end of a marriage just isn't something you can get over quickly, especially when it's a particularly painful and messy breakup. I'm doing pretty well, but it takes time to get all the poison out of your system."

"Well, if you're still bummed out about it, why don't you just go get neutered?" he offered helpfully.

"Neutered!" I squealed. "Are you out of your mind?!"

Steve added indignantly, "Hey, don't knock it till you've tried it—it worked for me! When a bitch walks by now, I couldn't care less."

"'Bitch'? That's not a very 'PC' way of putting it, Steve."

"I'm speaking *zoologically*, man, gimme a break. I mean 'bitch' as in 'female dog'!" he explained.

"Well, that isn't how most people take it," I chided.

"Hey! *We* had that word first, you know. You humans think you own everything. And where do you get off being so high and mighty about *my* language? I've heard you call her worse than that yourself!"

"Okay, point taken," I reasoned, not wishing to hear Steve go through a litany of all the things he'd heard me call my ex in recent months, "but I still don't think I'm desperate enough to consider getting neutered."

"Fine, that's your choice. But don't come crying to me the next time some woman dumps on you," he barked.

"I'll try to remember that," I replied.

"And if you should ever change your mind, let me know. I can recommend an excellent vet with *very* good hand skills. You'll be up and around the next morning."

I shuddered at the thought and said, "You'll be the first to know, Steve, I promise. But I don't think I'll ever be quite *that* desperate. Not everything about this situation is bad, you know. It was a very rough year, but there's a lot of good that came from it, too. I learned an awful lot about myself as a result of all this upheaval, and my life makes a lot more sense now."

Steve recognized that I was about to launch into one of my long-winded, boy-and-his-dog speeches about life, so he crawled up into my lap and settled in. I don't know if he's ever really all that interested in what I have to say or if he just likes the opportunity to utilize his greatest skill, being a lapdog, and curl up into a furry little ball in my lap while I pontificate.

"One of the most important things I learned, Steve," I began, "is that happiness, or contentment, or whatever you want to call it, doesn't come in the form of fame, or success, or awards, or accolades, or public admiration. If it's anywhere, it's in family and friends, personal relationships, liking yourself from the inside out, not for what you have accomplished but for who you are."

"Forgive me for saying so, Dan," he interrupted, "but that sounds like nineties, pop psychology bullshit." (The papillon is an insightful and candid breed.)

"Yes, it does, Steve, and that's exactly what it is," I confessed. "But that doesn't make it any less true. Just because something is corny, it doesn't necessarily mean it isn't valid. You see, Steve, we Americans have such a high standard of living that we take much for granted and have a great deal of spare time. A lot of people spend that time worrying about whether or not they are getting their fair share of happiness from life. But I think what you miss when you approach it that way is that there's nothing 'fair' about life in the first place. Happiness is a *choice*, it isn't a *right*. It isn't *owed* to you, and it can't be *caught*, no matter how hard or long you pursue it."

"Just like squirrels, right?" Steve asked. He was bright, but he was still a dog.

"Y-e-eah, I guess so," I replied, trying not to lose my train of thought. "The point is it's not something you can catch or create. It's a side effect of doing the right thing by people. If you behave responsibly and considerately toward others, you'll find that you like and respect yourself and it leads to happiness. If you dump on people, and waste your time and energy chasing happiness, you find it very difficult to respect yourself and practically impossible to be happy. Do you see what I mean, Steve? It isn't *out there*," I said, gesturing toward the distance, "it's *in here*." I pointed dramatically to my heart.

Steve seemed a little puzzled as he looked out the window in the direction I'd been pointing. "It isn't out in the yard, it's here in the house?" he asked.

"No, it's not in the world *around* you, it's in your *heart* . . . or mind, or soul, or whatever you want to call it," I explained.

"But where does that leave *me*? A lot of people think dogs don't have souls," he mused, cocking his head and perking up his enormous ears.

"But a lot of people think they do. Ever heard the expression 'Bless the beasts and the children'? What good is blessing something without a soul? You might as well say 'bless the bologna and the oven-cleaner spray.'"

"But they don't specifically mention *dogs* in that expression," Steve complained.

"Dogs come under the heading of 'beasts,'" I reasoned.

"You are *so* condescending," he growled.

"Okay." I decided to try a different tack. "What about 'All dogs go to heaven'? Ever heard that one?"

"Yes, but that's clearly a myth," Steve countered. "There's no way in hell that vicious, garbage-eating, car-chasing beast next door is going to heaven."

"I don't really think that's for you to judge, Steve, and besides, we're way off the point," I pointed out. "Do you even remember what I was talking about?"

Steve didn't miss a beat: "So what you were saying, in essence," he expounded, "is that the riches and adoration of the entire world fall pathetically short in comparison to the companionship of your family and loved ones. 'Happiness' can't be manufactured by manipulating your surroundings or changing your appearance, or filling your life with people who adore you. Rather, one must peer inside oneself and accept what one finds, behave considerately and responsibly toward other people and their community, have the discipline to delay ones own comfort or gratification in deference to the common good and long-range repercussions, thus building one's self-respect, and the respect of one's peers. What we call 'happiness' is then a side effect, a 'fringe benefit' if you will, of discipline, responsibility, consideration, and strong, moral character."

"Well . . . yeah. Exactly." I was astounded by Steve's insight and understanding and was actually becoming a little choked up. "My little doggy's growing up," I thought.

"Good boy, Steve. Good boy," I said softly, stroking his head.

"And you learned all this from your fans on the road?" Steve asked innocently.

"Well, uh, yes, partly there and partly from the demise of my marriage, I guess. All my adult life I think I had been basing my opinion of myself on the world's opinion of me. If my cartoon was popular, I was a great guy. If someone else's was *more* popular, he was a *better* guy. I had spent the past year thinking that if I knocked myself out promoting my cartoon and could gain some ground in the marketplace, I would be happier and more content. I had done what I set out to achieve: got some press, sold some books, got nominated for an award. But in the end all these accomplishments were utterly hollow in light of the family life I'd lost."

Steve perked up with a sudden look of canine Gestalt on his face. "Just like Dorothy in *The Wizard of Oz!*" he announced.

"How so?"

"She searched all over the world for a better life till she finally realized 'there's no place like home,'" he explained. "Only she did it with music, pigtails, and a blue gingham dress."

"I suppose I see your point," I surrendered.

"So what's Princess Narcissa's story? How does she figure into this?" Steve inquired.

"Princess Narcissa?" I asked.

"Your ex-wife. That's what I've been calling her," he explained.

I chuckled and attempted to field his question. "There was a time when I would have gladly expounded for hours on the exact nature of the Princess' psyche, Steve, but it's not really for me to say. You can never know for sure what's inside another person's head, no matter how long you've known them, but I think she's always been a very unhappy person and has spent her entire adult life looking for what was missing from her life. Before she knew what was happening, she was in way over her head."

"Why didn't you see it coming? I could've told you a long time ago she had one foot out the door," he boasted.

I was a little irritated at his 20/20 hindsight and snapped back sarcastically, "Well, Steve, if only more people had the sense to confer with their dogs about the state of their marriage, the world would be a much happier place. But then a lot of marriage counselors would be out of business, wouldn't they?"

"Damn right, homey," he shot back.

"I didn't see it coming because I believe a relationship should be built on trust. I trusted her completely, and it simply never occurred to me that our marriage wouldn't last forever," I elucidated. "But looking back from this side of the fence, yes, I see a million things that indicated that this was bound to happen sooner or later. I've always known she was a person with a lot of emotional baggage, but, as hard as I tried, I could never get her to deal with it. She was great at advising everyone else to get help, but she would never get any for herself."

Steve chimed in indignantly, "Yeah! She certainly didn't hesitate to send me to that puppy POW camp because of that little housebreaking problem I had!"

"The floors were practically warping from the water damage, Steve. Furniture was floating out into the street! We *had* to do something!" I asserted.

"'Physician, heal thyself!' That's all I've got to say," he added indignantly.

"What's done is done, let's just drop it," I said. "You know, sometimes I think you've got as much emotional baggage as she does."

Steve looked away thoughtfully for a brief second, then offered wisely, "I guess some people, for whatever reason, would rather run away and start over than look inward and deal with the *reason* they're miserable. But emotional baggage is an interesting thing, Dan. No matter how much you travel, you simply can't lose it—it just keeps popping up on the luggage carousel with your name on it. And even if you try to ignore it and don't pick it up, it gets delivered right to your hotel room. There is simply no escaping it until you unpack it."

"Then why don't more people just unpack it and get it over with?" I wondered aloud.

"I guess they just don't want to face their dirty laundry, Dan. They'd rather knock themselves out dragging locked steamer trunks around all their life than bear the smell of their own socks," he mused as he lifted his back foot and scratched behind his ear. "Undergarments can be a painful thing, pal."

Didn't I know it? I had spent enough time lately going through my own dirty laundry (and paying a shrink to go through it with me) to know exactly what Steve was talking about. He was a sissy-looking little spaniel, but he had uncanny insight into human nature. And while everybody has a little emotional baggage to drag around behind him, my ex-wife had always had a seemingly endless amount and just kept adding to it all the time. At last count it was an eighteen-piece set, made entirely of titanium steel, each piece padlocked and handcuffed to her wrist on a chain like a CIA courier. As many times as she had changed her surroundings, appearance, activities, and entourage, you could still hear it scraping along the ground behind her. No matter how heavy it got, she still wouldn't even look for the keys to unlock it, let alone unpack any of it.

Impressed by Steve's wisdom, I asked him, "How is it that a dog can be so emotionally healthy and well adjusted?"

"We're taken away from our parents at a very early age," he quipped. "They don't have time to ruin us."

"I suppose that makes some sense, but I don't think the Princess and I can blame *all* our problems on our parents," I said.

"Don't *ever* take your parents for granted, Dan!" Steve scolded. "I can only barely remember my mother, and I never even knew my father. I've had to take complete responsibility for all of my actions since I was six weeks old and, believe me, I'd give *anything* to have my parents' ineptitude to blame for my misbehavior! You humans don't know how good you've got it!"

I continued hesitantly, "So you think I should blame my parents for my depression and anxiety attacks during my book tour?"

"Why not? It's worth a try," he snapped.

"But placing blame doesn't *solve* the problem," I reasoned.

"All right then, try this: The real reason for your depression and anxiety was *Koyaanisqatsi*," he said ominously.

"What the hell is that?"

"It's the name of a strange, artsy movie that came out a few years ago," Steve explained. "I think it's an American Indian word meaning 'life out of balance.' Either that or it's a Yiddish expression that means 'very long, pretentious art film.' I can't remember."

"So which is it in my case?" I asked.

"'Life out of balance,' of course," he replied. "I think you placed your focus on all the wrong things. You've said it yourself; you put too much emphasis on career success and other people's opinions of you, while your relationship with your wife was shallow and dependent. I think your depression was a sort of subconscious barometer that was warning you of impending meltdown if you didn't set things right. The tour put pressure on all the weakest points in your life, the things that were making you unhappy in the first place, until they finally snapped. Now you can rebuild your life into what it ought to be."

"Now look who's pooping out the psychobabble, my little furry Freud," I teased.

He countered, "Just because it's trite doesn't mean it isn't true."

"You know, Steve," I admitted as I put him down on the floor and strolled leisurely toward the door, "you might have something. I'm reminded of Sajak's constant admonition to 'spin the wheel.' But the more I spun the wheel, the more things started falling apart. But they *needed* to fall apart to be put back together the way they should have been all along."

"I think that's a good observation," Steve added as he followed me out into the hall. "After all, Pat had learned that same lesson himself, as you may recall, with his short-lived foray into the talk-show arena, only to return to his own backyard, *Wheel of Fortune.* We all knew it was where he belonged all along, but he couldn't appreciate it until it was gone."

"Wow," I mused aloud. "Even the great Sajak has played the part of Dorothy."

Steve expounded with the wisdom of Confucius, "Each person, in his turn, must put on the pigtails and blue gingham dress, Dan."

We paused a moment and looked at each other. "Once again, your acumen amazes me, Steve," I told him honestly. "You know, for a toy breed, you've really got a lot to say. How is it that you never talked to me like this *before* the Princess left?"

"You were never lonely enough to listen," he replied.

Together we walked into the bathroom. I stood before the mirror and pulled a long pair of scissors out of a drawer as Steve watched from his usual perch atop the toilet tank. I methodically snipped at the long, dark shocks of curly hair dangling from my head.

"Are you ever going to *stop* talking to me, Steve?" I asked pathetically. "Will you ever abandon me like Sajak did?" I realized I was dangerously close to becoming codependent with my dog, and it scared me a little.

"Oh, I don't know," he offered comfortingly. "I suspect that once you get involved with another woman you'll have better things to do than sit around an empty house and talk to your dog. And since you refuse to take my advice on the neutering, it probably won't be long before that happens."

"Don't count on it, Steve. The last thing I want right now is another emotional crutch. Besides, I got married so young, I've never lived alone before and I'm actually starting to like it."

"But aren't you using *me* as an emotional crutch?" Steve asked as he watched the sink fill with my severed tresses.

"You're not big enough to be a crutch," I reasoned. "You're an emotional arch support at best." I had saved my treasured Salvador Dalí mustache for last and dramatically snipped each of the two protruding antennae off in turn. Putting the scissors down, I covered my head and beard with shaving cream.

Steve had been sitting silently for several moments, watching intensely. "Okay, I've gotta ask," he began, unable to contain his curiosity any longer. "What in the name of Hare Krishna are you doing? Shaving your head?"

"No," I answered coolly. "I'm shaving my entire body."

"Why?"

"Everything has changed, Steve," I said with a slight smile of inner peace and sense of resolution. "I'm a different person than I was a year ago, and I'm starting a whole new life. I want to be *reborn* the same way I was *born,* naked and bald."

"Did you also enter life without any furniture?" Steve asked, referring to the fact that I had emptied my entire eleven-room house of all its contents overnight.

"I don't remember how much furniture I had when I was born, but, yes, it is time to throw out the old and begin anew."

"And what did you *do* with all that furniture, Mr. Metamorphosis? Including my favorite chair," he added sarcastically as he followed me through the house to the back door.

"What did I do with it?" I repeated, my voice echoing through the hollow rooms as I stood looking out the window to the garden at the huge mound of freshly dug soil. Removing my clothing, I opened the door and stepped out into the sunshine and replied, "I buried it in the backyard."

The grass felt cool beneath my feet, and the sun warmed

my back as I crossed the yard and climbed the sixteen-foot-tall mound of earth. I sat atop it in the lotus position, closed my eyes, and took a deep, relaxing breath. A breeze as gentle as baby shampoo ran its diaphanous fingers across the stubble on my head, and as far as I could see in my little kingdom all was right with the world. Somewhere in the distance I could hear a small dog laughing.

Epilogue

A s I look back over the past year and a half, I am reminded of a saying I once heard: "A life can only be understood looking from the end of it backward, but we can only live it the other way around." I have taken comfort in those words on many occasions and have already begun to see that these traumatic events were but a springboard to a better understanding of myself and a more meaningful life.

And I have taken comfort in another common expression, too: "What doesn't kill us makes us stronger." If this is true, I think I will soon either be dead or be able to throw a Buick across a parking lot. Miserable as the past year has been, it didn't kill me, so I look forward to my new car-tossing skill with great anticipation. I don't know what purpose this ability will serve in my life, but, if nothing else, it will be easier to find a parking place.

Yet another saying goes: "If you find yourself talking to your dog and/or people on your television, and they are talking back, you might need serious professional help." I have also given much thought to these words, but have chosen to disregard them as the sentiments of a bitter and cynical person. I have considered telling my shrink about my relationship with Pat Sajak and my conversations with Steve but have decided that some of life's more mystical encounters are better kept to oneself, lest they lose their mystique.

Even now I can see that much good has already come from my experiences on the road and at home. I have conquered my fear of strangers to a large degree and realized that everyone has a little something to offer, some marvelous characteristic or quality or point of view that is uniquely his own. I have also been wrested from what had probably always been a detrimental marital relationship. It may be a long time before I can feel good about having lost something I cherished so much, but intellectually I can see that both my ex-wife and I have been liberated from a negative force in our lives that kept us perennially out of balance.

There was a time when I thought that the people "out there" were a threat. For years, based on that assumption, I hermited myself at home with my wife and kids. But my experiences of the past eighteen months taught me otherwise. People out there are just like people anywhere else; some are wonderfully kind and giving, a few are threatening, still others are as boring as watching a slide presentation of a golf tournament.

The one thing I know now, for certain, is that I don't really know much of anything. I don't know if my experiences with Pat Sajak and my papillon's sudden ability to speak were a manifestation of a higher power or just an hallucination brought on by stress. I don't know if I hate Melissa Etheridge's music for honest reasons or just because my ex-wife likes it so much. I don't know if I'll continue to draw *Bizarro* indefinitely or retire to an island in the South Pacific and hassle Marlon Brando.

I do know that you can make friends, enemies, lovers, and family along the road of life, but, in the end, you're really on your own. You'll encounter dangerous curves and unpredictable obstacles along the road, but, you'll never really know what you're made of until your back is against the wall. What so damned many walls are doing in the middle of the road of life in the first place, however, is a mystery I can't even begin to solve.

I used to envision the road as a slow, plodding journey

along a rocky path through deserts and mountains. But now it seems much more like running down a dark, cluttered alley in the middle of the night wearing gigantic, ill-fitting flippers and a blindfold and carrying a cream pie in each hand.

The thing I once feared most were the savages I might run into on the road, but now I know those fears were naive and misplaced (with the possible exception of Ken the Wacko). Frequently, the real dangers in life are much closer. In my case, the most dangerous savages were those in my own head.

I've not heard from Pat Sajak since our conversation over the car radio, and I don't expect to. I suppose he feels he has served his purpose in my life and, like an angel sent from Heaven in answer to a prayer, has moved on dutifully to his next assignment. The last time I spoke to him, he said I had already learned all I needed to know to solve the puzzle, and he was right. By that time the wheels were in motion and all that was left was the final collision. On some level, I think we both knew it was necessary that I go through it alone.

Pat's help was invaluable, though, and I feel certain he is still out there somewhere touching the lives of others with his cryptic puzzles and enigmatic presence even to this day. I suppose there are those who will say that life isn't a game show at all and there are no rules, just chaotic events in random order. They will argue that I just imagined the whole thing and Pat never guided me, spiritually or otherwise, and that I'm just another delusional nutbag. To those people I simply smile cordially and advise them to spin their *own* wheel and let me spin mine.

I once tried to call Sajak on the phone to thank him for all he had done for me, but, alas, he is unlisted. It is, to me, the final bit of evidence that his motives were purely altruistic. He doesn't need to be thanked; he doesn't need the public's adoration; he's already learned the hard lessons. He just keeps spinning the wheel and following the rules of the game the best way he knows how, and that is enough.

My hair is growing back now, and I've acquired a few pieces of furniture for the house. I've given up sitting nude atop the meditation mound in my backyard; the weather in Texas is just too unpredictable, and the neighbors were complaining. Some complained that they could see me from their house, some complained that they couldn't. There's just no pleasing everyone, I guess.

Instead, my dog, Steve, and I sit together in front of the television every night at six-thirty and watch *Wheel of Fortune.* We usually share a bowl of popcorn or a can of Vienna sausages and marvel at this classic game show that so accurately reflects the human condition. Like so many of the most valuable things in life, it is beautiful in its Zen-like simplicity: a consonant, a vowel, a question, a revelation. Before you know it, through the diligent spinning of the wheel and patient discernment of the symbols, Vanna reveals a few words of wisdom that enrich our lives forever. People can root for you, but you have to play the game all by yourself. If you're not careful, you could land on "Lose a Turn" or "Bankrupt" and have to start over. It hurts, and it takes a while to get back in the saddle, but, before you know it, it's your turn to spin again and you keep marching steadily toward solving the puzzle.

The people I met and stayed with during my book tour taught me that we all play the game together. In everyone's life there are a few savages, cream pies, lost turns, and bankruptcies, but if you just keep your eye on Vanna and keep spinning that wheel, the answer to the puzzle will eventually come. And if you're really lucky, you might even win prizes.

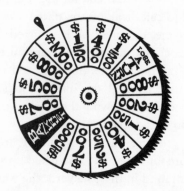